Latin to GCSE
Part 1

ALSO AVAILABLE FROM BLOOMSBURY

Essential GCSE Latin, John Taylor
Greek to GCSE: Part 1, John Taylor
Greek to GCSE: Part 2, John Taylor
Greek Beyond GCSE, John Taylor
Latin Beyond GCSE, John Taylor
Latin Language Tests for Levels 1, 2 and GCSE, Ashley Carter
Latin Momentum Tests for GCSE, Ashley Carter
Latin Stories: A GCSE Reader, Henry Cullen, Michael Dormandy and John Taylor
Latin to GCSE: Part 2, Henry Cullen and John Taylor

Supplementary resources for *Latin to GCSE: Parts 1 and 2* can be found at
www.bloomsbury.com/Cullen-Taylor-Latin-to-GCSE

Please type the URL into your web browser and follow the instructions to access
the Companion Website. If you experience any problems, please contact
Bloomsbury at contact@bloomsbury.com

Latin to GCSE: Part 1

By
Henry Cullen
John Taylor

Bloomsbury Academic
An imprint of Bloomsbury Publishing Plc

B L O O M S B U R Y
LONDON · OXFORD · NEW YORK · NEW DELHI · SYDNEY

Bloomsbury Academic
An imprint of Bloomsbury Publishing Plc

50 Bedford Square	1385 Broadway
London	New York
WC1B 3DP	NY 10018
UK	USA

www.bloomsbury.com

BLOOMSBURY and the Diana logo are trademarks of Bloomsbury Publishing Plc

First published 2016
Reprinted 2016 (four times), 2017 (three times)

© Henry Cullen and John Taylor, 2016

British Library Cataloguing-in-Publication Data
A catalogue record for this book is available from the British Library.

ISBN: PB: 978-1-78093-440-2
       ePub: 978-1-47428-562-9
       ePDF: 978-1-47428-563-6

Library of Congress Cataloging-in-Publication Data
A catalog record for this book is available from the Library of Congress.

Typeset by RefineCatch Limited, Bungay, Suffolk
Printed and bound in India

CONTENTS

ILLUSTRATIONS

PREFACE

The authors have become increasingly aware of the need for a new Latin textbook that takes students efficiently from scratch to GCSE, enabling them to begin reading Latin as quickly as possible but without compromising on the fundamentals of grammar. Many existing textbooks are excessively long and unwieldy, or pay insufficient attention to grammar, or both. Others not aimed specifically at GCSE introduce material that many students and teachers do not have time to cover. Many teachers share these frustrations; we hope that this course provides a useful new option.

Latin to GCSE aims to be both traditional and up-to-date. We do not apologise for the fact that it takes grammar seriously: grammatical understanding is essential for both progress in and enjoyment of Latin. It cannot simply be glossed over; nor (regrettably) is it something that students absorb by osmosis. At the same time, the needs of today's students are borne constantly in mind. We have tried to focus on things that students find difficult and that often cause mistakes at GCSE; we concentrate on the understanding of principles, in both accidence and syntax, so that the need for rote learning is reduced. The stories have been selected both for the intrinsic interest of their subject matter and for their importance in Roman history: amongst them are many old favourites, which students of Latin should not reach GCSE without having covered.

We should like to thank Deborah Blake for the initial invitation to write the book, and Alice Wright, Commissioning Editor for Classical Studies and Archaeology at Bloomsbury, for her constant help and encouragement, and not least her patience. The boys of Tonbridge School proved willing guinea-pigs for several early drafts of Part 1, and our former colleagues there offered valuable feedback at several stages. We are particularly grateful to Chris Burnand and Katy Waterfield who commented in detail on a penultimate version of the text, to its considerable advantage. We also wish to thank the several anonymous readers provided by Bloomsbury. The practice papers in Chapter 12, in the style of the new GCSE (9-1) for examination in 2018 onwards, have been adapted from recent past papers by kind permission of OCR. The book is directed primarily at the OCR GCSE, but we hope it may also be useful to pupils studying for the WJEC examination, and more broadly to learners of Latin of any age.

Henry Cullen would like in addition to thank Ed and Patte Sullivan. It was his tutoring of them that provided the initial inspiration for this project; revising the final sections of Part 1 at their home in Portland, Oregon, in August 2015 made for satisfying ring composition.

We have read and commented on successive drafts of each other's work, but Henry Cullen remains responsible for Part 1 and John Taylor for Part 2.

An answer key and other supplementary resources are available at www.bloomsbury.com/Cullen-Taylor-Latin-to-GCSE

Henry Cullen
John Taylor
October 2015

VOCABULARY AND GLOSSING

The chapter vocabularies for Part 1 and Part 2 cover the GCSE Defined Vocabulary List. In passages, GCSE words are underlined and glossed in blue when they first occur. The underlining is repeated for words that recur in the same passage: they should then be learned. They can be checked in the chapter vocabularies, or in the Latin-English vocabulary in the back of the book.

Non-GCSE words are underlined and glossed, again with the underlining repeated. Proper names are normally underlined and glossed at their first occurrence in a passage, but the underlining is not repeated.

In the glossed vocabulary underneath a passage, nouns are given with genitive singular and gender. 2-1-2 adjectives are given with feminine and neuter endings. Third declension adjectives are given with the neuter nominative singular if (like for *tristis*) it is different from the masculine/feminine, or with the genitive singular if (like for *ingens*) the neuter nominative singular is the same as the masculine/feminine. Verbs are given with principal parts (present tense, infinitive, perfect tense) to the extent that those principal parts are required to translate the form that appears in the passage.

e.g.	puella -ae *f*	girl
	laetus -a -um	happy
	tristis -e	sad
	ingens -entis	huge
	porto -are -avi	I carry

NOTE ON ENGLISH TO LATIN MATERIAL

English to Latin sentences are included throughout the book to provide practice in working that way round (once more an option at GCSE) and because the authors think that translating into Latin is invaluable for consolidating the language.

The requirements of the English to Latin section of the GCSE are explained after Chapter Six on pages 212–15; here you will find exam-style practice sentences.

Given the limited range of the vocabulary and syntax required for this section of the exam, many of the English to Latin exercises in this book go well beyond what candidates might find on an actual GCSE paper (they use, for example, wider vocabulary or more complex accidence and syntax). Where this is the case you will see the Stretch & Challenge (S&C) sign. Sometimes this sign appears part way through an exercise; this indicates that the sentences from that point onwards go beyond the requirements of the English to Latin section of the exam. We hope that students will not be deterred from attempting those sections marked S&C.

ABBREVIATIONS

abl	ablative
acc	accusative
adj	adjective
adv	adverb
conj	conjunction
dat	dative
f	feminine
fut	future
gen	genitive
imperat	imperative
indecl	indeclinable (does not change its endings)
inf	infinitive
irreg	irregular
lit	literally
loc	locative
m	masculine
n	neuter
nom	nominative
num	numeral

pl   plural

prep   preposition

pron   pronoun

qu   question

refl   reflexive

sg   singular

tr   translate

usu   usually

voc   vocative

1, 2, 3   first, second, third person; first, second, third etc. declension

1st, 2nd, 3rd   first, second, third etc. conjugation

Note also two abbreviations of Latin expressions that are common in English, and frequently used in the explanations of grammar in this book:

   e.g.   *exempli gratia*   for (the sake of) example

   i.e.   *id est*   that is (*introducing further explanation*)

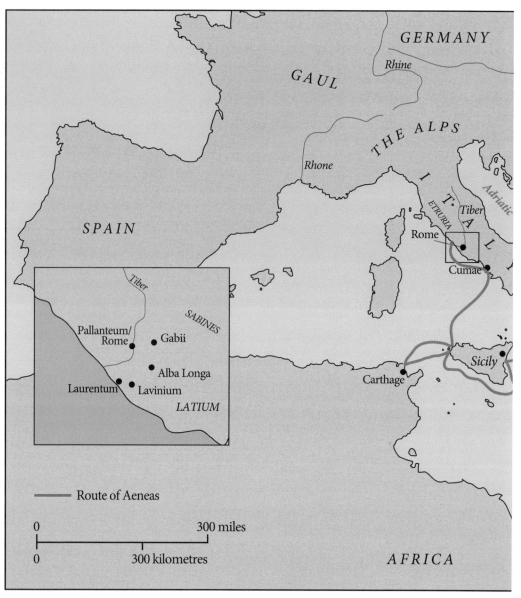

GERMANY

GAUL

Rhine

THE ALPS

Rhone

Tiber

Adriatic

SPAIN

ETRURIA

Rome

Tiber

ITALY

Cumae

Tiber

SABINES

Pallanteum/
Rome

Gabii

Alba Longa

Laurentum

Lavinium

LATIUM

Carthage

Sicily

Route of Aeneas

0	300 miles
0	300 kilometres

AFRICA

The Ancient World with the route of Aeneas. Inset: the environs of Rome.

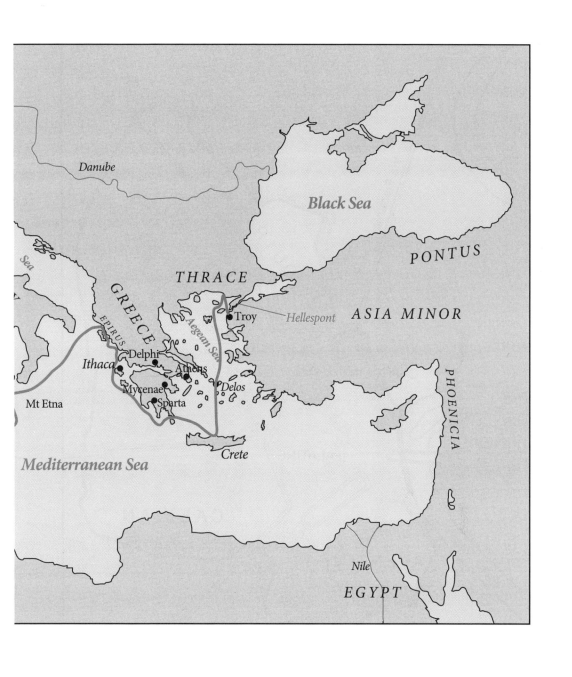

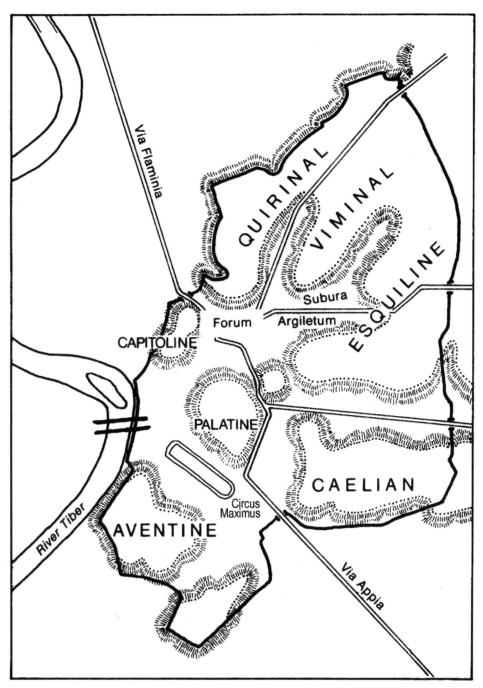

The seven hills of Rome, showing its early stone walls and the location of the later Circus Maximus.

Chapter One

THE LATIN ALPHABET

The Latin alphabet is the one that English still uses, with the following exceptions:

- No *j*   *i* is used as two different letters, a vowel like our *i* and a consonant with a *y* sound. English has often turned the consonant form of *i* into a *j*. e.g. *Iuppiter* = Jupiter (king of the gods).

- No *v*   *u* was also originally used as both a vowel and a consonant, performing the roles of both *u* and *v*. Hence the word *servus* (slave) was once (and still could be) written as *seruus*. Modern convention however is to use separate *u* and *v*.

- No *w*   there is no letter *w* (see below under 'Pronunciation').

There are therefore twenty-three letters in the Latin alphabet, though this book will use twenty-four (including *v*); *k*, *y* and *z* are very rare.

CAPITAL LETTERS

Latin texts would originally have been written in capital letters; the lower case forms that are familiar to us only started to be used in the Middle Ages.

By modern convention Latin (unlike English) does not use capital letters to begin a sentence or direct speech. Capital letters are therefore only used for proper nouns or adjectives, e.g. *Iuppiter* (Jupiter) or *Romanus* (Roman).

Most modern texts print capital *u* as U, though in some older texts and many carved inscriptions you will see capital *u* written as V (e.g. *SERVVS*).

PUNCTUATION

Classical Roman authors made limited use of punctuation. Words or phrases were sometimes separated by a *punctum* (point), hence the English term *punctuation*. Paragraph breaks were also sometimes made. Some later Roman writers used a wider range of punctuation marks, including the comma, though many texts were written with no punctuation at all. Modern versions of Latin texts are, however, printed with the same range of punctuation marks that English uses.

PRONUNCIATION

This is an issue that has been much debated. Both during and after the Roman Empire fashions changed over time and different pronunciations were used in different places. It is best not to complicate matters too much. Key points are as follows:

- Latin words are pronounced *phonetically* (as they are spelled) with every letter sounded. There are no silent letters. e.g. the word *nocte* (at night) is two syllables.
- One exception, however, is that certain pairs of consecutive vowels form *diphthongs*, which are single syllables and make single sounds. Common examples are -*ae*- (sounded like *eye*) and -*au*- (sounded like the *ou* in h<u>ou</u>se), e.g. the word *portae* (gates) is two syllables.
- In words of two syllables, the stress is normally on the first syllable.
- In words of three or more syllables, the stress is normally on either the penultimate (next to last) syllable or the one before that. This is normal in English too, so doesn't require much conscious thought.
- *c* and *g* are always hard in Latin (as in English *cat* and *get*).
- *i*, when being used as a consonant, sounds like an English *y*, as in *yet*. e.g. *ianua* (door) is pronounced '*yanua*'.
- Latin *v* (the consonant version of *u*) was pronounced *w* until the first century AD, when a *v* sound started to take over. So the word *servus* (slave), for example, would have been pronounced *ser-wus* in earlier times and *ser-vus* later on. Choose to pronounce *v* as a *w* or as a *v*, as you wish.
- The vowels are long in some places and short in others, but there are only a few places where this affects how a word should be translated, and we'll note them as we go along.

LATIN IN ENGLISH

The development of English has been heavily influenced by Latin. Almost 60 per cent of English words come from Latin, either directly or via French. About 25 per cent of English words have Germanic origins. The remaining English words come from many sources, including Greek.

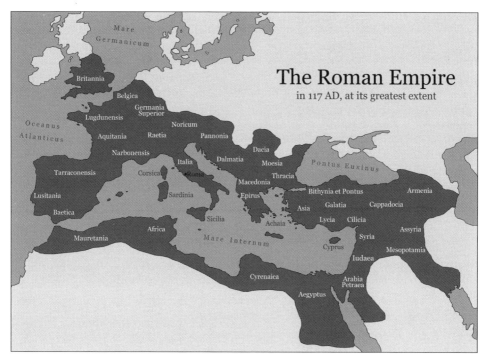

Figure 1.1 *The extent of Roman rule at the height of the Empire.*
Accessed via iStock, Copyright: PeterHermesFurian.

The high proportion of *Latinate* (Latin-derived) words in English means that Latin vocabulary comes much more naturally than you might expect, even when you are starting from scratch.

In order to demonstrate this, three lists of Latin words are below, arranged alphabetically. The first column contains words that English has taken directly from Latin; the second contains words that English has changed only slightly; the third contains Latin words that are the roots of many English words: i.e. we source, or *derive*, many English words (*derivatives*) from them. See how many you recognise or can guess the meanings of.

Directly used	Slight change	Root word (gives *derivatives*)
audio	ascendo	aqua
bonus	brevis	bene
consul	consumo	credo
data	defendo	dominus
ego	exspecto	equus
forum	flumen	femina
gladiator	gravis	gratus
honor (*USA*)	habito	hortus
index	invito	intellego
labor (*USA*)	legio	locus
minimum	maior	mater

Directly used	Slight change	Root word (gives *derivatives*)
nil	navigo	nox (noct-)
omnibus	offero	optimus
plus	praemium	pater
quasi	quantus	quaero
ratio	respondeo	rex (reg-)
senator	saluto	scribo (script-)
terminus	taberna	terra
ultra	ultimus	urbs
villa	validus	verbum

ABBREVIATIONS AND PHRASES

Many Latin phrases, often in abbreviated form, either are still in regular use in English or have become well-known sayings. Note the following:

e.g.	exempli gratia	for the sake of example
etc.	et cetera	and the other things
N.B.	Nota Bene	note well
i.e.	id est	that is [to say. . .]
p.s.	post scriptum	something written later
a.m.	ante meridiem	before midday
p.m.	post meridiem	after midday

Figure 1.2 *Drawing of a coin depicting Julius Caesar with the title* DICT[ATOR] PERPETUO, *issued after his assassination by the moneyer (mint director) Lucius Mussidius Longus.* (Photo by: Photo12/UIG via Getty Images)

veni, vidi, vici.	I came, I saw, I conquered.	(Julius Caesar, a general)
carpe diem.	Seize the day!	(Horace, a poet)
cogito ergo sum.	I think therefore I am.	(Descartes, a philosopher)

INFLECTION (1): WORD ORDER AND ENDINGS

Consider the following two English sentences:

1   The slave greets the woman.

2   The woman greets the slave.

The nouns in these examples swap roles between the two sentences: the *slave* is doing the action in (1), but on the receiving end in (2) – and *vice versa* for *woman*. The spelling of the nouns, though, remains the same. We can only work out the meaning of each sentence from the word order.

In English, the meaning is shown by the word order.

Latin works differently. Unlike English, most of the information about a word's role in a Latin sentence comes from looking at the word's ending. In Latin, the two sentences would be:

1   serv<u>us</u> femin<u>am</u> salutat.   The slave greets the woman.

2   femin<u>a</u> serv<u>um</u> salutat.   The woman greets the slave.

Note how the spelling of the nouns, *servus* (slave) and *femina* (woman), changes in the two sentences, depending on whether the nouns are doing the action (the *subject*) or suffering the action (the *object*).

In Latin, the verb (*salutat* in the above examples) tends to come at the end, but this pattern can be broken. In the Latin sentences above, it just so happens that the *subject* and the *object* come in the same order as in the English, but this doesn't always need to be the case. The first example could have been written in various ways:

servus feminam salutat.
feminam servus salutat.
salutat servus feminam.

These different versions emphasise different words by putting them first (e.g. if *feminam* comes first, the point is that it's the *woman* being greeted rather than anyone else). All the versions, however, essentially mean the same thing: *the slave greets the woman*. The word endings tell us who is doing what in the sentence. Whilst the Latin word order *can* sometimes resemble English word order, you cannot rely on this.

In Latin, the meaning is shown by the word endings.

These endings give the vital information required to translate the sentence correctly. They change depending on what is happening in the sentence. The process by which these endings change is called *inflection*. Latin relies upon this principle of inflection.

A noun's ending tells us:

- the noun's role in the sentence
- whether the noun is *singular* (i.e. just one) or *plural* (i.e. more than one).

A verb's ending tells us:

- who is doing the action of the verb
- when the action is happening.

INFLECTION (2): MODERN LANGUAGES

English has largely abandoned the principle of inflection. Word endings only change rarely. Here are a few examples where they still do:

- Plurals: English often adds -*s* or -*es*. Note exceptions like *children*, *mice*, *sheep*, *fish*, *women*.

- Pronouns: e.g.

I (subject)	*me* (object)	*mine* (possession)
he	*him*	*his*
she	*her*	*hers*
they	*them*	*theirs*
who	*whom*	*whose*

- Very irregular verbs, e.g. *to be*:

I		*am*	
you (*sg*)		*are*	
he/she/it		*is*	etc.

Other European languages, by contrast, have retained much more inflection.

- Consider a regular French verb, *aimer* (to like), whose endings change a lot:

j'aim<u>e</u>	*I like*	nous aim<u>ons</u>	*we like*
tu aim<u>es</u>	*you (sg) like*	vous aim<u>ez</u>	*you (pl) like*
il/elle aim<u>e</u>	*he/she likes*	ils/elles aim<u>ent</u>	*they like*

- The word for *the* has different forms in several modern European languages, whereas in English it stays the same:

French:	le / la / les
Spanish:	el / la / los / las
German:	der / die / das (and other forms)

VERBS: PERSON ENDINGS

As noted above, Latin verbs change their endings according to who is doing the action and when the action is happening.

This is different from English, which uses extra words before the verb to convey the information: pronouns (I, you, he, etc.) reveal who is doing the action and words like *will*, *was*, or *had* reveal when the action happens. Latin verb endings provide an efficient way of getting this information across; Latin often only needs one word where English needs two, three or even more.

The *person* is the grammatical name for the subject of the verb (i.e. who is doing the action).

The *person endings*, which appear in several different tenses and are therefore extremely important, are as follows:

sg	*1*	-o (*sometimes* -m)	I
	2	-s	you (*sg*)
	3	-t	he/she/it
pl	*1*	-mus	we
	2	-tis	you (*pl*)
	3	-nt	they

sg stands for *singular* and *pl* stands for *plural*.
1, *2* and *3* stand for *first person*, *second person* and *third person*.

There is a logic to the person order: the persons start with 'I' as the speaker and then refer to someone increasingly far away:

1st person	I myself *or* we ourselves
2nd person	someone I/we are talking to (i.e. you *sg* or *pl*)
3rd person	someone I/we are talking about (i.e. he, they)

A verb is often described as e.g. 'first person plural' (we) or 'third person singular' (he/she/it).

PRESENT TENSE: *porto*

A Latin verb attaches these person endings onto its stem, usually inserting a vowel between the stem and the person ending. The verb *porto* (carry) demonstrates one common pattern.

When new grammatical forms are met, hyphens will initially be used to show you where the stem (the part that stays the same) finishes and the ending begins.

carry

sg	1	port-o	I carry	*or*	I am carrying
	2	port-as	you (*sg*) carry		you (*sg*) are carrying
	3	port-at	he/she/it carries		he/she/it is carrying
pl	1	port-amus	we carry		we are carrying
	2	port-atis	you (*pl*) carry		you (*pl*) are carrying
	3	port-ant	they carry		they are carrying

- The whole verb is made up of the stem (*port-*), the letter -*a*- (in five bits out of six), and the person ending (-*o*, -*s*, -*t*, *etc.*).

- There used to be an -*a*- in the first person singular, too: the verb began as *portao*, but the -*a*- disappeared over time, leaving *porto*. Such changes are a common feature in the development of any language.

When you meet the verb, the stem *port-* tells you that someone is *carrying* something. You then need to look at the ending to work out who is doing the action:

          port-   carry
               -a<u>s</u>   you (*sg*)
so: portas =   you (*sg*) carry

          port-   carry
               -a<u>nt</u>   they
so: portant = they carry

Verbs like *porto* belong to the *first conjugation*. A *conjugation* is a family of verbs formed in the same way. The term comes from the Latin verb *coniugo* (I bind together, I yoke) and literally means the *binding together* of different verbs into a formal grouping. Latin has four conjugations; we shall meet the other three in Chapter 2.

Here are ten more verbs that go like *porto*:

ambulo	I walk
amo	I love, I like
clamo	I shout
laboro	I work, I toil
navigo	I sail
neco	I kill
paro	I prepare
pugno	I fight
saluto	I greet
voco	I call

Exercise 1.1

Give an English derivative (a word which uses the Latin) from:

1. navigo
2. clamo
3. laboro
4. ambulo
5. voco

Exercise 1.2

Translate into English:

1. salutatis
2. portamus
3. parant
4. necat
5. ambulas
6. voco
7. clamamus
8. navigant
9. laboratis
10. pugnat

Exercise 1.3

Change from singular to plural or vice versa, keeping the same person, then translate into English:

1. vocatis
2. laboramus
3. portat
4. navigo
5. amamus
6. necas
7. pugnatis
8. ambulant
9. saluto
10. paras

Exercise 1.4

Translate into Latin:

1. They greet.
2. We walk.
3. You (*sg*) are working.
4. We kill.
5. They are calling.
6. You (*pl*) carry.
7. She likes.
8. I prepare.
9. He shouts.
10. You (*sg*) sail.

NOUNS: DECLENSION, GENDER, CASE

Just as there are fixed patterns of verb endings (conjugations), so there are fixed patterns of noun endings, which we call *declensions*. Initially we shall meet nouns in the first and second declensions.

All Latin nouns have a *gender*, as in many modern European languages like French, Spanish or German. This isn't really a feature of modern English, though we might say, about a ship, that <u>she</u> *is sailing well*. The great majority of Latin nouns are either *masculine* or *feminine*, but some are *neuter* (literally 'neither').

Almost all nouns in the first declension are feminine.

Most nouns in the second declension are masculine, though some are neuter.

There are different endings for different noun cases. A *case* is the form of a noun that shows the job it does in the sentence. Initially we shall meet two cases:

nominative   used when the noun is the subject (doing the action).
The term *nominative* comes from the Latin verb *nomino* (I name): this is the case used to *name* the subject of the sentence.

accusative   used when the noun is the object (on the receiving end of the action).
The term *accusative* comes from the Latin verb *accuso* (I accuse): we can think of the accusative case being used when something is *accused* or targeted.

We say that nouns *decline* as they change their endings depending on case.

The term *decline* comes from the Latin *declino* (I bend away, I deviate): the nominative is envisaged as being the default case, with other cases *deviating* from this as the noun declines.

The term *case* comes from the Latin *casus* (a fall): the various other cases *fall away* from the nominative as the noun declines.

FIRST AND SECOND DECLENSION NOMINATIVE AND ACCUSATIVE SINGULAR

Here are the nominative and accusative singular of the first two declensions:

		1st declension	2nd declension
		girl	master
		f(eminine)	m(asculine)
sg	nom	puell-a	domin-us
	acc	puell-am	domin-um

- Note the distinctive -*m* ending in the accusative of both declensions.

Exercise 1.5

Identify the case of each noun, and translate into English:

1. puella laborat.
2. dominus clamat.
3. puellam voco.
4. dominum necatis.
5. dominus puellam salutat.

Exercise 1.6

Translate into Latin:

1. The girl is shouting.
2. You (*sg*) greet the girl.
3. The master is working.
4. We kill the master.
5. The girl calls the master.

'THE' OR 'A'?

Unlike modern European languages (and classical Greek), Latin has no word for 'the' (the *definite article*).

When you see a noun, you need to decide whether it is appropriate to translate it using *the*. It may be better to translate it using *a/an* (the *indefinite article*), or even to use no word at all. You can often work this out from the context. Sometimes several translations are equally valid. Use your judgement.

e.g.   puellam amo.
       I love the girl.   *or*   I love a girl.

Look again at the sentences in Exercise 1.5 (above). Are there any places where *a/an* could be used instead of *the*?

SUPPLYING A POSSESSIVE ADJECTIVE (*MY, YOUR*, ETC.)

Latin does have words for *my*, *your*, *our*, *his*, *her* and *their* (possessive adjectives); we shall meet these in later chapters.

Often however the possessive adjective is omitted if the identity of the possessor is clear enough from the context.

We can *supply* a possessive when we translate into English, inserting the correct adjective to fit the subject of the sentence. Use common sense.

   e.g. dominum amo.
        I like the master.   *or* I like *my* master.

        dominum amamus.
        We love the master.   *or* We love *our* master.

        puella dominum amat.
        The girl loves the master. *or* The girl loves *her* master.

WORD ORDER: HOW TO TACKLE A LATIN SENTENCE

In Latin, as you will have spotted, the verb tends to come at the end. The subject, if present, usually comes first. The object, if present, is normally sandwiched in between.

   e.g.   puella dominum amat.

   Word order: *subject – object – verb*

   literally: *The girl – the master – (she) loves.*
   so: The girl loves the master.

When translating look for things in this order: SUBJECT – VERB – OBJECT. Following this will help you to work out the grammatical 'shape' of the sentence. No matter how complicated the sentence seems, apply this order and it will become clearer.

There is usually a noun present in a sentence as the subject, in the nominative case. In this situation, the verb will naturally be third person.

   e.g. dominus puellam vocat.
        The master calls the girl.

If you cannot see a nominative noun at the start of the sentence:

1   Look to see if the nominative noun comes later on:

    e.g.   pugnat dominus.
                 The master is fighting.

Here the verb (*pugnat*) comes first, for emphasis.

2   If there is no nominative noun at all, the subject must be contained within
the verb, so start with that. You usually need to go to the end to find the
verb.

You cannot start translating a sentence with an accusative.

If the sentence starts with an accusative, you know that something must be
happening to that noun. In this situation, you need to look at the rest of the
sentence to work out what is going on.

    e.g.   dominum vocas.
          You (*sg*) call the master.

          puellam amo.
          I love the girl.

In these two examples there is no noun acting as the subject. The subject is
only revealed by the ending of the verb.

Exercise 1.7

Translate into English:

1. puellam vocamus.

2. puella dominum vocat.

3. ambulat dominus.

4. dominum puella necat.

5. dominus puellam portat.

REVISION CHECKPOINT

Make sure you know:

*   the present tense of *porto*
*   the meanings of the verbs listed on p9
*   the nominative and accusative singular of *puella* and *dominus*
*   the principles of Latin word order

Here are eight first declension nouns that go like *puella*:

ancilla	slave-girl, slave-woman
dea	goddess
epistula	letter
femina	woman
insula	island; block of flats*
pecunia	money
Roma	Rome
villa	house, country villa

* *insula* usually means *island*; the other meaning is not as odd as it seems, since a *block of flats* is thought of as being like an island within the sea of the city, with streets all around.

Exercise 1.8

Identify the case of:

1. feminam
2. pecunia
3. ancilla
4. Romam
5. deam

Exercise 1.9

Identify the case of each noun, and translate into English:

1. deam amo.
2. ancilla epistulam portat.
3. laborat ancilla.
4. puella insulam amat.
5. villam amamus.
6. femina ancillam vocat.
7. Romam amat dea.
8. feminam salutatis.
9. puella dominum necat.
10. pecuniam portant.

Exercise 1.10

Translate into Latin:

1. The woman greets the girl.
2. A slave-woman is shouting.
3. The master is carrying a letter.
4. We call the woman.
5. You (*pl*) carry the money.

Here are eight second declension nouns that go like *dominus*:

amicus	friend
cibus	food
deus	god
equus	horse
gladius	sword
hortus	garden
nuntius	messenger
servus	slave

Exercise 1.11

Give an English derivative from:

1. equus
2. insula
3. servus
4. hortus
5. villa
6. deus
7. dominus
8. gladius
9. femina
10. amicus

Exercise 1.12

Identify the case of:

1. deum
2. cibus
3. hortum
4. gladium
5. servus

Exercise 1.13

Identify the case of each noun, and translate into English:

1. servus nuntium necat.
2. deum amamus.
3. equus dominum portat.
4. hortum amant.
5. epistulam nuntius portat.
6. amicus feminam amat.
7. paras gladium.
8. dominus servum vocat.
9. servus cibum parat.
10. nuntius puellam salutat.

Exercise 1.14

Translate into Latin:

1. The slave is carrying food.
2. You (*pl*) greet your* friend.
3. The messenger is shouting.
4. The slave-girl carries the money.
5. I am calling the slave.

* Remember that no word for *your* is required here: see p13.

FIRST AND SECOND DECLENSION
NOMINATIVE AND ACCUSATIVE PLURAL

So far we have only met nouns in the *singular* (i.e. when there is just one of them). There are different forms for the *plural* (i.e. when there are two or more of them). The term *number* is used when talking about whether something is singular or plural.

Here are the nominative and accusative plural forms of the first two declensions. The singular forms are listed too, for revision:

		1st declension	*2nd declension*
		girl	master
		f	*m*
sg	nom	puell-a	domin-us
	acc	puell-am	domin-um
pl	nom	puell-ae	domin-i
	acc	puell-as	domin-os

- Note how the first declension keeps the *-a-* in all four bits.
- Note how the accusative plural ends in *-s* in both declensions.

Exercise 1.15

Identify the number (singular/plural) and case of:

1. hortos
2. insulae
3. deam
4. pecunia
5. equi
6. deos
7. villas
8. gladium
9. amicos
10. Roma

Exercise 1.16

Change from singular to plural or vice versa, keeping the same case. Then translate into English:

1. equos
2. femina
3. dominos
4. servus
5. ancillam
6. dei
7. deam
8. puellas
9. epistulae
10. nuntium

Exercise 1.17

Give the Latin (paying attention to the number of each noun) for:

1. house (*acc*)
2. slave-women (*nom*)
3. letters (*acc*)
4. food (*nom*)
5. goddesses (*nom*)
6. islands (*acc*)
7. messenger (*nom*)
8. friends (*nom*)
9. women (*acc*)
10. sword (*acc*)

Exercise 1.18

Translate into English:

1. servi cibum parant.
2. equi nuntios portant.
3. amicos salutamus.
4. dei Romam amant.
5. laborant ancillae.
6. dominos necamus.
7. nuntii epistulas portant.
8. servus gladios portat.
9. puellae pugnant.
10. hortos amatis.

Exercise 1.19

Translate into Latin:

1. I am carrying letters.
2. The friends kill the messengers.
3. You (*pl*) greet the women.
4. The slave-girls prepare the food.
5. The girls are shouting.

FIVE IMPORTANT WORDS

Here are two important conjunctions (joining words):

et	and
sed	but

Here are three important adverbs (words that describe or modify the verb):

non	not	(goes in front of the word which is being negated)
nunc	now	
semper	always	

nunc and *semper* often reinforce present tense verbs. When they are used it can be more natural to translate a present tense as (e.g.) *she is carrying* rather than *she carries*:

e.g.   servus nunc laborat.
       The slave *is* now *working*.   *or*   The slave now *works*.

       ancillae semper pugnant.
       The slave-girls *are* always *fighting*.   *or*   The slave-girls always *fight*.

Exercise 1.20

Translate into English:

1. villam et hortos amo.   *[handwritten: I love the house and the gardens]*
2. ancilla nunc laborat.   *[handwritten: The slave-girl now works]*
3. cibum semper paramus.   *[handwritten: We always prepare the food]*
4. nuntius ancillam amat sed ancilla nuntium non amat.
5. servus et ancilla semper laborant.*

* A combination of two or more singular subjects needs a plural verb.

Exercise 1.21

Translate into Latin:

1. The woman calls her* slaves and slave-girls.
2. You (*sg*) always prepare the food.
3. The master is now working.
4. We do not like the block of flats.
5. I love the girl but the girl loves the messenger.

* Remember that no word for *her* is required here: see p13.

REVISION CHECKPOINT

Make sure you know:

- the list of first declension nouns on p15
- the list of second declension nouns on p16
- the nominative and accusative plural of *puella* and *dominus*
- the new conjunctions and adverbs on p20

THE VERB *TO BE:* sum

In Latin, like in almost all modern European languages (including English), the verb *to be* is irregular. This is not surprising: the more often a word is used, the more likely it is that its form will be altered or corrupted when spoken or written.

Though irregular, this verb is so common that it will quickly become familiar. The present tense is:

		to be	
sg	*1*	sum	I am
	2	es	you (*sg*) are
	3	est	he/she/it is
pl	*1*	sumus	we are
	2	estis	you (*pl*) are
	3	sunt	they are

The Latin verb *sum* demonstrates clear similarities with the verb *to be* in French (*être*). This is unsurprising, given that French is a *Romance* language (i.e. it is a descendant of Latin).

Latin	French
sum	je suis
es	tu es
est	il/elle est
sumus	nous sommes
estis	vous êtes*
sunt	ils/elles sont

  * The circumflex (ê) indicates that an -s- has dropped out: it was originally *estes*, which bears an even closer resemblance to the Latin.

These similarities might help you recognise different bits of *sum* in Latin.

The verb *to be* is most commonly used to tell you what something is or what something is like (using an adjective – see Chapter 3).

When we are told what something is, the new noun goes into the nominative case and is called the *complement*. The nominative is used rather than the accusative because the verb *to be* is telling us more about the same person rather than describing something done to someone else.

  e.g.   nuntius sum.   I am a messenger.
          servi amici sunt.   The slaves are friends.

If *est* or *sunt* appear at the start of a sentence, it is often best to translate them not as *he/she/it is* or *they are* but *there is* or *there are*.

  e.g.   sunt dei.   There are gods (*or* the gods exist).

Exercise 1.22

Translate into English:

1. dominus sum; servi estis.
2. nuntius et servus amici sunt.
3. sunt dei, et dei Romam amant.
4. ancillae sumus; dominum non amamus.
5. puella ancilla est.

Exercise 1.23

Translate into Latin:

1. You (*sg*) are not a god.
2. The messenger is a slave.
3. The masters are friends.
4. There is a god.
5. The slave and the messenger are friends.

PREPOSITIONS (1): WITH THE ACCUSATIVE

Prepositions are words placed in front of nouns. They create phrases which provide more detail about the action happening in a sentence. They can tell you:

- location   e.g. in, on
- movement   e.g. to, from, into, out of
- a state or circumstance   e.g. with, without

All Latin prepositions require the noun to be in a particular case. Many prepositions take a noun in the accusative case. Five examples are:

ad	to, towards
circum	around
contra	against
in	into
per	through, along

Several of these express motion towards. This is a common role of the accusative – you might think of someone *targeting* a particular place (compare *I kick the ball* and *I walk to the station* as two different examples of a targeting action: both require an accusative noun). These prepositions focus the meaning that the accusative case already has.

e.g.   servi ad insulam navigant.
       The slaves sail to the island.

puella per villam ambulat.
The girl walks through the house.

Exercise 1.24

Translate into English:

1. per hortos ambulamus.
2. servi contra dominos semper pugnant.
3. amicus epistulam in villam portat.
4. ad insulas nunc navigamus.
5. nuntii circum insulam navigant.

Exercise 1.25

Translate into Latin:

1. The slave-women carry the money towards the house.
2. The girl is walking into the garden.
3. We do not fight against the gods.
4. I always sail around the islands.
5. The messenger and the master walk through the house.

Exercise 1.26

Translate into English. Unless a new subject is introduced, assume that the subject of the sentence is the same as the previous one:

1. ancillae sumus. semper laboramus. cibum paramus et epistulas portamus. dominum non amamus.
2. nuntius ad insulam navigat. epistulam portat. in villam ambulat. nuntium saluto. servos voco. servi cibum parant.
3. dominus servum non amat. servus contra dominum semper pugnat. dominus servum vocat. servus in villam ambulat. dominus servum necat.

REVISION CHECKPOINT

Make sure you know:

* the present tense of the verb *to be*
* how to translate prepositions that take the accusative case

SUMMARY OF CHAPTER ONE GRAMMAR

Nouns:

		1st declension	2nd declension
		girl	master
		f	*m*
sg	*nom*	puell-a	domin-us
	acc	puell-am	domin-um
pl	*nom*	puell-ae	domin-i
	acc	puell-as	domin-os

Verbs:

1st conjugation

carry

sg	*1*	port-o	I carry	*or*	I am carrying
	2	port-as	you (*sg*) carry		you (*sg*) are carrying
	3	port-at	he/she/it carries		he/she/it is carrying
pl	*1*	port-amus	we carry		we are carrying
	2	port-atis	you (*pl*) carry		you (*pl*) are carrying
	3	port-ant	they carry		they are carrying

to be (*irregular*)

sg	*1*	sum	I am
	2	es	you (*sg*) are
	3	est	he/she/it is
pl	*1*	sumus	we are
	2	estis	you (*pl*) are
	3	sunt	they are

Prepositions:

- precede nouns

- some take an accusative noun:

    ad, circum, contra, in, per

CHAPTER ONE VOCABULARY

ad (+ *acc*)	to, towards
ambulo	I walk
amicus	friend
amo	I love, I like
ancilla	slave-girl, slave-woman
cibus	food
circum (+ *acc*)	around
clamo	I shout
contra (+ *acc*)	against
dea	goddess
deus	god
dominus	master
epistula	letter
equus	horse
et	and
femina	woman
gladius	sword
hortus	garden
in (+ *acc*)	into, onto
insula	island; block of flats
laboro	I work, I toil
navigo	I sail
neco	I kill
non	not
nunc	now
nuntius	messenger
paro	I prepare
pecunia	money
per (+ *acc*)	through, along
porto	I carry
puella	girl
pugno	I fight
Roma	Rome
saluto	I greet
sed	but
semper	always
servus	slave
sum	I am
villa	house, country villa
voco	I call

40 words

Chapter Two

NOUNS: MORE CASES

Sentences would get rather boring if the only noun cases were nominative and accusative. In addition to these, there are three other main cases:

genitive	used to show possession	e.g. the house <u>of the girl</u>
dative	translated *to* or *for*	e.g. I give the book <u>to the master</u>
ablative	translated *by*, *with* or *from*	e.g. we fight <u>with swords</u>

We'll meet each of these in turn.

GENITIVE CASE

The *genitive* case is used to demonstrate possession. It is the possessor that goes into the genitive, not the thing they possess (e.g. in the phrase *the house of the master*, the *master* goes into the genitive).

The term *genitive* is linked to the word *genesis* (origin). You might think of things that are *owned* by somebody as (in a sense) *originating from* them.

Here are *puella* and *dominus* with the genitive added in:

		1st declension	2nd declension
		girl	master
		f	*m*
sg	*nom*	puell-a	domin-us
	acc	puell-am	domin-um
	gen	puell-ae	domin-i
pl	*nom*	puell-ae	domin-i
	acc	puell-as	domin-os
	gen	puell-arum	domin-orum

- In both *puella* and *dominus* the genitive singular and the nominative plural are identical. You need to work out which one you're dealing with from the context (what is happening in the rest of the sentence).

- Note how *puella* continues to use -a- in its endings.

- Note how the genitive plurals are very similar, but use a different vowel: -*arum* / -*orum*.

The genitive is translated into English using *of* or *'s* (*s'* for a plural).

> e.g.   villam amicorum amamus.
>   We like the house of the friends.
> *or*   We like the friends' house.

Remember that it is the possessor that goes into the genitive case, not the thing they possess (so, in the above example, *friends* is genitive).

The genitive noun tends to come immediately after the thing possessed: e.g. gladius domini (*the master's sword*).

Use any available clues to help you work out the number and case of a word with an ending that is *ambiguous* (could be more than one thing):

> e.g.   servus domini non laborat.
>   The slave of the master is not working.
> *or*   The master's slave is not working.

The verb *laborat* is singular, so you know that the subject of the sentence must be singular. The subject must be *servus*, so *domini* must be genitive singular (the other option, that *domini* is nominative plural, is impossible because it would need a plural verb).

When a noun is listed in a wordlist, the genitive singular (either in full or just the ending) is given too, as well as the gender. The declensions have different genitive endings, so you can work out which declension the noun belongs to (and therefore all the noun's endings):

> e.g.   puella -ae *f*   girl   genitive ending -*ae*, therefore 1st declension
>   dominus -i *m*   master   genitive ending -*i*, therefore 2nd declension

As you meet new items of vocabulary you will always be given enough information (e.g. the genitive of a noun) to enable you to work out what you are dealing with: e.g. a noun that goes like *puella*, or a verb that goes like *porto*, etc.

Exercise 2.1

Translate into English, identifying the genitive nouns:

1. servus domini semper laborat.
2. dominus insularum nunc es.
3. puellae equum nuntii amant.
4. contra amicos Romae non pugnamus.
5. ancilla gladios nuntiorum in hortum portat.

Exercise 2.2

Translate into Latin:

1. We greet the master of the house.
2. The slave-girl always carries the woman's letters.
3. You (*sg*) are carrying the girls' money.
4. The girl does not greet the slaves of the master.
5. I am calling the slaves' master.

DATIVE CASE

The *dative* case is used when a noun is the indirect object. The indirect object is a noun that is affected by the action of a sentence but is not the direct object of the verb:

e.g. I give the money (*direct object*) to the slave (*indirect object*).

In this example, *money* would be accusative (since it is on the receiving end of the verb) and *slave* would be dative.

The term *dative* comes from the Latin verb *do* (I give): one use of the dative is when one person *gives* a thing *to* someone else.

Here are *puella* and *dominus* with the dative added in:

		1st declension	*2nd declension*
		girl	master
		f	*m*
sg	*nom*	puell-a	domin-us
	acc	puell-am	domin-um
	gen	puell-ae	domin-i
	dat	puell-ae	domin-o
pl	*nom*	puell-ae	domin-i
	acc	puell-as	domin-os
	gen	puell-arum	domin-orum
	dat	puell-is	domin-is

- For *puella* the dative singular is identical to the genitive singular (and the nominative plural). You need to decide which one it is from the context.

- Note that the dative plural is the same for both *puella* and *dominus*.

- *dea* has an irregular form in the dative plural, *deabus*: this is to distinguish it from the dative plural of *deus* (*deis*).

The dative is usually translated with *to* or *for*.

    e.g. cibum domino paramus.
         We prepare the food for the master.

Note the new verb *do* (I give), which goes like *porto* (i.e. *do, das, dat, damus, datis, dant*).

    e.g. pecuniam domino damus.
         We give money to the master.

If in English you put the indirect object first, the word *to* is omitted:

      We give the master money (i.e. we give money to the master).

Exercise 2.3

Translate into English, identifying the dative nouns:

1. puella cibum feminae dat.
2. servi equum domino nunc parant.
3. ancilla epistulas servo dat.
4. equos nuntiis paramus.
5. feminae cibum deis et deabus dant.

Exercise 2.4

Translate into Latin:

1. I prepare swords for the messengers.
2. Masters do not prepare food for slaves.
3. The girl gives the woman a letter.
4. You (*pl*) always give food and money to the goddess.
5. We give the woman's money to the slaves.

ABLATIVE CASE

The remaining one of the five main cases is the *ablative*. This case has a range of uses and meanings.

If it appears by itself (without a preposition) it can mean *by*, *with* or *from*.

The term *ablative* comes from part of a Latin verb meaning *I take away*. This captures one important thing the ablative expresses: the idea of *separation*.

Here are *puella* and *dominus* with the ablative added in:

		1st declension girl *f*	*2nd declension* master *m*
sg	*nom*	puell-a	domin-us
	acc	puell-am	domin-um
	gen	puell-ae	domin-i
	dat	puell-ae	domin-o
	abl	puell-a (long *a*)	domin-o
pl	*nom*	puell-ae	domin-i
	acc	puell-as	domin-os
	gen	puell-arum	domin-orum
	dat	puell-is	domin-is
	abl	puell-is	domin-is

- The -*a* in the ablative singular of *puella* is pronounced long (whereas the -*a* in the nominative singular is short).
- Note that the dative and ablative singular of *dominus* are identical.
- The dative and ablative plural are the same for both *puella* and *dominus*.

In all instances where a word could be several different cases (e.g. *puellae* could be *gen sg*, *dat sg* or *nom pl*), judge which one it is from the context.

You will need to think carefully about which translation out of *by*, *with* or *from* is best when you see a word in the ablative.

> e.g.   servus nuntium gladio necat.
> The slave kills the messenger with a sword.

More commonly, however, an ablative noun does not appear by itself but instead follows a preposition that takes the ablative case.

PREPOSITIONS (2): WITH THE ABLATIVE

In Chapter One we met five prepositions that are followed by a noun in the accusative case: *ad, circum, contra, in, per*.

Prepositions can also be followed by the ablative case. Some important examples are:

a/ab*	from, away from
e/ex*	from, out of, out
cum	with (i.e. *accompanied by*)
in	in, on

> * *a* and *e* when the next word begins with a consonant.
> *ab* and *ex* when the next word begins with a vowel or *h*.

Once again, the prepositions often serve to reinforce or focus the meanings that the case already has. Two out of four of the prepositions listed above are to do with *going away* from a place: we saw above that *from* is one of the ablative's main meanings.

> e.g.   ancillae dominum e villa portant.
> The slave-girls carry the master out of the house.
>
> nuntius ab insula navigat.
> The messenger sails away from the island.

in can be followed by either the accusative or the ablative. There is an important difference in meaning:

> in + *acc* = in<u>to</u>   (motion towards)
> in + *abl* = in/on (staying put in a place)

> e.g.   dominus in hortum ambulat.
> The master walks into the garden.   (i.e. *he enters it*)

dominus in horto ambulat.
The master is walking in the garden.   (i.e. *he is strolling in it*)

cum means *with* in the sense of *accompanied by* (e.g. *a person*). To say *with* in the sense of *using a thing* the ablative is used by itself, without a preposition (we call this the *instrumental* use):

e.g.   cum puella ambulo.
       I walk with the girl.

       amicum gladio neco.
       I kill my friend with a sword.

Exercise 2.5

Identify the ablative nouns and translate the sentences into English:

1.   est nuntius in villa.
2.   puellae feminam gladiis necant.
3.   amicus ab insula nunc navigat.
4.   ex horto cum amicis ambulatis.
5.   servi dominum e villa portant.
6.   non sunt villae in insula.
7.   feminae in hortum cum puellis ambulant.
8.   dominus contra amicum gladio pugnat.
9.   in horto semper laboras.
10. puella a villa nunc ambulat.

Exercise 2.6

Translate into Latin:

1. There are messengers in the garden.
2. The slaves are preparing food with the slave-girls.
3. I walk into the garden with my friends.
4. We sail away from the island with our master.
5. The friends are now walking out of the house.

S&C

NOUN CASES: A SUMMARY

nominative   subject (doing the action)

accusative   direct object (on the receiving end of the action)
                      or used with specific prepositions

genitive   shows possession (*of* or *'s / s'*)

dative   indirect object (*to* or *for*)

ablative   *by*, *with* or *from*
                      or used with specific prepositions

REVISION CHECKPOINT

Make sure you know:
- the roles of the genitive, dative and ablative cases
- the endings of *puella* and *dominus* in all five cases, singular and plural
- how to translate prepositions that take the ablative

Exercise 2.7 (Revision)

Identify the number and case of the following:
1. pecunia (*two answers*)
2. amicos
3. dei (*two answers*)
4. gladiis (*two answers*)
5. puellarum
6. nuntio (*two answers*)
7. villae (*three answers*)
8. deam
9. hortorum
10. insulis (*two answers*)

Group

SECOND DECLENSION: *vir, puer, liber*

Most masculine nouns in the second declension go like *dominus*.

A few, however, such as *vir* (man), *puer* (boy) and *liber* (book) have a nominative singular ending in *-r*.

All their other endings are the same as those of *dominus*. In effect these nouns decline as if they had a nominative singular ending *-us*, which has disappeared.

Look at the tables below. Note how *puer* keeps the *-e-* in its stem in all cases, whereas *liber* drops the *-e-* from the accusative singular onwards, reflecting how the word would have been pronounced.

		vir *man*	puer *boy*	liber *book*
		m	*m*	*m*
sg	nom	vir	puer	liber
	acc	vir-um	puer-um	libr-um*
	gen	vir-i	puer-i	libr-i
	dat	vir-o	puer-o	libr-o
	abl	vir-o	puer-o	libr-o
pl	nom	vir-i	puer-i	libr-i
	acc	vir-os	puer-os	libr-os
	gen	vir-orum	puer-orum	libr-orum
	dat	vir-is	puer-is	libr-is
	abl	vir-is	puer-is	libr-is

* drops the *-e-* from its stem.

Note too another noun that goes like *liber* (dropping the *-e-* from the accusative singular onwards):

ager (*acc* agrum, *gen* agri, etc.)   field

Exercise 2.8

Identify the number and case of:

1. pueri (*two possible answers*)
2. librorum
3. puerum
4. agri (*two possible answers*)
5. viro (*two possible answers*)

Exercise 2.9

Translate into English:

1. pueri per agros cum nuntiis ambulant.
2. vir est dominus servorum.
3. femina libros pueris dat.
4. in agris cum servis semper laboro.
5. servus gladios virorum in hortum portat.

Exercise 2.10

Translate into Latin:

1. There are men in the house.
2. The slave-girls are preparing food for the men.
3. He is now working in the field with the boys.
4. I give the book to my friend.
5. We carry the boys' books into the house.

SECOND DECLENSION NEUTER

We have already met the concept of gender: the nouns we have met that go like *puella* are first declension feminine, and those that go like *dominus* (plus *vir, puer, liber* and *ager*) are second declension masculine.

In Latin there is a third gender, though it is rarer than the other two. This is called *neuter* (literally *neither* in Latin). Neuter nouns are *neither* masculine nor feminine. Neuter noun endings are a slightly modified version of the masculine endings.

There are no neuter nouns in the first declension, but plenty in the second. Because of the extensive overlap with the masculine endings there is not much new learning required.

Here is the second declension neuter noun *bellum* (war) in full. The three places where the endings differ from the masculine are underlined.

war

neuter (not masculine or feminine.)

sg	nom	bell-<u>um</u>	} same
	acc	bell-um	
	gen	bell-i	
	dat	bell-o	
	abl	bell-o	
pl	nom	bell-<u>a</u>	} same
	acc	bell-<u>a</u>	
	gen	bell-orum	
	dat	bell-is	
	abl	bell-is	

- Note that the nominative is the same as the accusative in both singular and plural. This is always true for neuter nouns.

- The neuter nominative and accusative plural end in -*a*. This too is always true for neuter nouns.

- The genitive, dative and ablative endings are the same as those of a masculine noun like *dominus*.

Here are six second declension neuter nouns that go like *bellum*:

auxilium	help
donum	gift
periculum	danger
templum	temple
verbum	word
vinum	wine

Note too a neuter second declension noun that goes like *bellum* but only exists in the plural:

arma	weapons

It is easy to confuse the nominative and accusative plural of second declension neuter nouns with the nominative or ablative singular of first declension nouns. Compare, for example:

ancilla	*nom* or *abl sg*	1st declension (feminine)
verba	*nom* or *acc pl*	2nd declension neuter

To avoid muddling these forms you need to learn each noun's declension (and gender).

Exercise 2.11

Give an English derivative from:
1. vinum
2. donum
3. auxilium
4. arma
5. verbum

Exercise 2.12

Identify the number and case of:
1. templa (*two answers*)
2. vino (*two answers*)
3. periculorum
4. armis (*two answers*)
5. auxilii

Exercise 2.13

Translate into English:
1. vinum in horto est.
2. viri arma in villam portant.
3. semper sunt bella in insula.
4. amici dominum e periculo portant.
5. dona deis damus, sed dei auxilium non dant.

Exercise 2.14

Translate into Latin:

1. I am walking to the temple of the goddess.
2. The slaves are preparing the wine in the garden.
3. The messenger is always giving gifts to the slave-girl.
4. We like the woman's words.
5. The boys are fighting with* the weapons.

* Remember that no word for *with* is needed here:
   with (accompanied by)   *cum* (+ *abl*)
   with (using a thing)   just use the ablative by itself

REVISION CHECKPOINT

Make sure you know:

* how *vir*, *puer*, *liber* and *ager* decline
* the endings of *bellum* and the list of neuter nouns on p37

Background: the Trojan War

The Romans borrowed most of their myths about gods and heroes from the Greeks. Even the part of their mythology that is distinctly *Roman* – the story of their founding hero Aeneas – begins with the Trojan War, the ten-year siege of Troy by the Greeks.

The legend of the Trojan War may have been loosely based on a real (but unidentified) historical war, perhaps over trade: Troy was strategically located at the mouth of the Hellespont, a narrow strait that gives access to the Black Sea from the Aegean Sea. The same region was fought over bloodily, for much the same strategic reasons, during the Gallipoli campaign during the First World War. The traditional date for the Trojan War is about 1200 BC. Archaeological evidence from the site of Troy (first excavated in the 1870s by the German Heinrich Schliemann) suggests that the city was indeed violently destroyed on several occasions. One of these may have given rise over time to the legend of the Trojan War. The war and the subsequent homeward journeys of its participants are narrated in the Greek epic poetry of Homer, a poet of unknown date (scholars cautiously suggest the late eighth century BC). Homer is credited with having composed two long works, the *Iliad* and the *Odyssey*.

The *Iliad* describes a period of several days in the final year of the war during which some key events occur. Agamemnon, the king of Argos and Mycenae, and in overall command of the Greek forces, falls out with the best Greek warrior, Achilles. Achilles withdraws from the fighting, and only re-enters the battle after the death of his best friend Patroclus at the hands of the Trojan prince Hector. Achilles then kills Hector, thus guaranteeing the eventual fall of Troy. The fall of Troy itself (including the famous story of the Wooden Horse) is not narrated in the *Iliad*, which also stops short of describing Achilles' own death, though both events are known to be inevitable.

The *Odyssey* describes the ten-year return journey of the Greek hero Odysseus to his home on the island of Ithaca in north-west Greece, where his wife Penelope and son Telemachus are fending off a crowd of suitors who are eager to marry Penelope and acquire power on the island. Odysseus, after encounters with gods, monsters and hostile cities, as well as a journey to the Underworld, finally returns home and kills the suitors, reclaiming his palace and his wife in one go.

The rest of this chapter includes short passages that describe several of the key events before and during the Trojan War.

All unfamiliar words are underlined, as are proper nouns when they first occur. Meanings are given in the wordlists that follow the paragraphs. In the wordlists, nouns that go like *puella*, *dominus* or *bellum* will be listed as below:

puella -ae *f*	girl
dominus -i *m*	master
bellum -i *n*	war

The details that follow the nominative singular are the genitive singular ending and the gender. Remember how the genitive ending shows the declension (*-ae* for 1st, *-i* for 2nd).

Once you know which declension a new noun belongs to you can work out the case and number of the noun as it appears in the passage.

To apply the ending given after the hyphen, remove the last syllable of the existing word (to get back to the stem) and attach the new ending: e.g. *puella; puell-; puellae.*

Note that Latin often breaks up direct speech by inserting a verb between the quoted words:

e.g.　dominus 'sunt pueri' clamat 'in horto.'
　　　The master shouts 'There are boys in the garden.'

Exercise 2.15

The birth of Paris

The king and queen of Troy receive an ominous prophecy about their unborn son but are thwarted in their desire to kill him when he is born.

Priamus rex Troiae est, Hecuba regina. dei somnium Hecubae dant. in somnio Hecuba facem parit. postridie Hecuba ad templum ambulat. in templo sacerdos 'somnium' inquit 'nuntius a deis est. puer tuus periculum portat. puer exitium Troiae est.'

	Priamus -i *m*	Priam
	rex	king (*nom sg*)
	Troia -ae *f*	Troy
	Hecuba -ae *f*	Hecuba
1	regina -ae *f*	queen
	somnium -i *n*	dream
	facem	torch, fire-brand (*acc sg*)
	parit	(she) gives birth to
	postridie	on the next day
2	sacerdos	priest (*nom sg*)
	inquit	(he) says (*usually interrupts quoted speech*)
	tuus	your (*nom sg*)
	exitium -i *n*	destruction, ruin

5 Hecuba puerum mox parit. Priamus servum vocat. Priamus puerum servo dat. 'puerum gladio neca!' inquit. servus puerum ad montem portat sed puerum non necat. puerum relinquit. sed ursa puerum nunc invenit. ursa puerum amat et curat. servus ad montem redit. puerum invenit. 'puer' clamat 'vivit! puer donum deorum est.' servus puerum ad villam in pera portat. servus 'puerum' inquit 'in
10 pera porto: puerum Paridem voco.' servus Paridem nunc curat.

	mox	soon
	neca	kill! (*an order*)
	montem	mountain (*acc sg*)
	relinquit	(he) abandons
7	ursa -ae *f*	bear
	invenit	(he/she) finds
	curo	I look after (*goes like* porto)
	redit	(he) returns
	vivit	(he) is alive
9	pera -ae *f*	backpack
	Paridem	Paris (*acc; believed to be derived from* pera)

SECOND CONJUGATION VERBS

So far we have only met verbs in the first conjugation. These verbs go like *porto* and feature an *-a-* as the characteristic vowel in their endings.

Now we shall meet the second, third and fourth conjugations.

All the conjugations use the same person endings (*-o, -s, -t, -mus, -tis, -nt*).

The major difference is that they use different characteristic vowels in these endings (compare French, which has *-er*, *-ir* and *-re* verbs; French inherited this system of different verb conjugations from Latin).

Verbs in the second conjugation use an *-e-* in their endings:

2nd conjugation
warn, advise

sg	1	mon-eo	I warn	*or*	I am warning
	2	mon-es	you (*sg*) warn		you (*sg*) are warning
	3	mon-et	*etc.*		*etc.*
pl	1	mon-emus			
	2	mon-etis			
	3	mon-ent			

- Note that *porto* originally started as *portao* in the first person singular and lost the *-a-* over time, whereas *moneo* has kept its characteristic *-e-* in the first person singular, rather than contracting to *mono*.

Here are five second conjugation verbs that go like *moneo*:

habeo	I have, I hold
sedeo	I sit
terreo	I frighten
timeo	I fear, I am afraid
video	I see

Exercise 2.16

Give an English derivative from:

1. sedeo
2. timeo
3. terreo
4. video
5. moneo

Exercise 2.17

Change from singular to plural or vice versa, keeping the same person, then translate into English:

1. timet
2. videmus
3. terretis
4. sedes
5. habent

Exercise 2.18

Translate into English:

1. pueri in agro cum puellis sedent.
2. villam in insula habemus.
3. ancilla equum domini timet.
4. verba domini puerum terrent.
5. nuntios <u>de</u> periculo monetis.

de (+ *abl*)   about (*also* from, down from)

Exercise 2.19

Translate into Latin:

1. I have the master's letter.
2. You (*pl*) do not fear the gods.
3. The messengers' swords frighten the woman.
4. We are sitting in the house with our friends.
5. You (*sg*) warn the girl about the boy.

THIRD CONJUGATION VERBS

Here is the present tense of *traho* (I drag), a verb in the third conjugation:

		3rd conjugation drag			
sg	1	trah-o	I drag,	*or*	I am dragging
	2	trah-is	you (*sg*) drag		you (*sg*) are dragging
	3	trah-it	*etc.*		*etc.*
pl	1	trah-imus			
	2	trah-itis			
	3	trah-unt			

- As you will realise from the above table, it is harder to identify a characteristic vowel for the third conjugation. We shall see later that in other parts of the third conjugation an -*e*- is used.

- Note that the third person plural is *trahunt* not, as you might expect from the other endings, *trahint*.

Here are five third conjugation verbs that go like *traho*:

bibo	I drink
duco	I lead
lego	I read; I choose
mitto	I send
scribo	I write

Exercise 2.20

Give an English derivative from:

1. duco
2. bibo
3. scribo
4. lego
5. mitto

Exercise 2.21

Change from singular to plural or vice versa, keeping the same person, then translate into English:

1. scribunt
2. mittis
3. trahimus
4. ducitis
5. legit

Exercise 2.22

Translate into English:

1. libros de deis semper scribis.
2. dominus epistulam legit et mittit.
3. feminae pueros e periculo ducunt.
4. auxilium ad insulam nunc mittimus.
5. viri vinum in <u>taberna</u> bibunt, pueri <u>aquam</u>.

taberna -ae *f*   inn, shop
aqua -ae *f*   water

Exercise 2.23

Translate into Latin:

1. The slaves are drinking wine in the fields.
2. We send a messenger to the temple.
3. The boys drag the horse out of the garden.
4. I am reading the girl's letter now.
5. The master sees the weapons and chooses a sword.

REVISION CHECKPOINT

Make sure you know:
- how to use the grammatical details given about a noun in a wordlist
- the endings of the second and third conjugations (*moneo* and *traho*)
- the new verbs listed on p42 and p44

Exercise 2.24

The Judgement of Paris

Figure 2.1 *An illustration from an edition of Homer's* Iliad, *showing the Judgement of Paris*. (Photo by Kean Collection/Archive Photos/Getty Images)

Paris, now an adult, is asked to judge a dispute between three goddesses. His decision has far-reaching consequences.

Paris cum servo <u>prope</u> <u>Troiam</u> nunc <u>habitat</u>. in agris semper laborat. <u>olim</u> deae <u>Minerva</u> et <u>Iuno</u> et <u>Venus</u> disputant.
deae ad Paridem <u>veniunt</u>. '<u>quis</u>' inquiunt 'est <u>pulcherrima</u>? <u>iudex</u> es.'

	Paris (*acc* Paridem)	Paris
	prope (+ *acc*)	near, near to
	Troia -ae *f*	Troy
	habito	I live (*goes like* porto)
1	olim	one day
	Minerva -ae *f*	Minerva (*goddess of wisdom*)
	Iuno *f*	Juno (*queen of the gods*)
	Venus (*acc* Venerem)	Venus (*goddess of love*)
	disputo	I argue (*goes like* porto)
3	veniunt	(they) come
	quis . . .?	who?
	inquiunt	(they) say (*usually interrupts quoted speech*)
	pulcherrima	the most beautiful
	iudex	judge (*nom*)

Minerva <u>sapientiam</u> <u>promittit</u>. Iuno pecuniam et <u>imperium</u> <u>promittit</u>. Venus
5 feminam <u>pulcherrimam</u> <u>promittit</u>. Paris Venerem legit. Venus Paridem ad
<u>Graeciam</u> ducit. in Graecia Paris <u>Helenam</u> videt. Helena femina <u>pulcherrima</u> est.
Paris Helenam amat et Helena Paridem amat. Paris Helenam e Graecia ducit.
<u>Troiam</u> navigant. <u>Graeci</u> <u>iratissimi</u> sunt et <u>Troiam</u> navigant. bellum <u>incipit</u>.

	sapientia -ae *f*	wisdom
	promitto	I promise (*goes like* traho)
	imperium -i *n*	power
	Graecia -ae *f*	Greece
6	Helena -ae *f*	Helen
	Troiam	to Troy
	Graeci -orum *m pl*	the Greeks
	iratissimi	very angry (*nom pl*)
	incipit	(it) begins

FOURTH CONJUGATION VERBS

Verbs in the fourth conjugation use an *-i-* in their endings:

4th conjugation
hear, listen to

sg	*1*	aud-io	I hear	*or*	I am hearing
	2	aud-is	you (*sg*) hear		you (*sg*) are hearing
	3	aud-it	*etc.*		*etc.*
pl	*1*	aud-imus			
	2	aud-itis			
	3	aud-iunt			

- Note that the third person plural keeps the *-i-*, so *they hear* is *audiunt*. Compare *trahunt* (they drag) in the third conjugation.

Here are five fourth conjugation verbs that go like *audio*:

custodio   I guard
dormio   I sleep
invenio   I find
punio   I punish
venio   I come

Exercise 2.25

Give an English derivative from:
1. dormio
2. audio
3. invenio
4. custodio
5. punio

Exercise 2.26

Change from singular to plural or vice versa, keeping the same person, then translate into English:
1. invenis
2. audit
3. custodimus
4. puniunt
5. venitis

Exercise 2.27

Translate into English:

1. nuntius puerum in horto invenit.
2. dei Romam nunc puniunt.
3. verba deorum audimus.
4. viri et feminae insulam armis custodiunt.
5. puella in villam venit. epistulam portat.

Exercise 2.28

Translate into Latin:

1. The girls are sleeping in the temple.
2. The boys are not listening to the slave.
3. The master comes into the house with the slave-girls.
4. We guard Rome with swords.
5. On the island the messenger finds a house.

THE INFINITIVE

The *infinitive* captures the basic meaning of a verb and is translated *to X* (to carry, to warn, etc.). It describes an action in a general (*non-finite*) sense, rather than dealing with a *finite* action done by a specific person on a specific occasion.

The infinitive is common and easy to spot since it has a distinctive *-re* ending. This is added to the stem and the characteristic vowel for the conjugation.

The infinitives for each conjugation are as follows:

1st	*2nd*	*3rd*	*4th*
port-are	mon-ere	trah-ere	aud-ire
to carry	*to warn*	*to drag*	*to hear*

- We noted that it is hard to pin down the characteristic vowel for the third conjugation. Here in the infinitive, and (as we shall see) in some other places, it uses *-e-*.

- Though the ending of the infinitive looks the same in the second and third conjugations (*-ere*), the pronunciation is different: in the second conjugation the first *e* of *-ere* is long, in the third it is short.

The infinitive of *sum* is *esse* (to be).

The infinitive follows some verbs naturally:

    e.g.   epistulam legere timeo.   I am afraid to read the letter.

             legere amo.   I like to read. *or* I like reading.

Note also an important second conjugation verb:

    iubeo   I order

This verb takes an accusative object (the person being ordered) and an infinitive (the action they are being ordered to do):

    e.g.   servos sedere iubemus.   We order the slaves to sit (down).

PRINCIPAL PARTS (1)

When a verb is listed in a vocabulary list or dictionary it is given with its *principal parts*.

    Principal parts are a way of plotting key information about a verb. There are four items altogether; we have now met the first two.

    The first principal part is the first person singular of the present tense, e.g. *porto*.

    The second principal part is the infinitive, e.g. *portare*.

    Sometimes only the ending is given for the infinitive, e.g. *porto -are*. This ending needs to be attached to the present stem.

    By looking at the first two principal parts you can work out which conjugation a verb belongs to:

	present tense ending	*infinitive ending*
1st	-o	-are
2nd	-eo	-ere
3rd	-o	-ere
4th	-io	-ire

- Note that if the present tense of a verb ends in -o, the verb could be either first or third conjugation; looking at the infinitive will tell you which it is (-*are* for first, -*ere* for third).

- Note too that -*ere* is the infinitive ending of both the second and the third conjugation, but a second conjugation verb is easily recognised by the distinctive -*eo* ending in the present tense.

When you meet a new verb in the wordlist below a passage, ensure that you take the time to look at the grammatical information and to work out which conjugation the verb belongs to (e.g. *sedeo -ere*: therefore 2nd conjugation).

When you know a verb's conjugation you can work out all its endings.

Exercise 2.29

Give the infinitive of (checking the conjugation of each verb):

1. habeo
2. voco
3. bibo
4. punio
5. saluto
6. mitto
7. invenio
8. terreo
9. duco
10. clamo

Exercise 2.30

Translate into English:

1. feminae ancillas in hortum venire iubent.
2. nuntii ad insulam navigare timent.
3. in horto cum amicis sedere amamus.
4. dominus servos cibum parare iubet.
5. libros legere et epistulas scribere amo.

Exercise 2.31

Translate into Latin:

1. The slaves like to drink wine.
2. The girl is afraid to walk into the temple.
3. I order the slave-girl to guard the money.
4. You (*pl*) like to walk through the fields.
5. We order the boys to carry the gift into the house.

S&C

TO, FROM, AND *IN* CITIES

We have seen how prepositions are used to describe motion to or away from places:

e.g. ad insulam   to the island   (motion to – accusative)
      a templo   away from the temple   (motion from – ablative)

When the name of a city is involved, no preposition is used. Instead, the name is used by itself in the appropriate case (accusative or ablative: i.e. the case that the preposition would have needed if one had been used).

e.g. Romam venio.   I come to Rome.   (using *acc*)
      Roma navigamus.   We sail from Rome.   (using *abl*)

A further surprising rule is that when an action happens *in* a city, you do not use the preposition *in* + *abl*, as you would expect. Instead, a special case is used. This is called the *locative*, because it *locates* the action (in Latin, *locus* = place). For now the only locative you need to recognise is that for Rome.

      Romae   in/at Rome

e.g. Romae cum amico sum.   I am in Rome with a friend.

• Often, as here, the locative is the same as the genitive: when translating you need to work out which it is from the context.

Exercise 2.32

Translate into English:

1. dominus amicos Romam venire iubet.
2. villam Romae habemus.
3. nuntii Roma ad insulas veniunt.
4. dei amicos Romae semper custodiunt.
5. Romae in taberna cum amicis sedere amo.

Exercise 2.33

Translate into Latin:

1. We are now sailing to Rome.
2. I do not have a house in Rome.
3. The gods are friends of Rome.
4. The horse carries the messenger away from Rome.
5. The master orders the slave to carry the letter to Rome.

> ## REVISION CHECKPOINT
>
> Make sure you know:
> - the endings of the fourth conjugation (*audio*)
> - the ending of the infinitive for each conjugation, and its use
> - how to recognise which conjugation a verb is by looking at the present tense and the infinitive (the principal parts)
> - that phrases involving *motion to/from* or *location in* cities do not use prepositions

Romam = to Rome

Roma = from Rome

Romae = in/at Rome

Exercise 2.34

The wrath of Achilles and the deaths of heroes

A quarrel between the Greeks about a girl has far-reaching consequences.

Graeci et Troiani decem annos pugnant. olim templum capiunt. in templo puellam inveniunt. Graeci puellam ad Agamemnonem trahunt, sed dei pestilentiam ad Graecos mittunt. Graeci deos timent et iubent Agamemnonem puellam Troianis dare. Agamemnon puellam ad Troianos mittit, sed puellam
5   Achillis nunc capit. Achilles iratus est et pugnare cum Troianis non iam vult. Graeci et Troiani pugnant sed Achilles in casa sedet.

	Graeci -orum *m pl*	the Greeks
	Troiani -orum *m pl*	the Trojans
	decem annos	for ten years
	olim	one day
1	capiunt	(they) capture, take
	Agamemnon (*acc* -onem)	Agamemnon (*leader of the Greeks*)
	pestilentia -ae *f*	plague
	Achilles (*gen* -is)	Achilles (*the best Greek warrior*)
	capit	(he) takes
5	iratus	angry (*nom sg*)
	non iam	no longer
	vult	(he) wants
	casa -ae *f*	hut

sed <u>Patroclus</u>, amicus Achillis, pugnare <u>vult</u>. Achilles Patroclum de periculo
monet sed Patroclus verba Achillis non audit. Patroclus et <u>Hector</u> pugnant.
Hector <u>dux</u> Troianorum est. Patroclus arma Achillis habet, sed Hector auxilio
10   deorum Patroclum necat. Achilles audit et <u>lacrimat</u>. amicos <u>iterum</u> pugnare
iubet. Hectorem punire nunc <u>vult</u>. Hector timet et circum <u>muros</u> <u>Troiae</u> <u>fugit</u>,
sed Achilles auxilio deae <u>Minervae</u> Hectorem necat. Hectorem circum <u>muros</u>
et ad <u>castra</u> Graecorum trahit.

	Patroclus -i *m*	Patroclus
	Hector (*acc* -orem)	Hector
	dux	leader
	lacrimo -are	I cry
10	iterum	again
	murus -i *m*	wall
	Troia -ae *f*	Troy
	fugit	(he) flees
	Minerva -ae *f*	Minerva (*goddess of wisdom*)
13	castra -orum *n pl*	camp (*sg meaning but only found in pl form*)

TIME EXPRESSIONS (1): 'TIME HOW LONG'

To say how long an action goes on for, a time expression in the accusative case is
used.
    Two new words are now required:

annus -i *m*   year
hora -ae *f*   hour

These words give many derivatives: *annual, annually, anniversary* (and French *an*, or
Spanish *año*); the word *hour* itself (and French *heure*, or Spanish *hora*).
    A word for a period of time (e.g. hours, years) is naturally accompanied by a
number. Here are two:

quinque   five
decem   ten

These two words do not change their endings (they are *indeclinable*).

    e.g.   puellae quinque horas dormiunt.
           The girls sleep for five hours.

           dominus decem annos navigat.
           The master sails for ten years.

The preposition *per* (through) can be used about time, as well as space. It has the
sense of *for the whole time* and is used for extra emphasis.

    e.g.   puellae per quinque horas dormiunt.
    lit   The girls sleep through five hours (i.e. for five whole hours).

Exercise 2.35

Translate into English:

1. contra Romam decem annos pugnamus.
2. puer quinque horas in agro dormit.
3. femina quinque epistulas Romam mittit.
4. amici vinum in taberna per decem horas bibunt.
5. dominus Romae quinque annos laborat.

Exercise 2.36

The Trojan Horse and the fall of Troy

After ten years of fighting the Greeks capture Troy by ingenious means.

Hector <u>mortuus</u> est sed <u>Graeci</u> <u>victoriam</u> non habent. <u>Ulixes</u>, <u>callidissimus</u> vir, <u>consilium capit</u>. iubet Graecos equum <u>ligneum</u> <u>aedificare</u> et <u>Troia</u> navigare. Graeci equum <u>aedificant</u>; Troia navigant. <u>Troiani</u> 'Graeci' inquiunt 'nunc <u>fugiunt</u>. equus donum deis est. <u>victoriam</u> habemus.' Troiani equum in muros Troiae
5 trahunt. vinum bibunt et <u>gratias</u> deis <u>agunt</u>.

	Hector	Hector (*nom*)
	mortuus	dead (*nom sg*)
	Graeci-orum *m pl*	the Greeks
	victoria -ae *f*	victory
1	Ulixes	Ulysses (*nom*; *Latin name for Odysseus*)
	callidissimus	very clever, very cunning (*nom sg*)
	consilium capit	(he) makes a plan
	ligneum	wooden (*acc sg*)
	aedifico -are	I build
2	Troia -ae *f*	Troy
	Troiani -orum *m pl*	the Trojans
	fugiunt	(they) flee
	gratias ago -ere	I give thanks to (+ *dat*)

sed sunt Graeci in equo! <u>media nocte</u> <u>dum</u> Troiani dormiunt Graeci de equo <u>descendunt</u> et <u>portas</u> <u>aperiunt</u>. <u>ceteri</u> Graeci Troiam navigant et per <u>portas</u> veniunt. est <u>caedes</u>. Graeci <u>victoriam</u> habent. <u>plurimos</u> Troianos necant sed <u>unus</u> vir, <u>Aeneas</u>, cum <u>familia</u> et <u>simulacris</u> deorum Troia <u>effugit</u>.

	media nocte	in the middle of the night
	dum	while
	descendo -ere	I descend, come down
	porta -ae *f*	gate
7	aperio -ire	I open
	ceteri	the other, the rest of (*nom pl*)
	caedes	slaughter (*nom sg*)
	plurimos	very many (*acc pl*)
	unus	one (*nom*)
9	Aeneas	Aeneas (*nom*)
	familia -ae *f*	family
	simulacrum -i *n*	holy image, statue
	effugit	(he) escapes

THE WOODEN HORSE OF TROY

Figure 2.2 *Engraving depicting the Trojan Horse.* (Photo by Kean Collection/Archive Photos/Getty Images)

SUMMARY OF CHAPTER TWO GRAMMAR

First and second declension noun endings:

		1f	2m	2n
sg	nom	-a	-us (or -r)	-um
	acc	-am	-um	-um
	gen	-ae	-i	-i
	dat	-ae	-o	-o
	abl	-a	-o	-o
pl	nom	-ae	-i	-a
	acc	-as	-os	-a
	gen	-arum	-orum	-orum
	dat	-is	-is	-is
	abl	-is	-is	-is

Present tense verb endings:

conj		1st	2nd	3rd	4th	
sg	1	-o	-eo	-o	-io	
	2	-as	-es	-is	-is	
	3	-at	-et	-it	-it	
pl	1	-amus	-emus	-imus	-imus	
	2	-atis	-etis	-itis	-itis	
	3	-ant	-ent	-unt	-iunt	
infinitive		-are	-ere	-ere	-ire	esse = to be

- *principal parts* = present tense, then infinitive: e.g. *porto -are*
- look at the principal parts to help work out the conjugation of a verb

Prepositions:

- *+ acc*:   ad, circum, contra, in, per
- *+ abl*:   a/ab, cum, de, e/ex, in
- no prepositions used with names of cities; N.B. *Romae* = in/at Rome

'Time how long' phrases: use *acc* case e.g. *quinque horas* = for five hours

CHAPTER TWO VOCABULARY

From now on the chapter vocabulary lists will give grammatical details:

- for verbs, the infinitive ending, which can help to show the conjugation
- for nouns, the genitive ending to show the declension, and the gender
- prepositions are listed with the noun case they take

• a/ab (+ *abl*)	from, away from
ager agri *m*	field
annus -i *m*	year
aqua -ae *f*	water
arma -orum *n pl*	weapons
audio -ire	I hear, I listen to
auxilium -i *n*	help
bellum -i *n*	war
bibo -ere	I drink
cum (+ *abl*)	with
custodio -ire	I guard
de (+ *abl*)	about, from, down from
decem	ten
do dare	I give
donum -i *n*	gift, present
dormio -ire	I sleep
duco -ere	I lead, I take
e/ex (+ *abl*)	from, out of, out
• habeo -ere	I have, I hold
hora -ae *f*	hour
in (+ *abl*)	in, on
inquit *pl* inquiunt	he/she says, *pl* they say (*usually interrupts quoted speech*)
invenio -ire	I find
iubeo -ere	I order
lego -ere	I read; I choose
liber libri *m*	book
mitto -ere	I send
moneo -ere	I warn, I advise
murus -i *m*	wall
periculum -i *n*	danger
puer pueri *m*	boy
punio -ire	I punish
quinque	five
scribo -ere	I write
sedeo -ere	I sit
taberna -ae *f*	shop, inn

templum -i *n*	temple
terreo -ere	I frighten
timeo -ere	I fear, I am afraid
traho -ere	I drag
venio -ire	I come
verbum -i *n*	word
video -ere	I see
vinum -i *n*	wine
vir viri *m*	man, male

45 words

Chapter Three

VERBS: IMPERFECT TENSE

All the verbs we have met so far have been in the present tense, i.e. the action is described as if it is happening now. More usually, however, a story is set in the past.

To describe an action that happened in the past, and over a period of time, the *imperfect* tense is used.

The imperfect tense has the basic meaning *was/were X-ing*.

e.g.   I was carrying the food into the garden.

The term *imperfect* comes from the Latin *imperfectus*, which literally means *unfinished* (as opposed to the normal modern sense of *imperfect* as *faulty*): an action *was* happening, but it was interrupted, and so unfinished (as in *I was writing the letter when . . .*). The imperfect is often used to give background to a story.

The imperfect tense has its own set of endings. It uses a distinctive syllable *-ba-* onto which are attached the basic person endings we met in Chapter One (underlined in the list below):

sg	*1*	-ba<u>m</u>	I was X-ing
	2	-ba<u>s</u>	you (*sg*) were X-ing
	3	-ba<u>t</u>	he/she/it was X-ing
pl	*1*	-ba<u>mus</u>	we were X-ing
	2	-ba<u>tis</u>	you (*pl*) were X-ing
	3	-ba<u>nt</u>	they were X-ing

- In this instance, the first person singular uses *m* rather than *o* as the basic person ending.

These endings are attached to the verb stem, with the characteristic vowel(s) for the conjugation inserted in between (here the 4th conjugation uses *-ie-*, not just *-i-* as it does in the present tense and the infinitive):

conj		1st	2nd	3rd	4th
		porto	moneo	traho	audio
infinitive		portare	monere	trahere	audire
		carry	warn	drag	hear
sg	1	porta-bam	mone-bam	trahe-bam	audie-bam
	2	porta-bas	mone-bas	trahe-bas	audie-bas
	3	porta-bat	mone-bat	trahe-bat	audie-bat
pl	1	porta-bamus	mone-bamus	trahe-bamus	audie-bamus
	2	porta-batis	mone-batis	trahe-batis	audie-batis
	3	porta-bant	mone-bant	trahe-bant	audie-bant

Exercise 3.1

Translate into English:

1. iubebamus
2. salutabam
3. mittebatis
4. veniebat
5. scribebas
6. dabant
7. puniebam
8. bibebamus
9. clamabas
10. terrebat

Exercise 3.2

Convert these verbs from present tense to imperfect (checking the conjugation as necessary), then translate into English:

1. dormit
2. moneo
3. vocas
4. ducimus
5. custoditis
6. timemus
7. inveniunt
8. sedet
9. laboratis
10. habent

Exercise 3.3

Translate into Latin (checking the conjugation as necessary):

1. I was fighting.
2. We were hearing.
3. She was writing.
4. They were greeting.
5. You (*sg*) were walking.
6. She was giving.
7. I was drinking.
8. He was punishing.
9. We were preparing.
10. You (*pl*) were reading.

Exercise 3.4

Translate into English:

1. viri equum ex horto trahebant.
2. ancilla amicos per agros ducebat.
3. dei et deae pugnabant.
4. amicos de periculis belli monebatis.
5. pueri in templo dormiebant.
6. femina iubebat ancillas in horto laborare.
7. pecuniam gladiis custodiebamus.
8. puella equos timebat.
9. nuntii in templo deae sedebant.
10. librum de bello scribebam.

TRANSLATING THE IMPERFECT TENSE

As well as the basic meaning *was/were*, the imperfect tense can be translated with a simple past tense (*I X-ed*) or with *used to*.

Some verbs, e.g. *habeo* or *amo*, sound very odd if they are translated with *was* or *were* when they occur in the imperfect tense. Often they are best translated with the simple past tense. This can still convey the sense of an ongoing action:

e.g. villam Romae habebam.   equum amabam.
I had a house in Rome.   I loved my horse.

The translation *used to* often introduces a contrast between the past and the present. Even if this contrast is not explicit, the translation *used to* suggests that something was once the case but no longer is.

e.g. cibum parabam; nunc epistulas domini scribo.
I used to prepare the food; now I write the master's letters.

Romae cum amicis in taberna semper sedebam.
In Rome I always used to sit in the inn with my friends.
(i.e. this is no longer the case)

An imperfect tense verb is often accompanied by a *time how long* expression, telling us the duration of the action.

e.g. quinque annos Romae laborabamus.
We were working in Rome for five years.
or We worked in Rome for five years.

Exercise 3.5

Translate into English:

1. decem annos villam Romae habebamus.

2. vinum semper bibebam; nunc aquam bibo.

3. quinque horas in agro sedebamus.

4. dominus dona servis dabat; nunc servos semper punit.

5. equum quinque annos habebam.

Exercise 3.6

Translate into Latin:

1. The master was sleeping in the house.

2. Men were walking to the walls of the temple.

3. We were dragging our friend out of the inn.

4. I used to sail to the islands.

5. You (*sg*) had a shop in Rome for ten years.

S&C

IMPERFECT TENSE OF *sum*

The imperfect tense of *sum* (I am) is listed below. *sum* is much more regular in the imperfect than it is in the present. The endings echo (and rhyme with) the *-bam*, *-bas*, *-bat* . . . of the usual imperfect endings, but lack the *-ba-* that other verbs have in this tense.

imperfect of sum

sg	1	eram	I was	or	I used to be
	2	eras	you (sg) were		etc.
	3	erat	he/she/it was		
pl	1	eramus	we were		
	2	eratis	you (pl) were		
	3	erant	they were		

Exercise 3.7

Translate into English:

1. servi eramus sed <u>liberti</u> nunc sumus.
2. pueri amici erant.
3. ancilla decem annos eras et nunc <u>domina</u> es.
4. erant in horto quinque nuntii.
5. puella in templo erat.

libertus -i *m*	freedman, ex-slave*
domina -ae *f*	mistress

* Slaves could be freed by their masters in return for loyal service in a process known as *manumission*. Freedmen were allowed to become citizens, hold property and vote. Many went on to become successful and wealthy.

Exercise 3.8

Translate into Latin:

1. The girls were not in danger.
2. The freedman and the master were friends.
3. We were on the island for ten hours.
4. You (*pl*) used to be friends but now you always fight.
5. In Rome I was a slave in the temple.

THE VERB *I CAN*: *possum*

possum (I can, I am able) is a *compound* (a combination of different words). Originally it consisted of the adjective *potis* (able, capable) and the verb *sum*, but the first half contracted over time, reflecting how the word was pronounced in practice, to leave the prefix *pot-*.

The present and imperfect tenses of *possum* are formed by sticking *pot-* onto the corresponding part of *sum*.

When the part of *sum* starts with an *s-* the prefix changes from *pot-* to *pos-*, so the final form is (e.g.) *possum* rather than *potsum*. This change happened over time, once again reflecting pronunciation (*-ts-* starts to sound like *-ss-*, which is easier to say). The places where this occurs are underlined below:

		present	*imperfect*
		I can, I am able	I could, I was able
sg	*1*	po<u>ss</u>um	pot-eram
	2	pot-es	pot-eras
	3	pot-est	pot-erat
pl	*1*	po<u>ss</u>umus	pot-eramus
	2	pot-estis	pot-eratis
	3	po<u>ss</u>unt	pot-erant

The infinitive of possum is *posse*, a compound of *pot-* and *esse* (the infinitive of *sum*). *possum* is naturally accompanied by an infinitive:

e.g.   dormire possum.
        I am able to sleep.   *or*   I can sleep.*

        domina servum invenire non poterat.
        The mistress could not find the slave.

* Note how the infinitive is translated differently depending on whether you translate *possum* as *I am able (to X)* or *I can (X)*.

The verb *possum*, and different parts of it, give many derivatives in English: *(im)possible, potential, potent,* and ultimately (via French) *power*.

Exercise 3.9

Change from singular to plural or vice versa, keeping the same person and tense, then translate into English:

1. possumus
2. potes
3. poteratis
4. potest
5. poteram

Exercise 3.10

Translate into English:

1. nunc dormire potestis.
2. feminae dona invenire non poterant.
3. in templo verba deorum audire possumus.
4. amici ad insulam navigare non possunt.
5. servus epistulam legere non poterat.

Exercise 3.11

Translate into Latin:

1. We are able to guard the temple.
2. I cannot hear the messenger.
3. I was not able to drink the wine.
4. The slaves could not carry the master.
5. The messenger can see the house of his friend.

REVISION CHECKPOINT

Make sure you know:

- how the imperfect tense is formed in all four conjugations
- the different translations of the imperfect: *was/were*, *used to* or a simple past tense
- the imperfect of *sum*
- the present and imperfect of *possum*

TEN NEW VERBS

Here are ten more verbs, listed with their infinitive endings and grouped according to conjugation:

1st   aedifico -are   I build
         festino -are   I hurry *to the festival*
         habito -are   I live *in a habitat*

2nd   debeo -ere   I ought, I should, I must, I owe (+ *infinitive*)* *debit card*
         maneo -ere   I remain, I stay

3rd   consumo -ere   I eat | *consume*
         curro -ere   I run – *courir*
         discedo -ere   I depart, I leave
         quaero -ere   I search for, I look for, I ask | | *query – ask*

4th   advenio -ire   I arrive – *advent*

* In a phrase involving *debeo* that is about the past, English uses a past tense infinitive e.g. *I ought to have stayed*. Latin works differently (and more logically), putting *debeo* into the past tense and continuing to use a present infinitive after it:

    e.g. manere debeo.
          I ought to stay.   *or*   I must/should stay.

          manere debebam.
    lit   I ought-ed to stay.
    i.e. I ought to have stayed.   *or*   I should have stayed.

Exercise 3.12

Give an English derivative from:

1. curro
2. habito
3. consumo
4. advenio
5. quaero

Exercise 3.13

State the conjugation of each verb and translate into English:

1. aedificamus
2. discedunt
3. debebamus
4. advenitis
5. quaeris

Exercise 3.14

Translate into Latin:

1. He remains.
2. I was living.
3. I used to have.
4. She runs.
5. We eat.

Exercise 3.15

Translate into English:

1. libertus ad* villam advenit.
2. pueri in templum festinare debent.
3. nuntii Roma nunc discedunt.
4. librum in horto quaerebas.
5. Romae quinque annos habitabam; in insula nunc habito.
6. verba nuntii audire debebatis.
7. amici domini cibum consumebant et vinum bibebant.
8. decem horas in taberna manebamus.
9. dominus villam in insula aedificabat.
10. servi per agros cum ancillis currunt.

* *ad* (+ *acc*) can also mean *at*

Exercise 3.16

Translate into Latin:

1. Men are arriving at the house.
2. The slaves were building the walls of the temple.
3. The women and girls are staying on the island.
4. We must run away from the danger.
5. You (*pl*) used to live in Rome in a block of flats.

Background: Aeneas and the origins of Rome

In Roman tradition, the fall of Troy (c.1200 BC) led to a quest by the Trojan hero Aeneas to find a new land for those who had survived the devastation. This new land turned out to be Italy. Virgil, a Roman epic poet writing during the time of the first Roman emperor, Augustus (ruled 31 BC – AD 14), narrates this quest in the *Aeneid* (the poem is named after its hero).

Aeneas endures both a troubled journey from Troy to Italy and a new war upon his arrival in Italy. The Roman *Aeneid* thus heavily alludes to the Greek *Odyssey* and *Iliad* (but in reverse order, in that the journeying 'Odyssean' section comes first and the warring 'Iliadic' section comes second). After surviving both his voyage and the conflict, Aeneas founds a new city, Lavinium, and establishes a new royal dynasty, which will go on to produce the twins Romulus and Remus. This pair famously quarrel, with Romulus triumphing and founding a new city named after himself – Rome (with a traditional foundation date of 753 BC).

Virgil's great challenge – and achievement – is to re-brand a defeated Trojan hero, Aeneas, as a glorious and virtuous founding father of the race that will, one day, be called Roman.

- From now on the following words will not be glossed: Aeneas -ae *m* (*acc* Aenean): Aeneas; Troia -ae *f*: Troy; Troiani -orum *m pl*: Trojans; Graeci -orum *m pl*: Greeks.

Figure 3.1 *The famous 'Prima Porta' statue of Augustus.* Braccio Nuovo, Vatican Museums, Rome. Statue of the emperor Augustus discovered in 1863 at the Villa of Livia in Rome. (Photo by Liszt Collection/Heritage Images/Getty Images)

Exercise 3.17

Aeneas and Creusa

Figure 3.2 *Denarius coin issued by Julius Caesar showing Aeneas carrying his father Anchises and the holy icons of Troy.* (Photo by DeAgostini/Getty Images)

Aeneas is fleeing from Troy with his father on his back and holding his son's hand. His wife Creusa is following on behind. Disaster suddenly strikes.

Aeneas et <u>familia</u> per <u>vias</u> Troiae currunt. periculum timent sed ad <u>portam</u>
adveniunt et in agros festinant. <u>ibi</u> <u>sistunt</u>. Aeneas <u>respicit</u>. <u>Creusam</u> non videt.
'Creusa! Creusa!' clamat. sed Creusam invenire non potest. Troiam <u>iterum</u> currit.
per <u>portam</u> festinat, per <u>vias</u> villas<u>que</u> Creusam quaerit. feminam videt. Aeneas
5   'Creusa,' clamat 'discedere nunc debemus! Graeci Troiam habent. manere non
possumus!'

	familia -ae *f*	family
	via -ae *f*	road, street
	porta -ae *f*	gate
	ibi	there
2	sisto -ere	I halt
	respicit	he looks back
	Creusa -ae *f*	Creusa
	iterum	again
	-que	and (*translate before word it is attached to*)*

sed femina non est Creusa: <u>umbra</u> Creusae est. <u>umbra</u> 'dei' inquit 'Creusam manere iubent. Graeci Creusam non habent: dei Creusam custodiunt. iubent Aenean <u>patriam</u> Troianis invenire. <u>consilium</u> habent; Aenean Troianos<u>que</u>
10 custodiunt. nunc <u>vale</u>!' <u>ter</u> Aeneas <u>umbram</u> <u>comprendit</u>; <u>ter</u> <u>umbra</u> <u>evanescit</u>. Aeneas <u>lacrimat</u>. Graecos nunc audit. ad <u>portam</u> festinat Troia<u>que</u> discedit. ad <u>familiam</u> amicos<u>que</u> currit.

	umbra -ae *f*	ghost, shade
	patria -ae *f*	country, homeland
	consilium -i *n*	plan
	vale!	goodbye!
10	ter	three times
	comprendo -ere	I grasp, I clutch at
	evanesco -ere	I vanish, I disappear
	lacrimo -are	I weep, I cry

*　Note this important idiom, and always translate *-que* <u>before</u> the word it is attached to: e.g. *man and woman* is *vir femina<u>que</u>* (or *vir et femina*).

ADJECTIVES (1): *laetus -a -um*

Adjectives are words used to describe nouns, with the term *adjective* deriving from the Latin verb *adicio* (I throw onto). We might think of an adjective *throwing* or attaching a characteristic *onto* a noun (e.g. the *big* house).

Like a noun, an adjective has different endings according to number and case, but whereas a noun has one fixed gender, an adjective has forms in all three genders, since it needs to be able to describe nouns of any gender.

One very common type of adjective uses the endings you have already met for the nouns *dominus*, *puella* and *bellum*, so there is no new learning to be done.

Here is *laetus* (happy). The conventional order when presenting the different genders is *m – f – n*.

happy

		m	*f*	*n*
sg	*nom*	laet-us	laet-a	laet-um
	acc	laet-um	laet-am	laet-um
	gen	laet-i	laet-ae	laet-i
	dat	laet-o	laet-ae	laet-o
	abl	laet-o	laet-a (long *a*)	laet-o
pl	*nom*	laet-i	laet-ae	laet-a
	acc	laet-os	laet-as	laet-a
	gen	laet-orum	laet-arum	laet-orum
	dat	laet-is	laet-is	laet-is
	abl	laet-is	laet-is	laet-is

Because the endings of *laetus* exactly match the endings of 2nd declension masculine, 1st declension feminine, and 2nd declension neuter nouns, this type of adjective is often called a *2-1-2* adjective. This is shorthand for *2m – 1f – 2n*. (Note how the order of presenting the genders overrides the declension order.)

When an adjective like *laetus* is given in a wordlist the masculine is written out in full, followed by the feminine and neuter, often in abbreviated form: e.g. *laetus -a -um*.

Here are nine more adjectives that decline like *laetus*:

bonus	good
iratus	angry
magnus	big, large, great
malus	bad, evil
multus	much, *pl* many
novus	new
parvus	small
Romanus	Roman
stultus	stupid, foolish

Exercise 3.18

Give an English derivative from:

1. multus
2. novus
3. bonus
4. magnus
5. iratus

Exercise 3.19

Identify the number, gender and case of:

1. mala (*four possible answers*)
2. stulti (*three possible answers*)
3. parvarum
4. Romanum (*three possible answers*)
5. laetis (*six possible answers*)

Exercise 3.20

Give the Latin for (noting the required number, gender and case):

1. new (*n gen sg*)
2. many (*f acc pl*)
3. angry (*f gen sg*)
4. large (*m dat pl*)
5. foolish (*n nom pl*)

USING ADJECTIVES (1)

An adjective must *agree* with the noun it describes in *number*, *gender* and *case*, i.e. if the noun is masculine nominative singular, any adjective describing it must also be masculine nominative singular, and so on.

Because *laetus* uses the same 2-1-2 endings as most of the nouns we have met there is often a convenient 'rhyme': e.g. *ancilla laeta*. This is not the same as *agreement*, though: e.g. *puer* and *bonus* agree, but do not 'rhyme'.

An adjective normally follows the noun it describes, but those concerning size or quantity (and *novus*, out of those we have met) usually come first.

Exercise 3.21

Identify the number, gender and case:

1. liberti irati (*two possible answers*)
2. puer laetus
3. magna templa (*two possible answers*)
4. vino bono (*two possible answers*)
5. novos gladios

Exercise 3.22

Give the Latin for (working out the required case if it is not indicated):

1. for the good friend
2. the small houses (*abl*)
3. many years (*acc*)
4. of the happy slaves
5. with much money

An adjective is used to give more information about a noun or to specify which noun is being talked about.

e.g. magnam villam aedificamus. servus stultus discedit.
  We are building a big house. The foolish slave departs.

An adjective can also be used with the verb *sum* to tell us what a noun is like.

e.g. servus stultus est.
  The slave is foolish.

If a masculine noun and a feminine noun are described by one adjective, the adjective needs to be masculine. This is true even if the masculine noun is heavily outnumbered (e.g. one man and fifty women still need a masculine adjective).

e.g. vir et femina laeti sunt.
  The man and the woman are happy.

Exercise 3.23

Translate into English:

1. taberna parva est et vinum malum est.
2. pecuniam nuntiis laetis damus.
3. ancillae novum consilium habent.
4. vinum Romanum amatis.
5. sunt multi dei et multae deae.
6. pueri et puellae stulti sunt.
7. servi muros magni templi aedificabant.
8. novus dominus multos annos servus erat.
9. vir iratus servum malum per hortum trahebat.
10. insula parva erat sed amicum invenire non poteramus.

USING ADJECTIVES (2)

Much less frequently an adjective can act as a noun. In this situation we often need to supply a word such as *man/men*, *woman/women*, *things* or *people* in our translation, depending on the number and gender of the adjective. Most of the time this sort of adjective appears in the plural.

e.g. dei malos puniunt.	The gods punish evil people.
in templo multa audio.	I hear many things in the temple.
stultus deos non timet.	The foolish man does not fear the gods.

Romanus often acts as a noun, normally in the plural:

Romani -orum *m pl*   the Romans

Note two subtly different uses of *multi* (many), the plural of *multus*:

e.g.   multi Romani in insula sunt.
        Many Romans are on the island.

        multi Romanorum servos habent.
        Many of the Romans have slaves.

The second example uses a genitive (*many of the Romans*). Although this sort of phrase is often simply a different way of saying (e.g.) *many Romans*, it can also be used to tell us what part of a certain group are doing something (e.g. *many of the slaves are fighting*). We call this use of the genitive the *partitive* because it tells us *what part* is involved. The partitive genitive is also used with *multum*, the neuter of *multus*:

e.g.	servus multum cibi domino dat.
lit	The slave gives much of food to the master.
i.e.	The slave gives much food (*or* a lot of food) to the master.

Exercise 3.25

Translate into English:

1. dei bona Romanis semper dant.
2. boni deos amant et timent.
3. femina multum pecuniae ancillis dat.
4. Romae multi in insulis habitabant.
5. multi servorum in horto nunc laborant.

REVISION CHECKPOINT

Make sure you know:

- the meanings of the new verbs on p68 and adjectives on p74
- how an adjective like *laetus* declines, and what we mean when we say that an adjective is '2-1-2'
- that an adjective must agree in three ways with a noun it describes: number, gender and case
- the different ways in which adjectives are used
- how to translate a phrase that uses a partitive genitive e.g. *multum cibi*

Exercise 3.26

The journey begins

Aeneas sets sail with the Trojan survivors in a bid to find a new home.

Aeneas Troianos <u>reliquos</u> <u>colligit</u>. 'Graeci' inquit 'Troiam nunc habent. discedere debemus. dei Troianos iubent novam patriam invenire.' Troiani verba Aeneae audiunt. viri feminaeque clamant; pueri puellaeque lacrimant. Aeneas Troianos Troia ducit. Troiani <u>naves</u> <u>celeriter</u> aedificant et ad <u>Thraciam</u> navigant.

5 in Thracia Aeneas novos muros aedificat. sed dei <u>augurium</u> malum mittunt: <u>sanguis</u> de <u>arboribus</u> <u>cadit</u> et Aeneas <u>vocem</u> amici <u>mortui</u>, <u>Polydori</u>, audit. Polydorus Aenean iubet a Thracia discedere. verba Polydori Aenean terrent. Aeneas Troianos ad naves <u>celeriter</u> ducit et amicos a Thracia navigare iubet.

ad parvam insulam, <u>Delon</u>, adveniunt. <u>duo</u> dei, <u>Apollo</u> <u>Dianaque</u>, in insula
10 habitant. in templo Aeneas dona deis dat et verba deorum audit. dei 'Troiani' inquiunt 'ad <u>matrem</u> <u>antiquam</u> navigare debent. <u>ibi</u> est nova patria.' pater Aeneae verba audit et '<u>Creta</u>' clamat '<u>mater</u> <u>antiqua</u> Troianorum est. consilium nunc habemus. ad Cretam navigare debemus.'

	reliquus -a -um	remaining, surviving
	colligo -ere	I collect, I gather together
	naves	ships (*acc pl*)
	celeriter	quickly
4	Thracia -ae *f*	Thrace (*region on north coast of Aegean Sea*)
	augurium -i *n*	omen
	sanguis	blood (*nom sg*)
	arboribus	trees (*abl pl*)
	cado -ere	I fall
6	vocem	voice (*acc sg*)
	mortuus -a -um	dead
	Polydorus -i *m*	Polydorus
	Delon	Delos (*acc; sacred island in Aegean Sea*)
	duo	two
9	Apollo	Apollo (*god of archery and the sun*)
	Diana	Diana (*goddess of hunting and the moon*)
	matrem	mother (*acc sg*)
	antiquus -a -um	ancient
	ibi	there
12	Creta -ae *f*	Crete (*large island in Aegean Sea*)
	mater	mother (*nom sg*)

GENDER AND DECLENSION

Gender and declension are not the same, although they demonstrate a broad overlap in the material we have covered so far.

Almost all nouns in the first declension (e.g. *puella*) are feminine. Most nouns in the second declension are masculine (e.g. *dominus*), but some are neuter (e.g. *bellum*).

There are, however, some exceptions.

A few first declension nouns decline like *puella* but are masculine. These are mainly words for roles or jobs that were thought of as male activities. The only one you need to know for GCSE is *nauta* (sailor).

Other first declension masculine nouns (not required for GCSE) include *agricola* (farmer), *poeta* (poet) and *scriba* (clerk, secretary).

There are also a few second declension nouns that decline like *dominus* but are feminine. Some of these are names of trees (e.g. ficus -i *f*, fig tree) or islands. None are required for GCSE.

Although the endings of *nauta* make the word *look* feminine, do not be fooled. Any adjective describing it needs to be masculine because it has to agree in respect of gender (as well as of number and case).

e.g.   nauta stultus est.
       The sailor is foolish.

       nautae laeti in taberna sunt.
       The happy sailors are in the inn.

Here the endings of the noun and the adjective agree but do not look alike (i.e. there is no convenient 'rhyme').

Note that when we talk about '2-1-2' adjectives such as *laetus -a -um* we are (for these purposes) talking about gender and declension as if they were equated: the different genders of such adjectives take their endings from the declension where most nouns are that gender: second for masculine and neuter, first for feminine.

ADJECTIVES (2): *miser* and *pulcher*

All the 2-1-2 adjectives we have met so far decline like *laetus -a -um*. A few 2-1-2 adjectives, however, have a masculine nominative singular that ends in *-er*. These then subdivide – exactly like the equivalent nouns *puer* and *liber* (see p35) – into those that keep the *-e-* and others that drop it.

One example is *miser* (miserable, wretched, sad). The whole adjective declines as if *-us* has disappeared from the masculine nominative singular. *miser* (like *puer*) keeps the *-e-* throughout.

miserable, wretched, sad

		m	*f*	*n*
sg	nom	miser	miser-a	miser-um
	acc	miser-um	miser-am	miser-um
		etc.	*etc.*	*etc.*

pulcher (beautiful, handsome) declines similarly but, like *liber*, it drops the *-e-* from its stem after the masculine nominative singular:

beautiful, handsome

		m	*f*	*n*
sg	nom	pulcher	pulchr-a*	pulchr-um*
	acc	pulchr-um*	pulchr-am	pulchr-um
		etc.	*etc.*	*etc.*

* drops the *-e-* after masculine nominative singular

When *miser* or *pulcher* appear in the masculine nominative singular, noun-adjective agreement will likely be 'non-rhyming': e.g. *dominus miser*.

Exercise 3.27

Translate into English:

1. dominus dona pulchra dominae semper dat.
2. nautae irati in templo pugnabant.
3. nauta miser vinum in taberna bibebat.
4. patriam pulchram habemus.
5. verba misera nuntiorum audiebamus.

Exercise 3.28

S&C

Translate into Latin:

1. The miserable friend was not eating his food.
2. Many of the Romans lived in beautiful villas.
3. The wretched girl was crying for five hours.
4. The happy sailors were sailing to Rome.
5. We love to give beautiful gifts to the gods.

Exercise 3.29

The Trojans depart from Crete

Aeneas leads the Trojans to Crete but soon learns that it is their destiny to settle elsewhere.

Troiani laeti ad <u>Cretam</u> nunc navigant. in Creta <u>forum</u> et templa et villas aedificant. sed dei novum malum Troianis dant: <u>pestilentiam</u> malam mittunt. <u>pestilentia</u> multos Troianorum necat. in <u>somnio</u> Aeneas deos Troianos videt et audit. dei 'ad <u>terram</u> <u>aliam</u>' inquiunt 'navigare debetis. in Creta manere non

	Creta -ae *f*	Crete (*island to the south of mainland Greece*)
	forum -i *f*	forum, marketplace
	pestilentia -ae *f*	plague, disease
	somnium -i *n*	dream
4	terra -ae *f*	land, country
	aliam	other (*f acc sg*)

5   potestis. Creta non est <u>mater</u> Troianorum. est <u>terra</u> bona <u>procul</u>, <u>Hesperia</u>.
     <u>antiqua</u>, <u>valida</u>, pulchra est. Hesperia <u>prima</u> patria Troianorum erat. nunc <u>nomen</u>
     <u>terrae</u> <u>Italia</u> est. Troianos ad Italiam ducere debes.' Aeneas <u>ubi</u> verba audit miser
     est. Troianos a Creta navigare iubet.

	mater	mother (*nom sg*)
	procul	far away, far off
	Hesperia -ae *f*	Hesperia
	antiquus -a -um	ancient
6	validus -a -um	powerful
	primus -a -um	first
	nomen	name (*nom sg*)
	Italia -ae *f*	Italy
	ubi	when

DIRECT COMMANDS: THE IMPERATIVE

The *imperative* is a form of the verb used when a direct command is being given. The
term *imperative* comes from the Latin verb *impero* (I order).

e.g.   *Give the book to the slave!*

The imperative is normally found in the second person (i.e. *you sg/pl*). It has its own
distinctive set of endings, as follows:

conj	*1st*	*2nd*	*3rd*	*4th*
	carry	warn	drag	hear
you (*sg*)	port-a	mon-e	trah-e	aud-i
you (*pl*)	port-ate	mon-ete	trah-ite	aud-ite

- In three of the four conjugations the singular imperative ends with the
  characteristic vowel for the conjugation; the plural then adds -*te*.
- Note how the third conjugation uses an -*e* in the singular imperative and an
  -*i*- in the plural. (Compare how four bits of its present tense have an -*i*-
  whereas its infinitive ends -*ere* and its imperfect features an -*e*-; compare e.g.
  trah<u>i</u>s, trah<u>e</u>re, trah<u>e</u>bam).

e.g.   porta cibum ad forum
       Carry the food to the marketplace!   (*to one person*)

       equum ex horto trahite!
       Drag the horse out of the garden!   (*to more than one person*)

An imperative often comes earlier in the sentence than a Latin verb normally does.
It is modern convention to use an exclamation mark in both Latin and English
(though this was not actually used by ancient authors).

Exercise 3.30

Translate into English:

1. quaere!
2. venite!
3. manete!
4. da!
5. aedificatis
6. aedificate!
7. sede!
8. bibite!
9. punis
10. puni!

Exercise 3.31

Translate into English:

1. in hortum ambula!
2. monete libertum de magno periculo!
3. Roma discedite!
4. iube servos stultos laborare!
5. custodite templum gladiis!

VOCATIVE CASE

The *vocative* case is used when someone is being directly addressed. The term *vocative* is derived from the verb *voco*: someone is being *called*.

   e.g.   Messengers are arriving, master!

The vocative is always identical to the nominative in the plural, and usually in the singular, too, so there is very little new learning to do.

The only place where the vocative is different from the nominative is the singular of the second declension masculine:

- Nouns and adjectives ending -*us* (e.g. *dominus* and *laetus*) have a vocative singular ending -*e* (e.g. *domine laete*). *deus* is an exception: the vocative is still *deus*.

- Nouns ending -*ius* (e.g. *nuntius*) have a vocative singular ending -*i* (e.g. *nunti bone*).

- But nouns and adjectives ending -*r* (e.g. *puer* and *miser*) have a vocative that is identical to the nominative.

The vocative is often found accompanying an imperative verb. The person who is being given the order goes into the vocative.

    e.g. bibe vinum, amice!
           Drink the wine, friend!

In prayers to gods and in other formal contexts the word *o* often precedes the vocative noun. This can be left out when translating into English:

    e.g. custodite Romam, o dei!
           Guard Rome, (o) gods!

Exercise 3.32

Translate into English, identifying the words in the vocative case:

1. audite verba laeta nuntii, puellae!
2. veni Romam, o domine bone!
3. domina, nuntius ad villam nunc advenit.
4. nova arma puero da, nunti!
5. patriam custodite, o Romani!

Exercise 3.33

Translate into Latin:

1. Master, I cannot find the letter.
2. There is a messenger in the house, mistress.
3. Stay in the garden, boy!
4. Gods, guard the temple!
5. Drink the wine and eat the food, sailors!

REVISION CHECKPOINT

Make sure you know:

- the difference between gender and declension
- the gender and declension of the noun *nauta*
- how the adjectives *miser* and *pulcher* decline
- the forms and the function of imperative verbs
- the forms and use of the vocative case (usually identical to the nominative apart from in the singular of the second declension masculine, e.g. *domine*)

Exercise 3.34

Two contrasting receptions

The Trojans encounter the savage Harpies, but their fortunes then improve.

Troiani ad parvam insulam adveniunt. in insula habitant <u>Harpyiae</u>. Harpyiae <u>monstra</u> sunt. feminae sunt sed <u>alas</u> et <u>ungulas</u> habent. Troiani <u>cenam</u> parant. cibum consumunt vinumque bibunt. sed Harpyiae <u>advolant</u> et cibum <u>rapiunt</u>. Troiani lacrimant timentque. Aeneas viros iubet <u>monstra</u> gladiis <u>oppugnare</u>.

5 <u>monstra</u> <u>fugiunt</u> sed <u>regina</u> Harpyiarum 'navigate' clamat 'ad <u>Italiam</u>, Troiani stulti! <u>famem</u> malam <u>ibi</u> invenite! lacrimate! <u>etiam</u> <u>mensas</u> consumite!' verba Aenean terrent; amicos miseros navigare iubet.

	Harpyiae -arum *f pl*	the Harpies
	monstrum -i *n*	monster
	ala -ae *f*	wing
	ungula -ae *f*	claw
2	cena -ae *f*	dinner, meal
	advolo -are	I fly up, I fly near
	rapiunt	(they) snatch
	oppugno -are	I attack
	fugiunt	(they) flee
5	regina -ae *f*	queen
	Italia -ae *f*	Italy
	famem	hunger (*f acc sg*)
	ibi	there
	etiam	even
6	mensa -ae *f*	table

ad <u>Epirum</u> adveniunt. in Epiro Aeneas <u>alios</u> Troianos invenit. <u>hi</u> Troiani <u>Novam</u>
<u>Troiam</u> aedificant. <u>Helenus</u>, amicus Aeneae, Novam Troiam <u>regit</u>. Helenus
10 Aenean in villam <u>invitat</u>. Aeneas cum Heleno <u>diu</u> laetus* manet.

	Epirus -i *m*	Epirus (*kingdom in northwest Greece*)
	alios	other (*m acc pl*)
	hi	these (*m nom pl*)
	Nova -ae Troia -ae *f*	New Troy
9	Helenus -i *m*	Helenus (*prince of Troy*)
	rego -ere	I rule
	invito -are	I invite
	diu	for a long time

* *laetus* is being used here as an adverb, *happily*. Other adjectives can also be used like
this, e.g. *puella per viam misera ambulat*. (The girl walks sadly along the road.)

TIME ADVERBS (1)

Time adverbs give important information about when or how quickly the action in
a sentence is happening. Here are five very common examples:

deinde	then, next
diu	for a long time
statim	at once, immediately
subito	suddenly
tandem	at last, finally

e.g.   pueri stulti tandem discedunt.
       The stupid boys are finally departing.

       nuntius periculum statim videt.
       The messenger sees the danger at once.

Take particular care to distinguish between *statim* and *subito*; confusing these is a
very common mistake at GCSE.

Exercise 3.35

Translate into English:

1. insulam diu oppugnabamus.

2. epistulam statim mitte, domina!

3. dominus verba feminarum audit. deinde servum vocat.

4. amicus nunc discedit; dormire tandem possum.

5. libertus subito equos audit. 'puellae,' inquit 'amici nunc adveniunt.'

Exercise 3.36

Translate into Latin:

1. The sailors were drinking wine for a long time.
2. Suddenly a slave-girl runs into the field.
3. Write the letter at once, boy!
4. At last I was able to read the book.
5. We listen to the words of the messenger. Then we call the girls.

Exercise 3.37

Scylla and Charybdis

Helenus warns Aeneas about two formidable obstacles that lie ahead.

Troiani cum <u>Heleno</u> diu manent sed discedere tandem debent. Aeneas amicique <u>naves</u> parant. deinde Helenus Aenean de periculis monet: 'amici, circum <u>Siciliam</u> navigate! <u>inter</u> Siciliam et <u>Italiam</u> sunt magna pericula. <u>dextra</u> est <u>Scylla</u>. Scylla <u>pistrix</u> est, <u>parte</u> femina, <u>parte</u> <u>lupus</u>, <u>parte</u> <u>delphinus</u>. nautas subito <u>capit</u> et
5   consumit. periculum <u>sinistrum</u> <u>Charybdis</u> est. Charybdis <u>vortex</u> est. <u>ter per diem</u> <u>naves</u> nautasque <u>sugit</u> et <u>delet</u>. non <u>tutum</u> est navigare <u>inter</u> Scyllam et Charybdem: navigate circum insulam!'

	Helenus -i *m*	Helenus (*ruler of New Troy, in Epirus*)
	naves	ships (*acc pl*)
	Sicilia -ae *f*	Sicily
	inter (+ *acc*)	between
3	Italia -ae *f*	Italy
	dextra *adv*	on the right
	Scylla -ae *f*	Scylla
	pistrix	sea-monster (*nom sg*)
	parte	in part, partly
4	lupus -i *m/f*	wolf
	delphinus -i *m/f*	dolphin
	capit	she seizes, she captures
	sinister -ra -rum	on the left (*adj*)
	Charybdis (*acc* -dem)	Charybdis
5	vortex	whirlpool (*nom sg*)
	ter per diem	three times per day
	sugo -ere	I suck down
	deleo -ere	I destroy
	tutus -a -um	safe

deinde Helenus Troianos iubet: 'deam <u>Iunonem</u> semper amate!' Aenean iubet: 'in
Italia, quaere <u>Sibyllam</u>, feminam <u>sacram</u>!' Troiani tandem discedunt. viri et
10 feminae lacrimant. Helenus dona Aeneae dat. deinde Troiani ad Italiam navigant.
Siciliam tandem vident; circum insulam navigant; Scyllam et Charybdem
<u>diligenter</u> <u>vitant</u>.

	Iunonem	Juno (*acc*) (*queen of gods, hostile to Trojans*)
	Sibylla -ae *f*	the Sibyl (*a prophetess*)
	sacer -ra -rum	sacred, holy
	diligenter	carefully
12	vito -are	I avoid

SUMMARY OF CHAPTER THREE GRAMMAR

Imperfect tense:

- translate as *I was X-ing, I used to X*, or simple past tense (*I X-ed*)
- endings: *-bam, -bas, -bat, -bamus, -batis, -bant*
- added to present stem plus characteristic vowel(s) for conjugation:

		1st	*2nd*	*3rd*	*4th*
sg	1	port<u>a</u>-bam	mon<u>e</u>-bam	trah<u>e</u>-bam	aud<u>ie</u>-bam
	2	port<u>a</u>-bas	mon<u>e</u>-bas	trah<u>e</u>-bas	aud<u>ie</u>-bas
		etc.	*etc.*	*etc.*	*etc.*

- for *sum*:   eram, eras, erat, eramus, eratis, erant

possum (I am able, I can):

- = *pot-* (*pos-* before an *s*) + the relevant part of *sum*
- present: *possum, potes*, etc.
- imperfect: *poteram, poteras*, etc.

Imperatives (for direct commands):

	1st	*2nd*	*3rd*	*4th*
you (sg)	port-a	mon-e	trah-e	aud-i
you (pl)	port-ate	mon-ete	trah-ite	aud-ite

Adjectives:

- 2-1-2 adjectives like *laetus -a -um* use the endings of *dominus, puella, bellum*
- note *miser -era -erum* and *pulcher -chra -chrum* (*m* like *puer/liber*)
- must agree with noun in number, gender and case (e.g. *puella laeta*) but do not always 'rhyme' (e.g. *nauta bonus*)

Vocative case:

- identical to the nominative except in second declension masculine singular:
  - where nominative is *-us*, vocative is *-e* (e.g. *domine*)
  - where nominative is *-ius*, vocative is *-i* (e.g. *nunti*)

CHAPTER THREE VOCABULARY

advenio -ire	I arrive
aedifico -are	I build
bonus -a -um	good
cado -ere	I fall
cena -ae *f*	dinner, meal
consilium -i *n*	plan, idea, advice
consumo -ere	I eat
curro -ere	I run
debeo -ere	I ought, I should, I must, I owe (+ *infinitive*)
deinde	then, next
deleo -ere	I destroy
discedo -ere	I depart, I leave
diu	for a long time
domina -ae *f*	mistress
festino -are	I hurry
forum -i *n*	forum, marketplace
habito -are	I live, I dwell
inter (+ *acc*)	among, between
invito -are	I invite
iratus -a -um	angry
lacrimo -are	I weep, I cry
laetus -a -um	happy
libertus -i *m*	freedman, ex-slave
magnus -a -um	big, large, great
malus -a -um	bad, evil
maneo -ere	I remain, I stay
miser -era -erum	miserable, wretched, sad
multus -a -um	much, *pl* many
nauta -ae *m*	sailor
novus -a -um	new
oppugno -are	I attack
parvus -a -um	small
patria -ae *f*	country, homeland
porta -ae *f*	gate
possum posse	I can, I am able
pulcher -ra -rum	beautiful, handsome
quaero -ere	I search for, I look for, I ask
-que	and (*before word it is attached to*)
Romanus -a -um	Roman
statim	at once, immediately
stultus -a -um	stupid, foolish
subito	suddenly
tandem	at last, finally
terra -ae *f*	earth, ground, land, country
via -ae *f*	road, street, way

45 words

Chapter Four

VERBS: PERFECT TENSE

In the last chapter we met the imperfect tense: *I was, I used to*. This is used for actions that took place in the past and over a period of time.

When talking about actions that took place at a specific moment in the past (rather than going on for a long time), Latin uses the perfect tense. The term *perfect* comes from the Latin verb *perficio* (I complete): the action described by a perfect tense verb has been *completed*. (Compare the grammatical sense of *imperfect* as *unfinished*.) This is the most frequently used tense in Latin.

The perfect is usually translated with a simple past tense (e.g. *I carried*), but can be translated using *have/has* (e.g. *I have carried*).

As with other tenses, the perfect has its own set of person endings. In some places these resemble the present and imperfect endings, but they are generally quite different from other tenses.

These endings are added to the perfect stem. This consists of the basic verb stem that has been either slightly added to or modified.

sg	*1*	perfect stem + -i	I X-ed	*or*	I have X-ed
	2	-isti	you (*sg*) X-ed		you (*sg*) have X-ed
	3	-it	he/she/it X-ed		he/she/it has X-ed
pl	*1*	-imus	we X-ed		we have X-ed
	2	-istis	you (*pl*) X-ed		you (*pl*) have X-ed
	3	-erunt	they X-ed		they have X-ed

- Dintinguish carefully between the second person singular and plural: *-isti* and *-istis* are easily confused.
- Note too the distinctive third person plural ending, *-erunt*.
- The last four bits end with the usual letters that signify the person in other tenses: *-t, -mus, -tis, -nt*.

Most of the time the perfect tense is translated with a simple past tense. English normally adds *-ed* (e.g. *I carried*), though some verbs have irregular forms (e.g. *I ran*).

Alternatively, the perfect tense can be translated with *have/has: I have carried*. This translation suggests either that the action happened recently and/or that its effects are still continuing. We call this the true perfect. For example, compare:

simple past   I opened the window.
                   (i.e. simply stating what happened)

true perfect   I have opened the window.
                   (i.e. I did it just now *and/or* the window is still open)

Often one of these translations fits the context better than the other.

PERFECT TENSE: FIRST CONJUGATION

The perfect stem for the first conjugation uses the basic verb stem (e.g. *port-*) and a syllable consisting of the characteristic vowel *a* and the letter *v*: *portav-*.
    Hence:

sg	1	portav-i	I carried	*or*	I have carried
	2	portav-isti	you (*sg*) carried		you (*sg*) have carried
	3	portav-it	*etc.*		*etc.*
pl	1	portav-imus			
	2	portav-istis			
	3	portav-erunt			

Exercise 4.1 (mixed tenses of *porto*)

Translate into English:

1. portavisti
2. portas
3. portabamus
4. portaverunt
5. portamus
6. portavi
7. portavistis
8. portatis
9. portate!
10. portavit

All of the first conjugation verbs you have met so far form their perfect tense like *porto*, with the execption of *do* (I give). Here is a revision list:

present tense	meaning	perfect tense	
aedifico	build	aedificavi	
ambulo	walk	ambulavi	
amo	love, like	amavi	
clamo	shout	clamavi	
do	give	dedi	(N.B. irregular stem)
festino	hurry	festinavi	
habito	live, dwell	habitavi	
invito	invite	invitavi	
laboro	work, toil	laboravi	
lacrimo	cry	lacrimavi	
navigo	sail	navigavi	
neco	kill	necavi	
oppugno	attack	oppugnavi	
paro	prepare	paravi	
porto	carry	portavi	
pugno	fight	pugnavi	
saluto	greet	salutavi	
voco	call	vocavi	

Exercise 4.2 (perfect tense)

Translate into English:

1. clamavit
2. oppugnavisti
3. paravi
4. necaverunt
5. lacrimavimus
6. invitavistis
7. vocavit
8. aedificavi
9. dedisti
10. festinavistis

Exercise 4.3 (mixed tenses)

Translate into English:

1. salutavimus
2. ambulabatis
3. dat
4. navigas
5. laboravisti
6. amaverunt
7. habitabant
8. necamus
9. pugnavi
10. aedificabam

Exercise 4.4 (mixed tenses)

Translate into Latin:

1. They gave.
2. We were calling.
3. He is crying.
4. You (*sg*) worked.
5. She has sailed.
6. I was hurrying.
7. They attacked.
8. You (*pl*) have killed.
9. We live.
10. They were carrying.

Exercise 4.5

Translate into English:

1. cenam bonam libertis paravistis.
2. dominus in magno bello pugnavit.
3. servum malum gladio necavi.
4. Romani novum templum in foro aedificaverunt.
5. nuntius epistulas dominae ad insulam portavit.

Exercise 4.6

Translate into Latin:

1. The messengers have sailed away from the homeland.
2. We immediately invited our new friends to dinner.
3. The small boy carried the wine into the garden.
4. The angry slaves attacked the walls of Rome.
5. Many of the girls have given gifts to the goddess.

REVISION CHECKPOINT

Make sure you know:

- the difference in meaning between the perfect and imperfect tenses
- the person endings for the perfect tense
- the subtle difference in meaning between the simple past tense (e.g. *I carried*) and the true perfect (e.g. *I have carried*)
- how first conjugation verbs form the perfect stem

PERFECT TENSE: SECOND, THIRD, FOURTH CONJUGATIONS

All four conjugations all use the same person endings in the perfect tense (*-i, -isti, -it, -imus, -istis, -erunt*). They differ, however, in the way in which they form the perfect stem.

Study the table below:

conj		1st	2nd	3rd	4th
		porto	moneo	traho	audio
infinitive		portare	monere	trahere	audire
		carry	warn	drag	hear
sg	*1*	portav-i	monu-i	trax-i	audiv-i
	2	portav-isti	monu-isti	trax-isti	audiv-isti
	3	portav-it	monu-it	trax-it	audiv-it
pl	*1*	portav-imus	monu-imus	trax-imus	audiv-imus
	2	portav-istis	monu-istis	trax-istis	audiv-istis
	3	portav-erunt	monu-erunt	trax-erunt	audiv-erunt

Note the various ways in which the perfect stem is formed:

- 1st and 4th conjugation verbs normally use the basic stem (*port-*, *aud-*) followed by a syllable with the characteristic vowel for the conjugation (*a* or *i*) and *v*: *portav-*; *audiv-*.

- 2nd conjugation verbs normally add a *u* to the basic stem: *monu-*. There are, however, some irregulars.

- 3rd conjugation verbs form their perfect stem in various ways; there is not one set rule, and perfect tenses of these verbs need to be learned. Many, like *traho*, have a stem that incorporates an *s* sound. This is sometimes in the form of an *x*, as in the case of *traho*: *trax-*.

Exercise 4.7 (perfect tense)

Translate into English:

1. traxit
2. monuimus
3. audivisti
4. monuistis
5. traxerunt
6. traxi
7. audivit
8. audivistis
9. monuerunt
10. traxisti

The following summary lists contain all the 2nd, 3rd and 4th conjugation verbs you have met so far, along with their perfect tenses. The lists are arranged to show the different ways a perfect stem can be formed.

2nd conjugation

present tense	meaning	perfect tense
most use -u-:		
debeo	ought	debui
habeo	have	habui
moneo	warn	monui
terreo	frighten	terrui
timeo	fear	timui

- some use -s-:

| iubeo | order | iussi |
| maneo | remain | mansi |

- some use the basic stem (usually lengthening the first vowel):

| sedeo | sit | sedi |
| video | see | vidi |

- a few use the basic stem and add the characteristic vowel *e* plus *v*:

| deleo | destroy | delevi* |

* On the analogy of 1st conjugation *portavi*, you might have expected many more 2nd conjugation verbs to have perfect tenses like *delevi*. *-ui* forms did, in fact, start off as *-evi* (i.e. *monevi*), but most contracted over time.

Exercise 4.8 (perfect tense)

Translate into English:

1. terruerunt
2. timuistis
3. mansimus
4. debuisti
5. habuit
6. delevimus
7. vidisti
8. iussi
9. sederunt
10. monuit

3rd conjugation (where things are most complicated)

| *present tense* | *meaning* | *perfect tense* |

- most use -s- (forming an -x- when combined with some consonants):

consumo	eat	consumpsi
discedo	depart	discessi
duco	lead	duxi
mitto	send	misi
scribo	write	scripsi
traho	drag	traxi

- some use the basic stem (usually lengthening the first vowel):

| bibo | drink | bibi (first *i* stays short) |
| lego | read; choose | legi |

- some double up the stem, adding an extra syllable at the start which repeats the initial consonant of the basic stem. This process is called *reduplication*:

| cado | fall | cecidi |
| curro | run | cucurri |

- some change more unpredictably:

| quaero | search for | quaesivi |

Exercise 4.9 (perfect tense)

Translate into English:

1. quaesivit
2. misimus
3. cucurristis
4. legisti
5. biberunt
6. discessi
7. duxisti
8. scripsit
9. ceciderunt
10. consumpsimus

4th conjugation

| *present tense* | *meaning* | *perfect tense* |

- most go like *audio*, adding to the basic stem a syllable with the characteristic vowel *i* plus the letter *v*:

audio	hear	audivi
custodio	guard	custodivi
dormio	sleep	dormivi
punio	punish	punivi

- *venio* uses the basic stem *ven-* (but lengthening the vowel), and compounds of *venio* do the same:

venio	come	veni
advenio	arrive	adveni
invenio	find	inveni

Exercise 4.10 (perfect tense)

Translate into English:

1. invenerunt
2. venistis
3. punivit
4. advenisti
5. dormivimus

Note also the perfect tenses of the two irregular verbs we have met:

present	*perfect*	
sum	fui	I was, I have been (on one occasion)
possum	potui	I could, I was able (on one occasion) (this was originally *pot + fui*)

Note the difference between the imperfect and perfect of these verbs:

e.g. dominus bonus erat.
  The master was a good man.   (ongoing: *erat*)

  dominus iratus fuit.
  The master was angry.   (on one occasion: *fuit*)

  servus legere non poterat.
  The slave could not read.   (ongoing: *poterat*)

  servus epistulam invenire non potuit.
  The slave could not find the letter.   (on one occasion: *potuit*)

The verb *inquit* (he/she says) does not change its form in the perfect tense; the same form can be translated as present or perfect, depending on the context. The plural form *inquiunt* (they say) is only used in the present tense.

Exercise 4.11 (mixed tenses)

Translate into English:

1. fuerunt
2. poteramus
3. potuisti
4. eras
5. fuistis
6. inquit (*two answers*)
7. es
8. fuit
9. poterat
10. potest

Exercise 4.12 (perfect tense)

Translate into Latin, checking the perfect stem as necessary:

1. You (*pl*) stayed.
2. We guarded.
3. He fell.
4. You (*sg*) have eaten.
5. They saw.
6. You (*pl*) departed.
7. They were able (*on one occasion*).
8. She has arrived.
9. I have frightened.
10. You (*sg*) were (*on one occasion*).

Exercise 4.13 (perfect tense)

Translate into English:

1. nuntius e villa cum liberto cucurrit.
2. servos cibum in hortum portare iussistis.
3. puer stultus de muro subito cecidit.
4. in templo librum pulchrum invenimus.
5. dominam de novo periculo monui.
6. amici ad villam tandem advenerunt.
7. verba domini audire non potuimus.
8. puellae laetae cibum consumpserunt vinumque biberunt.
9. feminam pulchram in via vidisti.
10. Romani villas templaque deleverunt.

Exercise 4.14

Translate into English:

1. epistulam legit et servo dedit.
2. multos libros de bello scripsisti.
3. decem horas laborabam. tandem dormivi.
4. domina irata puerum malum punivit.
5. nautae Romani circum insulam navigaverunt.
6. nuntium gladiis oppugnavimus.
7. magnam villam in parva insula aedificavistis.
8. arma domini puellam terruerunt.
9. verba dei audivi; bellum non timeo.
10. fuit Romae magnum periculum.

Exercise 4.15

Translate into Latin:

1. We led the women out of danger.
2. The friends have finally arrived.
3. I stayed in the temple with the girls.
4. The foolish men dragged the horse through the gate.
5. Call the master at once, boy! Messengers have come from Rome.

PRINCIPAL PARTS (2)

In Chapter Two we met the concept of verb principal parts. Principal parts are a way of plotting key information about a verb.

The first two principal parts are the first person singular of the present tense and the infinitive (e.g. *porto -are*).

The third principal part is the first person singular of the perfect tense (e.g. *portavi*). It is very important to look at this when you meet a new verb since you cannot necessarily predict how a verb will form its perfect stem by looking the first two principal parts alone.

If the perfect tense builds on the present stem, the information can be given in abbreviated form: e.g. *porto -are -avi*.

If the perfect tense changes more radically, it is written out in full: e.g. *iubeo -ere iussi*.

Remember that by looking at the first two principal parts you can work out which conjugation a verb belongs to. By looking at the third principal part you see how the verb forms its perfect stem. These pieces of information allow you to work out the other endings of a verb.

Here are some more examples of verbs listed with their principal parts:

timeo -ere -ui   *venio -ire veni*
cado -ere cecidi   *sum esse fui*
custodio -ire -ivi   *possum posse potui*

REVISION CHECKPOINT

Make sure you know:

- the different ways in which the perfect stem can be formed in the four conjugations
- the perfect tenses of the verbs we have met so far (see the lists on pp93–98)
- what we mean when we talk about a verb's 'third principal part'
- the order in which verb principal parts are normally written out

Exercise 4.16

Danger in Sicily (1)

Aeneas and his men encounter further horrors when they land in Sicily.

Aeneas Troianique circum <u>Siciliam</u> navigabant. ad terram venerunt et
cenam paraverunt. laeti erant: <u>prope</u> novam patriam tandem erant. sed
subito <u>strepitum</u> <u>horrendum</u> audiverunt: <u>Mons Aetna</u> erat. Aetna multas
horas <u>ignem</u> <u>vomebat</u>. <u>strepitus</u> Troianos terruit. Aeneas amicique dormire
5 non potuerunt. <u>mane</u> vir miser ad Troianos subito cucurrit. <u>macer</u> erat
et <u>vestimenta</u> <u>lacerata</u> habebat. '<u>servate</u> <u>me</u>, Troiani!' clamavit.

	Sicilia -ae *f*	Sicily
	prope (+ *acc*)	near, near to
	strepitus *m*	din, noise
	horrendus -a -um	dreadful
3	Mons Aetna -ae *f*	Mount Etna (*volcano in Sicily*)
	ignis -is *m*	fire
	vomo -ere	I spew up
	mane	in the morning
	silva -ae *f*	wood, forest
5	macer -cra -crum	thin, scrawny
	vestimenta -orum *n pl*	clothing
	laceratus -a -um	torn, ripped
	servo -are	I save, I protect
	me	me (*acc*)

'<u>Graecus</u> sum et <u>Troiae</u> pugnabam, sed miser et <u>solus</u> nunc sum. <u>post</u> bellum cum
<u>Ulixe</u> domino multos annos navigabam; ad Siciliam tandem advenimus. per terram
ambulavimus et <u>speluncam</u> invenimus. erat in <u>spelunca</u> multum cibi. laeti cibum
10 consumebamus sed subito advenit <u>Cyclops</u>, <u>monstrum</u> <u>horrendum</u> et <u>unoculum</u>.
Cyclops iratus multos viros consumpsit. sed Ulixes <u>monstrum</u> <u>hasta</u> <u>caecavit</u> et e
<u>spelunca</u> cucurrimus. Ulixes iussit nautas ab insula statim navigare sed stultus
<u>me</u> miserum <u>reliquit</u>. <u>servate</u> <u>me</u>! festinate! statim discedere debemus!'

	Graecus -a -um	Greek
	Troiae	at Troy (*locative*)
	solus -a -um	alone, lonely
	post (+ *acc*)	after, behind
8	Ulixes (*abl* Ulixe)	Ulysses (*Latin name for Odysseus*)
	spelunca -ae *f*	cave
	Cyclops	Cyclops
	monstrum -i *n*	monster, giant
	horrendus -a -um	dreadful
10	unoculus -a -um	one-eyed
	hasta -ae *f*	spear
	caeco -are -avi	I blind
	me	me (*acc*)
	relinquo -ere reliqui	I leave, I leave behind (i.e. abandon)
13	servo -are	I save, I protect

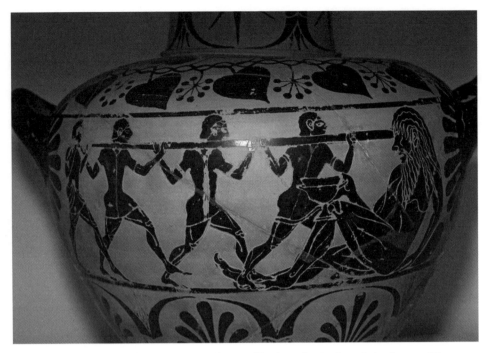

Figure 4.1 *Etruscan vase portraying Odysseus blinding the Cyclops Polyphemus.* (Photo by CM Dixon/Print Collector/Getty Images)

THIRD DECLENSION NOUNS

So far we have met first and second declensions nouns (i.e. nouns that decline like *puella*, *dominus* and *bellum*).

Now we meet the third declension. (In Part 2 we shall meet fourth and fifth declension nouns, but these are much less common; the vast majority of Latin nouns are first, second or third declension.)

If a noun is first or second declension its nominative singular will almost always end *-a*, *-us*, or *-um*. In the third declension, however, the nominative singular can end in many different ways. This means that it is impossible to assign a 'normal' ending for the third declension nominative singular. However, in all other bits of the third declension there is a standard set of endings, added to the stem (explained below):

		3rd declension endings
		m/f
sg	*nom*	(wide range of possibilities)
	acc	stem + -em
	gen	stem + -is
	dat	stem + -i
	abl	stem + -e

pl	nom	stem + -es
	acc	stem + -es
	gen	stem + -um (or -ium)*
	dat	stem + -ibus
	abl	stem + -ibus

* see note on pp108–109.

- The same endings are used for both masculine and feminine nouns in this declension.
- There is a neuter variant, which we shall meet later in this chapter; it differs from the masculine/feminine only in the nominative and accusative.
- The vocative is identical to the nominative for third declension nouns.

Here are some common third declension nouns. As you can see, there is a variety of possible endings in the nominative singular:

rex *m*	king
dux *m*	leader
frater *m*	brother
mater *f*	mother
miles *m*	soldier
nox *f*	night
pater *m*	father
senex *m*	old man
urbs *f*	city

The most important part of a third declension noun is, however, its genitive stem. When you know the genitive stem, all you then need to do to form the other cases is add the endings. You cannot predict the genitive stem by looking at the nominative alone (although you will become aware of some recurrent patterns), so it needs to be learned.

One way in which a third declension noun can form its genitive stem is to make a make a slight spelling change to the nominative singular, e.g. the genitive stem of *rex* is *reg-*. This means that the forms of *rex* are:

		king
		m
sg	nom	rex
	acc	reg-em
	gen	reg-is
	dat	reg-i
	abl	reg-e
pl	nom	reg-es
	acc	reg-es
	gen	reg-um*
	dat	reg-ibus
	abl	reg-ibus

* see note on pp108–109.

- A form ending *-es* could be nominative or accusative plural: judge which it is from the context of the sentence.
- Note how, if you didn't know that *rex* was third declension, you could mistake the genitive plural *regum* for the accusative singular of a noun like *dominus*, or the nominative or accusative singular of a noun like *bellum*.
- Likewise, the *-is* ending of the third declension genitive singular (pronounced with short *i*) is confusable with the *-is* ending of the first and second declension dative and ablative plural (long *i*).
- It is therefore very important to learn which declension each noun is.

The other third declension nouns listed above all make a slight spelling change to form their genitive stem:

dux ducis *m*	leader	*stem*	duc-
frater -tris *m*	brother		fratr-
mater -tris *f*	mother		matr-
miles -itis *m*	soldier		milit-
nox noctis *f*	night		noct-
pater -tris *m*	father		patr-
senex -is *m*	old man		sen-
urbs urbis *f*	city		urb-

- The genitive of monosyllabic nouns is normally written out in full in a wordlist.
- As well as being vital for forming other bits of the noun correctly, the genitive stem often provides lots of English derivatives (e.g. *reg-* gives us *regal*, *regicide*, *regalia*, etc.).

Exercise 4.17

Give an English derivative from:
1. pater
2. miles
3. urbs
4. frater
5. nox

Exercise 4.18

Identify the number and case of:

1. senibus (*two possible answers*)
2. urbem
3. milites (*two possible answers*)
4. patris
5. duce
6. noctes (*two possible answers*)
7. matrem
8. nox
9. militum
10. regi

Exercise 4.19

Change the following from singular to plural or vice versa, keeping the same case:

1. ducum
2. matre
3. fratribus (*dat*)
4. urbs
5. reges (*acc*)

There are two more main ways in which a third declension noun can form its genitive stem, as the words *navis* (ship) and *clamor* (shout) demonstrate. *rex* is also listed below, for comparison:

		king	ship	shout, shouting, noise
		m	*f*	*m*
sg	*nom*	rex	navis	clamor
	acc	reg-em	nav-em	clamor-em
	gen	reg-is	nav-is	clamor-is
	dat	reg-i	nav-i	clamor-i
	abl	reg-e	nav-e	clamor-e
pl	*nom*	reg-es	nav-es	clamor-es
	acc	reg-es	nav-es	clamor-es
	gen	reg-um*	nav-ium*	clamor-um*
	dat	reg-ibus	nav-ibus	clamor-ibus
	abl	reg-ibus	nav-ibus	clamor-ibus

* see note on pp108–109

navis forms its genitive stem by dropping the final syllable of the nominative singular (i.e. *nav-*). In this instance, the genitive singular ends up looking identical to the nominative singular. Another noun like this is:

    iuvenis -is *m*   young man   *stem*   iuven-

For *clamor* the whole of the nominative singular is the genitive stem (i.e. *clamor-*). Another noun like this is:

    amor -oris *m*   love   *stem*   amor-

A noun's gender does not dictate which of these methods it uses to form the stem.

As with nouns of all declensions, when a third declension noun is given in a wordlist its genitive singular and gender are listed too (this is especially important for the third declension, since the genitive stem can't easily be predicted from the nominative singular).

Sometimes the genitive is given in abbreviated form to save space, with the syllables that stay the same not being printed again. Removing the ending (*-is*) from the genitive will leave you with the genitive stem. You can then use this stem to form all the other bits of the noun.

    e.g. miles, militis *m*   soldier (*therefore stem* = milit-)
    or   miles -itis *m*   soldier

Remember that the genitive ending tells you which declension a noun is:

    -ae *first declension*
    -i   *second*
    -is *third*

Knowing the declension of a noun prevents you confusing the endings: e.g. *regum* must be genitive plural once you know that *rex, regis* is a third declension noun.

Genitive plural endings for third declension nouns:

- *-um* if the *gen sg* has one more syllable than the *nom sg* (i.e. if the noun 'increases' in the *gen sg*, it does not extend again in the *gen pl*): e.g. *clamor; clamoris; clamorum.*
- *-ium* if the *gen sg* and the *nom sg* have the same number of syllables (i.e. if the noun does not increase in the *gen sg*, it does in the *gen pl*): e.g. *navis; navis; navium.* Also *-ium* if the *nom sg* is a monosyllable ending in two consonants, e.g. *urbs, nox* (*x* counts as two consonants, = *cs* or *gs*): *urbs; urbis; urbium* (this sort increase twice).

However, these rules are sometimes broken:

- *pater, mater, frater, iuvenis, senex* (all, coincidentally, people you might find in a family) have *-um* in the *gen pl*, despite having the same number of syllables in the *nom sg* and *gen sg* (they should therefore increase to *-ium* in the *gen pl*).

- *rex*, as a monosyllable ending in two consonants (*x* counting as two), should have a genitive plural *-ium*, but in fact has *-um*.

Exercise 4.20

Translate into English:

1. noctem diu timebamus.
2. matres miserae in via lacrimabant.
3. dux multos milites in insula reliquit.
4. frater regis stultus et malus erat.
5. matrem patremque per vias urbis quaerebam.
6. libertus magnum amorem pecuniae habebat.
7. iuvenis per urbem cum militibus regis currebat.
8. pueri clamores senum non audiverunt.
9. senex iuvenes de periculis belli monebat.
10. nautae ad insulam in magna nave navigaverunt.

Exercise 4.21

Translate into Latin:

1. There are many cities on the island.
2. I did not hear my brother's shout.
3. The young man suddenly saw his mother and father.
4. The king's soldiers were guarding the money.
5. We must run to the ship at once, old man!

REVISION CHECKPOINT

Make sure you know:

- the endings of masculine and feminine third declension nouns
- the importance of the genitive stem in forming the other cases
- the different ways in which third declension nouns can form the genitive stem

Exercise 4.22

Danger in Sicily (2)

The Trojans soon come face to face with the one-eyed Cyclopes.

verba misera nautae Troianos terruerunt. Aeneas amicique statim <u>misericordiam</u>
habuerunt. clamorem subito audiverunt et <u>Cyclopem</u> viderunt. Cyclops <u>caecatus</u>
iratusque ad Troianos ambulabat. Aeneas statim Troianos et nautam miserum ad
naves currere iussit. subito <u>ceteri</u> Cyclopes advenerunt. Cyclopes Troianos
5 <u>lapidibus</u> <u>ramis</u>que oppugnaverunt. Troiani ad naves cucurrerunt et statim
discesserunt. Graecum miserum non reliquerunt.

	misericordia -ae *f*	pity
	Cyclops -opis *m*	Cyclops
	caecatus -a -um	blinded
	ceteri -ae -a	the other, the rest of
5	lapis -is *m*	stone
	ramus -i *m*	branch (of tree)

Troiani circum <u>Siciliam</u> ad novam patriam <u>lente</u> navigabant. sed dei novum <u>dolorem</u>
miserunt: senex <u>Anchises</u>, pater Aeneae, tandem <u>periit</u>. Aeneas miser diu lacrimabat
sed Troiani manere non poterant. dux <u>pius</u> nautas iussit naves in aquam <u>iterum</u>
10 <u>deducere</u>. 'ad naves,' inquit 'amici! <u>lacrimae</u> verbaque misera non <u>prosunt</u>.
patriam <u>petere</u> debemus!'

	Sicilia -ae *f*	Sicily
	lente	slowly
	dolor -oris *m*	grief, woe
	Anchises -is *m*	Anchises
8	periit	(he) perished, (he) died
	pius -a -um	dutiful
	iterum	again
	deduco -ere	I launch, I bring down
	lacrima -ae *f*	tear
10	prosum	I am of use
	peto -ere petivi	I seek, I make for (*also* I beg/ask for)

THIRD DECLENSION NEUTER

We have seen that in the third declension both masculine and feminine nouns use the same endings.

There is, however, a neuter variant. The neuter endings differ from the masculine and feminine endings in the nominative and accusative.

In the table below the neuter endings have been added on the right:

3rd declension endings

		m/f	*n*
sg	*nom*	(wide range)	(wide range)
	acc	stem + -em	(wide range, same as *nom*)
	gen	stem + -is	stem + -is
	dat	stem + -i	stem + -i
	abl	stem + -e	stem + -e
pl	*nom*	stem + -es	stem + -a
	acc	stem + -es	stem + -a
	gen	stem + -um (or -ium)	stem + -um (or -ium)
	dat	stem + -ibus	stem + -ibus
	abl	stem + -ibus	stem + -ibus

- As with the masculine and feminine forms, the nominative singular of third declension neuter nouns can end in various ways.
- As with all neuter nouns, the nominative and the accusative are always identical.
- The vocative is identical to the nominative.
- Any stem change for a third declension neuter noun will only kick in with the genitive singular (this is why we talk about the *genitive* stem for third declension nouns: the idea of a different *accusative stem* wouldn't work for neuter nouns). This genitive stem will be used in all subsequent bits of the noun.
- Like all neuter nouns, the nominative and accusative plural end in -*a*.
- The rules about whether the genitive plural ends -*um* or -*ium* govern the neuter, too (see note on pp108–109).

One common third declension neuter noun, *nomen* (name), is given below. Note how the stem changes from the genitive singular onwards.

		name	
		n	
sg	*nom*	nomen	
	acc	nomen	
	gen	nomin-is	(*stem* nomin-)
	dat	nomin-i	
	abl	nomin-e	
pl	*nom*	nomin-a	
	acc	nomin-a	
	gen	nomin-um	
	dat	nomin-ibus	
	abl	nomin-ibus	

- The ablative singular can mean *by name* (i.e. *called...*):

  e.g.   dux, Caesar nomine, in templo erat.
          The leader, called Caesar, was in the temple.

Three other common third declension neuter nouns are as follows; the genitive singular enables you to work out the stem:

caput -itis *n*	head	*stem*	capit-
iter -ineris *n*	journey		itiner-
mare -is *n*	sea		mar-

- *mare* is slightly irregular: its ablative singular is usually *mari* and its nominative and accusative plural are *maria*.

Exercise 4.23

Give an English derivative from:
1. caput
2. iter
3. mare
4. nomen

Exercise 4.24

Identify the number and case of:
1. nominum
2. capitibus (*two possible answers*)
3. itineris
4. maria (*two possible answers*)
5. capite

Exercise 4.25

Translate into English:

1. nomen urbis Roma est.
2. senex milites ad mare duxit.
3. rex nautas Romanos necavit et capita Romam misit.
4. iter <u>longum</u> erat sed dormire nunc possumus.
5. equus pulcher, Bucephalus nomine, magnum caput habet.*

   longus -a -um   long

* Bucephalus (literally 'Ox-head'), the horse of Alexander the Great (king of Macedon 336-323 BC), was so called because of his unusually large head. Bucephalus proved a faithful companion to Alexander as he conquered the known world; Alexander even named a city after him when he died.

Exercise 4.26

Translate into Latin:

1. The sailors feared the god of the sea.
2. The new slaves do not have names.
3. I carried the head of the evil young man to the king.
4. The leader gave the island a new name.
5. We have heard about the soldiers' journeys.

REVISION CHECKPOINT

Make sure you know:

*   the endings of neuter third declension nouns
*   the meaning and genitive stem of all the third declension nouns we have met so far
*   the use of *nomine* to mean *by name* (i.e. *called*)

Exercise 4.27

Storm and Prophecy

Juno, still smarting from the Judgement of Paris, engineers a terrible storm.

Aeneas Troianique novam patriam nunc petebant. sed <u>Iuno</u>, <u>regina</u> deorum,
Troianos punire <u>adhuc</u> <u>cupiebat</u>. naves Troianas irata <u>spectabat</u>. necare nautas et
naves delere <u>cupiebat</u>. ad <u>Aeolum</u>, regem <u>ventorum</u>, festinavit. dea Aeolum iussit
magnam <u>tempestatem</u> mittere. Aeolus <u>ventos</u> in <u>caelum</u> statim misit. <u>venti</u> mari
5   incubuerunt, <u>lux</u> e <u>caelo</u> discessit, aquae naves <u>oppresserunt</u>. Aeneas lacrimavit
<u>mortem</u>que timuit. sed <u>venti</u> et aquae tandem <u>resederunt</u>. multae naves, multi
nautae <u>amissi</u> nunc erant. Aeneas ad terram tandem navigavit. <u>Venus</u>, mater Aeneae,
periculum vidit. ad <u>Iovem</u> festinavit, lacrimavit, verba irata clamavit: '<u>promisisti</u>, rex
deorum, Troianis novum <u>regnum</u> novamque patriam! sed <u>tempestas</u> naves Troianas
10 nunc <u>oppressit</u> et dux bonus in magno periculo est. <u>cur</u> Aenean <u>adhuc</u> punis?' sed
Iuppiter <u>risit</u>. 'consilia deorum manent,' inquit. 'Troianos custodio. Aenean non
punio. pater novi <u>regni</u> Romani est; Romanis <u>imperium</u> <u>sine</u> <u>fine</u> dedi.'

	Iuno -onis *f*	Juno
	regina -ae *f*	queen
	adhuc	still
	cupiebat	(she) wanted
2	specto -are -avi	I look at, I watch
	Aeolus -i *m*	Aeolus
	ventus -i *m*	wind
	tempestas -atis *f*	storm
	caelum -i *n*	sky, heaven
5	incumbo -ere incubui	I throw myself upon (+ *dat*)
	lux lucis *f*	light
	opprimo -ere oppressi	I overwhelm
	mors mortis *f*	death
	resido -ere resedi	I settle down, I subside
7	amissus -a -um	lost
	Venus -eris *f*	Venus
	Iuppiter Iovis *m*	Jupiter
	promitto -ere -misi	I promise
	regnum -i *n*	kingdom
10	cur	why?
	rideo -ere risi	I smile, I laugh
	imperium -i *n*	empire
	sine (+ *abl*)	without
	finis -is *m*	end, border, limit

DIRECT QUESTIONS (1)

A direct question quotes the actual words of someone asking a question and ends in a question mark, e.g. *Are you happy?* There are two main types of question.

1. The first type asks if something is the case, and leads to a *Yes* or *No* answer.
    Any sentence in Latin can be turned into a question simply by adding a question mark.

	e.g.	laeti estis.	You (*pl*) are happy.
		laeti estis?	Are you (*pl*) happy?

More commonly, a question is signalled by adding *-ne* to the end of first word. The suffix *-ne* means '*is it the case?*', though it is clumsy to translate it like this. Adding *-ne* can make a familiar word look odd: remove the *-ne* to get back to the original word. When a statement is made into a question the word order is often changed, with the verb usually coming first; but another word that the author wants to emphasise can also be put first.

	e.g.	discesseruntne feminae?		Have the women left?
		fratremne necavit rex?		Did the king kill his *brother*?
			or	Was it his *brother* that the king killed?

Note how Latin can subtly shift the emphasis by manipulating the word order; English has to find other ways to achieve this effect.
    -*ne* is neutral, and does not point towards either *Yes* or *No* as the likely answer.
    Alternatively, the question can be slanted to suggest either *Yes* or *No* as the expected answer by using one of the following instead of *-ne*:

nonne . . . ?	Surely . . . ?	(expecting the answer *Yes*)
num . . . ?	Surely . . . not . . . ?	(expecting the answer *No*)

Note how *nonne* is simply *non* + *ne*: literally <u>*isn't*</u> *it the case. . . ?* (*Yes*)

	e.g.	nonne Romam amas?		Surely you (*sg*) like Rome?	(*Yes*)
			or	You (*sg*) do like Rome, don't you?	(*Yes*)
		num vinum amas?		Surely you (*sg*) do not like the wine?	(*No*)
			or	You (*sg*) don't like the wine, do you?	(*No*)

2. The second type of question requests a specific piece of information. As in English, various question words are used, five of which are listed below.

cur?	why?	
quando?	when?	
quo?	where . . . to?	(*whither?* in old-fashioned English)
ubi?	where?	
unde?	where . . . from?	(*whence?* in old-fashioned English)

Many Latin question words begin with *qu-* (and even *cur* used to be spelled *quor*), just as many question words in English begin with *wh-*:

    e.g. quando advenit rex?   quo curritis, pueri?
         When did the king arrive?   Where are you running (to), boys?

Note how in modern English we often simply say *where?* rather than *where to?* (e.g. *where are you going (to)?*); Latin is more precise, with *ubi* and *quo* having specific different meanings.

Exercise 4.28

Translate into English:

1.   mare amatis?
2.   habetne insula nomen?
3.   cur ridetis, pueri?
4.   quando discessit regina?
5.   nonne dei Romam amant?
6.   timetisne iter longum, puellae?
7.   num senex gladio pugnare potest?
8.   unde navigavistis, nautae?
9.   quo currebas, puer?
10. ubi nunc sumus, pater?

Exercise 4.29

Translate into Latin:

1   When did you find the money, slave-girl?
2   Why are you not working, boy?
3   You (*pl*) are able to read, aren't you?
4   Where is the mistress walking to?
5   Has the leader ordered the soldiers to make for the city?

Exercise 4.30

Dido and Aeneas (1)

Divine intervention helps the lost Aeneas find his way to Carthage.

Aeneas in terra nova <u>ignota</u>que nunc erat. miser erat et timebat. sed <u>Iuppiter</u> rex
deorum Aenean Troianosque <u>servabat</u>. terra <u>Carthago</u> erat, regina <u>Dido</u>. Iuppiter
<u>Mercurium</u>, nuntium deorum, ad <u>Poenos</u> Didonemque reginam misit. Mercurius
Poenis <u>mentem</u> <u>benignam</u> dedit. periculum igitur Troianis parvum erat. Aeneas
5 amicusque, <u>Achates</u> nomine, per agros <u>ignotos</u> miseri <u>errabant</u>. subito <u>Venus</u>, dea
amoris et mater Aeneae, de caelo ad terram <u>descendit</u> et ad Aenean venit. sed dea
<u>vestimenta</u> puellae <u>gerebat</u>: Aeneas matrem non <u>agnovit</u>.

	ignotus -a -um	unknown
	Iuppiter *gen* Iovis *m*	Jupiter
	servo -are	I save, I protect
	Carthago -inis *f*	Carthage
2	Dido -onis *f*	Dido
	Mercurius -i *m*	Mercury
	Poeni -orum *m pl*	Carthaginians
	mens mentis *f*	mind
	benignus -a -um	kind, friendly
5	Achates -ae *m*	Achates (*Trojan warrior*)
	erro -are	I wander, I roam
	Venus -eris *f*	Venus
	descendo -ere -i	I go down, I come down
	vestimenta -orum *n pl*	clothing
7	gero -ere	I wear
	agnosco -ere agnovi	I recognise

Venus viros salutavit: '<u>salvete</u>, viri! <u>qui</u> estis? cur <u>hic</u> erratis? unde venistis?'
Aeneas 'Troiani' inquit 'sumus, et Troia navigavimus. novam patriam petimus
10 sed dei <u>adversi</u> sunt: multa pericula et magnam <u>tempestatem</u> miserunt. nunc in
terra <u>ignota</u> sumus. sed <u>quis</u> es? deane es? num puella es? ubi sumus? <u>qui hic</u>
habitant? suntne viri <u>benigni</u>?'

	salvete!	greetings! hello! (to *pl*)
	qui	who (*pl*)?
	hic	here
	adversus -a -um	hostile
10	tempestas -atis *f*	storm
	quis?	who (*sg*)?

Venus 'tuti' inquit 'estis, Troiani. in terra Poenorum estis. Poeni viri boni sunt, et
Dido regina bona est. Poeni huc per maria navigaverunt; nuper advenerunt. urbem
15 nunc aedificant. non dea sed venatrix sum; vias agrosque scio. ad urbem nunc
festinate!' deinde dea passibus fulgentibus discessit: Aeneas matrem statim
agnovit. Aeneas Achatesque Carthaginem petiverunt. Venus viros nebula densa
velavit; nemo Aenean videre poterat.

	tutus -a -um	safe
	huc	to here
	nuper	recently
	venatrix -icis *f*	huntress
15	scio -ire	I know
	passibus fulgentibus	with radiant steps
	agnosco -ere agnovi	I recognise
	nebula -ae *f*	cloud, mist
	densus -a -um	thick
18	velo -are -avi	I cover, I veil
	nemo	nobody

ad novam urbem advenerunt. Poeni forum, muros, templa aedificabant. viri
20 feminaeque sicut apes laborabant. Aeneas Didonem pulchram subito vidit. erat
cum regina – mirabile dictu! – magna turba iuvenum Troianorum. Aeneas
Achatesque amicos laeti viderunt. deinde nebula subito evanuit. Aeneas in forum
turbamque ambulavit. Dido obstupefacta Aenean Troianum spectavit.

	sicut	just like
	apis -is *f*	bee
	mirabile dictu!	wondrous to say!
	turba -ae *f*	crowd
22	evanesco -ere evanui	I vanish, I disappear
	obstupefactus -a -um	amazed, astounded

- Note that Dido -onis *f* (Dido) and Poeni -orum *m pl* (Carthaginians) will not
  be glossed again.

MIXED CONJUGATION VERBS

So far we have met verbs in four different conjugations.

There are, however, a few verbs that fall between the third and fourth conjugations. These are called *mixed conjugation* verbs. They possess some features of either conjugation.

- In the present and imperfect these verbs go like the fourth conjugation.
- The present infinitive ends -*ere*, like the third conjugation (this means that they count as third overall, even though they have more in common with fourth).
- The way they form their perfect stem (vowel change or lengthening, and slight irregularity) aligns them with third.
- In the imperative they go like the third.
- In the vocabulary at the back of this book they are shown as '3rd*'.

Study the forms of *capio* (I take, I catch, I capture):

		present	*imperfect*	*perfect*
sg	1	cap-io	capie-bam	cep-i
	2	cap-is	capie-bas	cep-isti
	3	cap-it	capie-bat	cep-it
pl	1	cap-imus	capie-bamus	cep-imus
	2	cap-itis	capie-batis	cep-istis
	3	cap-iunt	capie-bant	cep-erunt

infinitive	cap-ere	
imperative	cap-e	(sg)
	cap-ite	(pl)

Two important mixed conjugation verbs that go like *capio* are:

facio -ere feci	I make, I do
fugio -ere fugi*	I flee, I run away

* *fugio* has a short *u* in the present tense and a long *u* in the perfect.

Note that *facio* can sometimes appear with two accusative nouns:

> e.g.   puerum ducem fecimus.
>   We made the boy our leader.

Note too a very common phrase involving *capio*:

| consilium capio | I make (*lit* I take) a plan |

Exercise 4.31

Translate into English:

1. faciunt
2. capiebatis
3. fuge!
4. facere
5. cepisti
6. fugerunt
7. facis
8. capitis
9. fugistis
10. consilium capite!

Exercise 4.32

Translate into Latin:

1. We were doing.
2. She fled.
3. To capture.
4. They have made.
5. He flees.

Exercise 4.33

Translate into English:

1. senes miseri iter longum Romam faciebant.
2. urbem ducemque tandem cepimus.
3. libertus 'num' inquit 'fugitis, nuntii?'
4. equum capite, pueri stulti!
5. Romani servum regem fecerunt.
6. fuge, o regina! urbem relinque!
7. duces Romanorum novum consilium capiebant.
8. ancillae ex horto subito fugerunt.
9. pater iuvenis vinum bonum facit.
10. <u>tempus</u> fugit.

tempus -oris *n*   time

Exercise 4.34

Translate into Latin:

1. We are making wine in the garden.
2. The slaves caught the evil boy.
3. Why did you not flee from the danger, old man?
4. The brothers were making a journey through the new land.
5. The soldiers have captured the walls and gates; we cannot flee.

REVISION CHECKPOINT

Make sure you know:

- how a sentence can be turned into a question
- how a question can be slanted to expect either *Yes* or *No* as the answer
- the list on p115 of question words requesting specific information
- how mixed conjugation verbs use the endings of the 3rd and 4th conjugations in different places

Exercise 4.35

Dido and Aeneas (2)

Dido gives Aeneas a royal welcome but Venus then hatches a fateful plan.

Aeneas ad reginam ambulavit. 'ducem' inquit 'militum Troianorum quaeris, o regina. ego, Aeneas, adsum. dedisti, Dido regina, Troianis magnum auxilium: nautas fessos in urbem invitavisti et gentem sparsam servavisti. o magni dei, servate Poenos et urbem et reginam bonam!' deinde Dido 'cur,' inquit 'dux, ad
5 terram Poenorum venisti? quid contra deos fecisti? cur dei Troianos oderunt? multas fabulas de Troianis et de Aenea audivi. ego quoque exsul sum: patriam reliqui et novam urbem nunc aedifico. gratissimi estis, Troiani. ad regiam venite!'

	ego	I (*nom*)
	adsum adesse	I am here, I am present
	fessus -a -um	tired
	gens gentis *f*	race, tribe, family
3	sparsus -a -um	scattered
	servo -are	I save, I protect
	quid	what (*acc*)?
	oderunt	(they) hate
	fabula -ae *f*	story, tale
6	quoque	also, too
	exsul -ulis *m/f*	exile, exiled person
	gratissimus -a -um	very welcome
	regia -ae *f*	royal palace

regina Troianos in regiam duxit. servos magnam cenam parare iussit. multum cibi ad naves amicosque Aeneae misit. Aeneas nuntium iussit <u>filium</u> <u>Ascanium</u> ad
10 urbem ducere. sed <u>Venus</u> novum consilium nunc cepit: non Ascanium sed <u>Cupidinem</u>, Ascanio <u>similem</u>, ad urbem misit. <u>dum</u> Poeni et Troiani <u>cenant</u>, Cupido <u>cor</u> Didonis amore Aeneae <u>incendit</u>.

	filius -i *m*	son
	Ascanius -i *m*	Ascanius
	Venus -eris *f*	Venus
	Cupido -inis *m*	Cupid (*assistant of Venus*)
11	similem	(*m acc sg*) resembling, looking like (+ *dat*)
	dum	while (+ *present tense verb, translate as imperfect*)
	ceno -are	I dine
	cor cordis *n*	heart
12	incendo -ere -i	I burn, I set on fire

TIME EXPRESSIONS (2): 'TIME WHEN'

In Chapter Two we saw that the accusative case is used in a expression that states how long an action lasts.

e.g. librum multos annos scribebam.
I was writing the book for many years.

To express *when* something happens the *ablative* case is used.
The following two new adjectives are frequently found in this context:

medius -a -um the middle (of)
primus -a -um first, the first

Note that *medius* is simply an adjective that agrees with the relevant noun. It usually has the sense *the middle of . . .* (e.g. *the middle of the forum*) rather than *the middle one of several* (as in *the middle child of three*). Both adjectives normally come before the nouns they describe.

e.g. Roma prima hora discessi.
I left Rome at the first hour.

urbem media nocte cepimus.
We captured the city in the middle of the night.

Exercise 4.36

Translate into English:

1. ad templum prima hora ambulavistis.
2. Romani primo anno insulas oppugnaverunt.
3. pueri in mediam turbam cucurrerunt.
4. senex fratrem gladio media nocte necavit.
5. multas villas primo anno aedificavimus.

Exercise 4.37

Dido and Aeneas (3)

The queen of Carthage and her Trojan guest grow ever closer.

post cenam Aeneas Didoni <u>fabulam</u> longam de <u>exitio</u> Troiae et itinere
Troianorum <u>narravit</u>. regina Poenique <u>obstupefacti</u> erant. media nocte <u>sagitta</u>
amoris Didonem <u>transfixit</u>: regina caput, <u>capillos</u>, <u>oculos</u> viri Troiani amavit.
<u>cotidie</u> Dido et Aeneas templa <u>visitabant</u>, dona deis dabant, per vias urbis
5   ambulabant. <u>Iuno</u> regina deorum <u>cupiebat</u> Aenean in terra Poenorum diu
manere. dea consilium cepit. Dido et Aeneas <u>venationem ducebant</u>; Iuno
magnam <u>tempestatem</u> misit. regina et Aeneas ad <u>speluncam</u> fugerunt: <u>hic</u>
manebant; <u>hic amaverunt</u>. Dido laeta nunc Aenean <u>maritum</u> vocabat.

	fabula -ae *f*	story, tale
	exitium -i *n*	destruction
	narro -are -avi	I tell, I narrate
	obstupefactus -a -um	amazed, astounded
2	sagitta -ae *f*	arrow
	transfigo -ere transfixi	I pierce (someone) through
	capilli -orum *m pl*	hair
	oculus -i *m*	eye
	cotidie	every day
4	visito -are	I visit
	Iuno -onis *f*	Juno
	cupio -ere	I want, I desire
	venationem duco	I lead the hunt, I lead the hunting packs
	tempestas -atis *f*	storm
7	spelunca -ae *f*	cave
	hic	here
	amaverunt	(*here*) they made love
	maritus -i *m*	husband

PERSONAL PRONOUNS AND POSSESSIVE ADJECTIVES (1): *ego, tu, meus, tuus*

Personal pronouns refer to specific people (I, you, he, etc.), and operate like nouns within sentences. Like nouns, they decline according to case.

Note how English has retained inflection (i.e. the changing of word endings to create meaning) for pronouns. Consider for example (subject, object, possessive): *I, me, mine*; *he, him, his*; *she, her, hers*.

Here are the forms of the first and second person singular personal pronouns, *I* and *you* (*sg*):

	I, me	you (*sg*)
nom	ego	tu
acc	me	te
gen	mei	tui
dat	mihi	tibi
abl	me	te

- There is no distinction made for the gender of the person referred to.
- *ego* and *tu* do not have plural forms: there are separate words for *we* and *you* (*pl*).
- There is no vocative of *ego*; for *tu* it is identical to the nominative.

e.g.   milites me ceperunt.   deus tibi multa dona dedit.
       The soldiers captured me.   The god has given you many gifts.

Personal pronouns in the nominative are normally only used to add emphasis, particularly in a question or in a contrast between two people. They can also mark a change of subject between sentences.

e.g.   ego mansi, sed tu fugisti.
       I stayed, but *you* (*sg*) fled.

In this sentence the subjects of the verbs are already revealed by the verb endings; the pronouns give greater weight to the contrast.

Personal pronouns can be used *reflexively* (i.e. to refer back to the subject):

e.g.   me cibum consumere iussi.
       I ordered myself to eat the food.

If a pronoun appears with the preposition *cum* (with), the two words join up, and the pronoun comes first, i.e. *mecum, tecum* rather than *cum me, cum te*.

e.g.   in hortum mecum ambula, pater!
       Walk into the garden with me, father!

A *possessive adjective* shows who an item belongs to: e.g. *my* book, *your* house.

The possessive adjectives *my* and *your* (belonging to you *sg*) are regular 2-1-2 adjectives like *laetus*:

meus -a -um	my
tuus -a -um	your, yours (belonging to you *sg*)

- The masculine vocative singular of *meus* is *mi* (in the other genders the vocative is the same as the nominative). There is no vocative of *tuus*.

A possessive adjective normally follows the noun it describes. Like any adjective, it needs to agree with the noun in number, gender and case. Note that the possessive adjective will have the gender of the thing owned, not the gender of the owner. Like other adjectives they can also be used on their own, acting like nouns.

We have already seen that when the possession is clear from the context, Latin doesn't normally use a possessive adjective. A possessive adjective is used for emphasis, or when the possession is not otherwise obvious.

e.g.	patrem amas.	patrem meum amas.
	You (*sg*) love your father.	You (*sg*) love my father.
	urbem meam amo.	pater tuus meum non amat.
	I love my city.	Your father does not like mine.

It is possible to use the genitive of the personal pronoun rather than the possessive adjective, e.g. *villa mei* (*lit* the villa of me) rather than *villa mea* (my villa). It is, however, much more common to use the possessive adjective.

Exercise 4.38

Translate into English:

1. unde venisti tu? ubi habitas tu?
2. mecum in agros meos ambulate, amici!
3. ego vinum bibi, tu aquam.
4. fratres mei tuos non timent.
5. materne mea donum tibi et patri tuo dedit?

Exercise 4.39

S&C

Translate into Latin:

1. Your husband gave me the weapons.
2. Kill yourself with the sword, brother!
3. They found my slave-girl in the temple.
4. Why are your slaves not with you, father?
5. Is my book in your house, freedman?

Exercise 4.40

Dido and Aeneas (4)

The gods remind Aeneas of his mission; the love affair cannot go on.

sed Aeneas cum Didone manere non poterat: <u>fatum</u> non erat. Troianos ad novam
patriam ducere debebat. <u>Iuppiter</u> iratus <u>Mercurium</u> ad Aenean media nocte misit.
Mercurius ad ducem in <u>somnio</u> venit. 'vir stulte,' inquit 'cur verborum Iovis non
<u>meministi</u>? patriam Troianis invenire debes. <u>hoc</u> regnum tuum non est. maritus
5 Didonis non es. statim discede! festina!' verba dei Aenean terruerunt. <u>postridie</u>
naves paravit et Troianos navigare iussit. Dido <u>ubi</u> consilium ducis Troianorum
<u>cognovit</u> misera et irata erat. lacrimavit, clamavit, Aenean manere iussit: sed <u>frustra</u>.
Aeneas ad naves festinavit et amicos a terra Poenorum navigare iussit. regina 'nunc'
clamavit 'Poeni <u>hostes</u> Troianorum sunt. o dei, Poenos <u>vindicate</u>! Troianos punite!'
10 Aeneas Troianique discesserunt; Dido regina <u>se</u> gladio <u>transfixit</u> et in <u>ignem</u> <u>iniecit</u>.

	fatum -i *n*	fate, divine will
	Iuppiter Iovis *m*	Jupiter
	Mercurius -i *m*	Mercury
	somnium -i *n*	sleep, dream
4	memini (*perfect form, but present meaning*)	I remember (+ *gen*)
	hoc	(*n nom*) this
	postridie	on the next day
	ubi	(*here*) when
7	cognosco -ere cognovi	I find out
	frustra	in vain
	hostis -is *m*	enemy
	vindico -are	I avenge, I take vengeance on behalf of
	se	(*acc*) herself
10	transfigo -ere transfixi	I pierce (someone) through
	ignis -is *m*	(*here*) funeral pyre
	inicio -ere inieci	I throw. . . onto

Figure 4.2 *A manuscript illustration of Dido killing herself on the pyre.* c.400 AD. Found in the collection of the Biblioteca Apostolica Vaticana. (Photo by Fine Art Images/Heritage Images/Getty Images)

SUMMARY OF CHAPTER FOUR GRAMMAR

Perfect tense:

- meaning: *I X-ed* (simple past) or *I have X-ed* (true perfect)
- endings: *-i, -isti, -it, -imus, -istis, -erunt*
- added to perfect stem (first person singular of perfect = third principal part)
- e.g. *portavi, monui, traxi, audivi*
- but perfect stem can be formed in various ways: see pp93–98
- perfect of *sum* = *fui*; of *possum* = *potui*

Mixed conjugation verbs:

- e.g. *capio, facio, fugio*
- go like 4th conjugation *audio* in present and imperfect
- go like 3rd conjugation *traho* in imperative and infinitive
- normal perfect tense endings applied to their perfect stem

Third declension nouns:

m & f

sg	nom	(wide range)	pl	stem + -es
	acc	stem + -em		stem + -es
	gen	stem + -is		stem + -um (or -ium)
	dat	stem + -i		stem + -ibus
	abl	stem + -e		stem + -ibus

- same set of endings for both *m* & *f*; in neuter, *acc sg* same as *nom sg*, and both *nom pl* and *acc pl* are stem + -a
- vital to know the *gen sg* stem and gender of each third declension noun
- for rules about *gen pl* ending see pp108–109
- e.g. *rex regis* m; *navis -is* f; *clamor -oris* m; *nomen -inis* n

Questions:

- some are answered by *Yes* or *No*:   *-ne, nonne, num*
- some ask for specific information: *cur, quando, ubi, quo, unde*

'Time when' expressions: use the ablative: e.g. *media nocte*; *primo anno*

Personal pronouns: *ego* and *tu*; they decline; can be used reflexively

Possessive adjectives: *meus* and *tuus* (both 2-1-2); function like other adjs

CHAPTER FOUR VOCABULARY

amor -oris *m*	love
caelum -i *n*	sky, heaven
capio -ere cepi	I take, I catch, I capture
caput -itis *n*	head
clamor -oris *m*	shout, shouting, noise
cur?	why?
dux ducis *m*	leader
ego mei	I, me
facio -ere feci	I make, I do
frater -tris *m*	brother
fugio -ere fugi	I run away, I flee
iter -ineris *n*	journey
iuvenis -is *m*	young man
longus -a -um	long
mare -is *n*	sea
maritus -i *m*	husband
mater -tris *f*	mother
medius -a -um	middle (of)
meus -a -um	my
miles -itis *m*	soldier
navis -is *f*	ship
-ne ... ?	(*makes a question, e.g.*) is it ... ?
nomen -inis *n*	name
nonne ... ?	surely ... ?
nox noctis *f*	night
num ... ?	surely ... not ... ?
pater -tris *m*	father
peto -ere -ivi	I seek, I beg/ask for, I make for
post + *acc*	after, behind
primus -a -um	first
quando?	when?
quo?	where to?
regina -ae *f*	queen
regnum -i *n*	kingdom
relinquo -ere reliqui	I leave, I leave behind (i.e. abandon)
rex regis *m*	king
rideo -ere risi	I laugh, I smile
senex -is *m*	old man
specto -are -avi	I look at, I watch
tu tui	you (*sg*)
turba -ae *f*	crowd
tuus -a -um	your (of you *sg*), yours
ubi?	where?
unde?	where from?
urbs urbis *f*	city, town

45 words

Chapter Five

VERBS: FUTURE TENSE

So far we have met three different verb tenses:

present	porto	I carry, I am carrying
imperfect	portabam	I was carrying, I used to carry
perfect	portavi	I carried, I have carried

We now meet the *future tense*, which describes actions that are yet to take place and has the basic meaning *I shall . . ., I am going to . . .*.

Since most stories are set in the past, the future tense is used less often than the other tenses we have met. Unless the author is talking about the future (which is unlikely), you will probably find a future tense verb within direct speech.

The future tense has two sets of endings. The 1st and 2nd conjugations use one set, and the 3rd, 4th and mixed conjugations use the other. You therefore need to know the conjugation of a verb in order to form and recognise its future tense correctly (remember how you can work this out by analysing the principal parts: see p50). The endings are:

conjugation		1st & 2nd	3rd, 4th & mixed	
sg	1	-bo	-am	I shall. . .**
	2	-bis	-es	you (*sg*) will. . .
	3	-bit	-et	he/she/it will. . .
pl	1	-bimus	-emus	we shall. . .**
	2	-bitis	-etis	you (*pl*) will. . .
	3	-bunt*	-ent	they will. . .

* Note the form *-bunt* rather than, as you might have predicted, *-bint*.
** Nowadays *will* is often used rather than *shall* for the first person. But in formal English there is a subtle difference: *I will* conveys determination or an order (*I will go to the city*), whereas *I shall* is neutral (*I shall go to the city*). Conversely for the second and third persons *will* is neutral whereas *shall* is used for an instruction: *you will learn* vs *you shall learn*. Reversing the *shall/will* norm for the person expresses an order.

You will recognise once again the distinctive person endings that we saw in the endings of the present and imperfect: -o (or -m), -s, -t, -mus, -tis, -nt.

The 1st and 2nd conjugations use endings similar to the -bam, -bas, -bat (etc.) of the imperfect tense; in the imperfect tense all the conjugations used the same endings, but this is not the case in the future.

Here in full are the future tense forms for each of the four main conjugations. Note once again how the characteristic vowels appear in the 1st (a), 2nd (e) and 4th (i) conjugations between the basic verb stem and the ending.

		1st *I shall carry*	2nd *I shall warn*	3rd *I shall drag*	4th* *I shall hear*
sg	1	porta-bo	mone-bo	trah-am	audi-am
	2	porta-bis	mone-bis	trah-es	audi-es
	3	porta-bit	mone-bit	trah-et	audi-et
pl	1	porta-bimus	mone-bimus	trah-emus	audi-emus
	2	porta-bitis	mone-bitis	trah-etis	audi-etis
	3	porta-bunt	mone-bunt	trah-ent	audi-ent

* Just as in the present and imperfect tenses, mixed conjugation verbs go like *audio* in the future tense: e.g. *capiam, capies, capiet,* etc.

Exercise 5.1 (future tense)

Translate into English:

1. timebo
2. fugient
3. bibes
4. ridebunt
5. punient
6. vocabimus
7. scribetis
8. habebitis
9. cadet
10. petam

A possible source of confusion is that the future tense of the 3rd conjugation (*traham, -es, -et*, etc.) resembles the present tense of the 2nd conjugation (*moneo, -es, -et*, etc.) in every bit apart from the first person singular. To translate the verb correctly you need to remember (or check) its conjugation.

e.g. mones   *2nd conjugation, therefore present:*   you *(sg)* warn
      trahes   *3rd conjugation, therefore future:*   you *(sg)* will drag

(The present tense of the 3rd conjugation here would be *trahis*.)

Exercise 5.2 (2nd and 3rd conjugations, mixed tenses)

Translate into English:

1. sedes
2. curres
3. videbis
4. relinquent
5. delent
6. ducebant
7. discedam
8. manebat
9. mittet
10. terrent

Exercise 5.3

Translate into Latin (checking the conjugation where necessary):

1. He will guard.
2. You *(sg)* will build.
3. He will leave behind.
4. You *(pl)* will capture.
5. They will give.
6. She is afraid.
7. She will depart.
8. We shall run.
9. We run.
10. They will stay.

Exercise 5.4

Translate into English:

1. dei viros bonos non punient.
2. num per urbem media nocte ambulabis?
3. maritus meus post cenam adveniet.
4. epistulas librosque in horto legam.
5. mater mecum in villa manebit.
6. decem annos Romae habitabimus.
7. invenietne patrem in magna turba?
8. ad insulam in quinque navibus navigabimus.
9. auxilium ad amicos statim mittemus.
10. dux stultus te in periculum ducet.

Exercise 5.5

S&C

Translate into Latin:

1. The soldiers will depart in the middle of the night.
2. Brother, where shall we build the city?
3. The young man will have to flee from Rome.
4. You (*pl*) will drink good wine in the inn.
5. Surely you (*sg*) will warn your friends about the danger?

'will have to': use future of *debeo* (+ *infinitive*)

Here are three more time adverbs that are often (but not only) found with future tense verbs:

cras	tomorrow
mox	soon
numquam	never

Exercise 5.6

Translate into English:

1.   rex cum multis militibus mox adveniet.
2.   dei Romam numquam relinquent.
3.   mater me ad forum cras mittet.
4.   puer stultus libros numquam legit.
5.   quaere me cras in foro, amice!
6.   clamores senum mox audivimus.
7.   frater meus ad villam tuam cras adveniet.
8.   urbem Romam numquam vidi.
9.   navigabitne mox dominus ad insulam?
10.   dux 'cras,' inquit 'milites, muros capiemus.'

FUTURE TENSE OF *sum* and *possum*

We have so far met *sum* and its compound *possum* in three tenses:

	I am	I can, I am able
present	sum	possum
imperfect	eram	poteram
perfect	fui	potui

Here are their forms in the future tense:

		I shall be	I shall be able
sg	*1*	ero	potero
	2	eris	poteris
	3	erit	poterit
pl	*1*	erimus	poterimus
	2	eritis	poteritis
	3	erunt*	poterunt*

* Note *(pot)erunt* rather than *(pot)erint*, as you might have predicted: compare *-bunt* rather than *-bint* in the future tense of the 1st and 2nd conjugations. Take care to distinguish the future *(pot)erunt* from the imperfect *(pot)erant*.

Note how *possum* once again simply sticks the prefix *pot-* onto *sum*.

Exercise 5.7

Translate into English:

1. cras, pueri, reginam videre poteritis.
2. frater meus 'num' inquit 'bellum erit?'
3. nunc lacrimatis, sed laeti mox eritis.
4. senes te in foro invenire non poterunt.
5. quinque horas Romae ero; deinde cum domino discedam.

Exercise 5.8

Translate into Latin:

1. Will the leader be angry?
2. You will be able to stay with your brother in Rome, boy.
3. I shall be in the city tomorrow, friends; seek me in the forum!
4. The soldiers will soon arrive; we shall not be able to flee.
5. The Romans are foolish; they will never be able to capture me.

REVISION CHECKPOINT

Make sure you know:

- the two sets of endings for the future tense, and which set is used for which conjugations
- the new adverbs *cras, mox, numquam*
- the future tense forms of *sum* and *possum*

Background: Aeneas and the Roman 'future'

Aeneas dutifully obeys divine will in abandoning Dido and Carthage, and takes to the seas once again. While sailing away from the African coast he spots smoke rising from the city; little does he realise that this comes from Dido's funeral pyre. Dido's final words contain the promise that the peoples of Rome and Carthage will be enemies for evermore, and a vow that one day a Carthaginian 'avenger' will punish Aeneas' descendants for his betrayal.

This scene illustrates the way in which the poet Virgil cleverly manipulates time as he tells the story of Aeneas' quest. Virgil composed the *Aeneid* in the 20s BC, by which time Rome had indeed fought and won three bitter wars against Carthage for control of the western Mediterranean (the Punic Wars in 264–241, 218–201 and 149–146 BC). Hannibal, the most formidable Carthaginian general, even occupied Italy itself for many years during the second war, before his eventual defeat: it is Hannibal to whom Virgil is likely referring when he describes Dido's wish for an 'avenger'. For Virgil's readers, therefore, the Punic Wars were already the familiar stuff of history, a key part of the story of Rome's unstoppable progress from tiny city to world superpower. In the world of Virgil's poem, however, the struggles between the descendants of Dido and Aeneas lie many years ahead. The events of myth are depicted as the root cause of later historical events. Virgil also uses his readers' knowledge of Roman history to add greater depth to Dido's tragedy. Not only does the queen herself suffer at Aeneas' hands, but her dying wish for Carthaginian revenge on Rome will not ultimately be fulfilled (as the readers well know, to their glee).

There are several other scenes where Virgil writes about known historical events as if they were in the distant Roman future. For example, even when Aeneas is in grave danger during the storm that drives him to Carthage, Jupiter reassures Venus with the words *imperium sine fine dedi* ('I have granted [the Romans] empire without end') – see Ex. 4.27. Here Virgil explains Roman territorial expansion as divine destiny, long ago set in stone: the empire that the Romans have by his day acquired was sanctioned by the gods from the very start.

When Aeneas lands once again in Sicily he organises games to celebrate the anniversary of the death of his father Anchises, who later appears to Aeneas as a ghost. Upon arrival in Italy, the ghost tells him, Aeneas must visit Anchises' soul in the Underworld, where he will learn more about his future. He will need to seek out the Sibyl as his guide for this descent (recall the words of Helenus that you read in Ex. 3.37). In the Underworld Aeneas will also see a parade of Roman heroes; these are the souls of great Romans yet to be born, amongst them Julius Caesar and the emperor Augustus, during whose reign Virgil was writing. Once again Virgil incorporates past and present figures into his poem in the form of prophecies about the 'future'.

When Aeneas finally reaches central Italy he finds himself searching for allies on the very spot where Rome will one day stand. Virgil describes cows grazing in what will later become the *Forum Romanum*, and again invites his readers to reflect on the workings of time. Many centuries later, long after the demise of the Roman Empire, the sight of the classical buildings in ruins prompted the historian Edward Gibbon (1737–1794), himself reflecting on the workings of time, to write the landmark *The History of the Decline and Fall of the Roman Empire* (1776–1788): all things eventually come full circle, as Virgil himself perhaps sensed.

Exercise 5.9

The Sibyl and the Underworld

Neptunus Troianis ventos bonos dedit. nimbi e caelo statim discesserunt. naves
per mare sine periculo navigaverunt et ad terram mox advenerunt. nautae e
navibus laeti cucurrerunt: in Hesperia tandem erant. pater Aeneas scopulos
ascendit; templum statim vidit. erat prope templum magnum antrum ubi
5 habitabat Sibylla. Sibylla Aenean subito vocavit: 'Troiane, precibus deos voca!
tum futura audies.' Aeneas 'o magni dei!' clamavit. 'magnae deae! Hesperiam
Troianis date! o Sibylla domina, futura Troianorum mihi monstra!'

	Neptunus -i *m*	Neptune
	ventus -i *m*	wind
	nimbus -i *m*	cloud
	sine (+ *abl*)	without
3	Hesperia -ae *f*	Hesperia (*the Trojans' promised land*)
	scopulus -i *m*	cliff
	ascendo -ere -i	I climb
	prope (+ *acc*)	near
	antrum -i *n*	cave
4	ubi	(*here*) where (*not as question*)
	Sibylla -ae *f*	the Sibyl
	preces -um *f pl*	prayers
	futura -orum *n pl*	the future (*lit* future things)
	monstro -are	I reveal, I show

Sibylla 'dux bone,' inquit 'Troiani Hesperiam habebunt. sed bella, horrida bella,
et Tiberim multo sanguine spumantem video. auxilium ab urbe Graeca pete!'
10 Aeneas 'tu, o vates,' inquit 'portam Averni custodis. permitte me patrem meum
videre perque terram mortuorum ambulare!' Sibylla 'est ramus aureus in silva'
inquit. 'tu ramum inveni! deinde ego tibi viam monstrabo.'

	horridus -a -um	dreadful
	Tiberis *acc* Tiberim *m*	the Tiber (*river in Rome*)
	spumantem	foaming (*m acc sg*)
	sanguis -inis *m*	blood
9	Graecus -a -um	Greek
	vates -is *f*	(*here*) prophetess
	Avernus -i *m*	the Underworld
	permitto -ere	I allow
	mortuus -a -um	dead
11	ramus -i *m*	branch, bough
	aureus -a -um	golden
	silva -ae *f*	wood

Aeneas in <u>silvam</u> statim festinavit. <u>ramum</u> <u>aureum</u> mox invenit et ad Sibyllam
portavit. deinde <u>vates</u> portam Averni Aeneae <u>monstravit</u>; Aeneas cum Sibylla per
15 portam in Avernum <u>descendit</u>. advenerunt ad <u>loca</u> <u>ubi</u> habitant <u>Morbus</u> et <u>Mors</u>
et Bellum et <u>Discordia</u>. mox ad <u>Stygem</u> venerunt et <u>portitorem</u> <u>Charontem</u>
viderunt. Sibylla Charonti <u>ramum</u> <u>aureum</u> <u>monstravit</u>. senex Aenean <u>vatemque</u>
<u>trans</u> Stygem portavit.

	descendo -ere -i	I descend, I go down
	locus -i *m (pl is n: loca)*	place, area, region
	Morbus -i *m*	Disease
	mors mortis *f*	death *(with capital letter, as a deity,* Death)
16	Discordia -ae *f*	Strife
	Styx Stygis *f*	the Styx *(river in the Underworld)*
	portitor -oris *m*	ferryman
	Charon -ontis *m*	Charon
	trans (+ *acc*)	across

magnum <u>latratum</u> subito audiverunt; <u>Cerberus</u> fuit. Cerberus, <u>canis</u> <u>triceps</u>,
20 Avernum custodiebat. Aeneas timebat sed Sibylla Cerbero cibum <u>soporatum</u>
dedit; Cerberus cibum laetus consumpsit et mox dormiebat. ad terram
<u>mortuorum</u> advenerunt. Aeneas Didonem vidit et 'egone,' inquit 'femina misera,
<u>mortis</u> tuae <u>causa</u> fui? per deos <u>iuro</u>, <u>invitus</u> ab urbe tua discessi: dei me navigare
iusserunt.' sed Dido <u>aversa</u> <u>tacebat</u>; mox fugit. 'cur' inquit Aeneas 'fugis? mecum
25 mane!' sed frustra: Dido discessit.

	latratum	barking (*m acc sg*)
	Cerberus -i *m*	Cerberus
	canis -is *m/f*	dog
	triceps	three-headed (*m nom sg*)
20	soporatus -a -um	sleep-inducing
	mortuus -a -um	dead
	causa -ae *f*	cause, reason
	iuro -are	I swear
	invitus -a -um	unwilling
24	aversus -a -um	having turned away
	taceo -ere	I am silent

ad <u>Elysium</u> tandem advenerunt. Sibylla et Aeneas multos Troianos viderunt. tum
<u>Anchisem</u> tandem invenerunt. Aeneas patrem salutavit et lacrimavit. tum
Anchises <u>posteros</u> Aeneae <u>monstravit</u>. '<u>ecce</u>!' inquit. 'hic sunt reges <u>Albae Longae</u>;
<u>hic</u> magnus <u>Romulus</u> et reges Romani; <u>hic</u> <u>Iulius Caesar</u>; <u>hic</u> <u>Augustus</u>, vir <u>divus</u>.
30 Augustus <u>imperium</u> Romanum <u>Oceano</u>, <u>famam</u> Romanam <u>astris</u> <u>terminabit</u>.
<u>posteri</u> tui, Aenea, terrarum domini erunt!'

Elysium -i *n*	Elysium (*land of the blessed*)
Anchises -is *m*	Anchises
posteri -orum *m pl*	descendants
monstro -are -avi	I reveal, I show

28	ecce!	look!
	hic ... hic ...	here ... here ...
	Alba -ae Longa -ae *f*	Alba Longa (*city, forerunner to Rome*)
	Romulus -i *m*	Romulus (*founder of Rome*)
	Iulius -i Caesar -aris *m*	Julius Caesar (*general and dictator*)
29	Augustus -i *m*	Augustus (*first emperor of Rome*)
	divus -a -um	godlike
	imperium -i *n*	empire
	Oceanus -i *m*	the Ocean (*thought to bound the known world*)
30	fama -ae *f*	fame, glory
	astrum -i *n*	star
	termino -are	I limit, I bound (X, *acc*) with (Y, *abl*)

TEN NEW VERBS (2)

Here are ten more verbs, grouped according to their conjugation and listed with their principal parts:

1st	rogo -are -avi	I ask, I ask for*
	supero -are -avi	I overcome, I beat
2nd	taceo -ere -ui	I am silent, I am quiet
	teneo -ere -ui	I hold
3rd	ascendo -ere -i	I climb
	defendo -ere -i	I defend
	pono -ere posui	I place, I put, I set up
	rego -ere rexi	I rule
	trado -ere -idi	I hand over, I hand down
	vinco -ere vici	I conquer, I win, I am victorious

* When *rogo* means *ask for (a thing)* it can take two accusatives: I ask X (*acc*) for Y (*acc*), e.g. *fratrem auxilium rogo* = I ask my brother for help.

Alternatively you can phrase this: I ask for X (*acc*) from Y (*a/ab* + *abl*), e.g. *auxilium a fratre rogo* = I ask for help from my brother. *peto* works similarly: *auxilium a fratre peto.*

Exercise 5.10

Translate into English:

1. tradidimus
2. vincebas
3. superant
4. tenebunt
5. ponite!
6. tacuistis
7. reximus
8. ascendet
9. rogabis
10. defendebam

Exercise 5.11

Give the Latin for:

1. Conquer (*sg*)!
2. They will hand over.
3. We used to ask.
4. He will be silent.
5. You (*pl*) rule.

Exercise 5.12

Translate into English:

1. patriam meam semper defendam.
2. parvus puer arma tenere non poterit.
3. montem multas horas ascendebamus.
4. Caesar 'veni, vidi, vici' scripsit.
5. multum cibi in navem posuistis.
6. dux 'Romanos' inquit 'mox superabimus, milites.'
7. rex bonus terram multos annos regebat.
8. senem cibum rogavimus.
9. epistulam legi et servo tradidi.
10. tacete, pueri! patrem audite!

mons montis *m*   mountain

Exercise 5.13

Translate into Latin:

1. The soldiers defended the gate for many hours.
2. I have climbed many mountains and seen many seas.
3. We shall ask the goddess for help.
4. Hand the money over to the king at once, boy!
5. I fought against you (*sg*) for a long time. Finally you overcame me.

TIME ADVERBS (2)

Here are five more adverbs connected with time:

heri	yesterday
hodie	today
olim	once, some time ago
saepe	often
tum	then (i.e. at that time)*

* Compare *deinde* = then (i.e. next).

Exercise 5.14

Translate into English:

1. pater me Romam saepe invitat.
2. olim dei ad terram saepe veniebant; nunc caelum numquam relinquunt.
3. servus miser sum: heri laboravi, hodie laboro, cras laborabo.
4. tum laetus eram; nunc puella mea me non amat.
5. te in via heri vidi: quo ambulabas?

Exercise 5.15

Translate these linked sentences into Latin:

1. The Romans were once attacking an island.
2. The leader often sent the soldiers into danger.
3. But the Roman soldiers were never victorious.
4. Then the leader heard a god's words.
5. 'Today the gods have given me help,' he said. 'Tomorrow we shall capture the island.'

LINKING SENTENCES: *FOR, THEREFORE, HOWEVER*

The following are often used to link sentences:

enim	for (i.e. because)
igitur	therefore, and so
tamen	however

None of these words can come first in a sentence; they normally come second, but are often translated as if they had come first.

enim is used to explain a previous sentence.

> e.g.   vinum bibimus. aqua enim mala est.
>   We are drinking wine. For the water is bad.

igitur is used when a second sentence describes the result of the first.

> e.g.   aqua mala est. vinum igitur bibimus.
>   The water is bad. Therefore we are drinking wine.

tamen is used to provide a contrast between two sentences.

> e.g.   servi laborant. ancillae tamen dormiunt.
>   The slaves are working. The slave-girls however are sleeping.

Exercise 5.16

Translate these linked sentences into English:

1. iuvenis in urbe non habitabat. in agris enim ambulare currereque amabat. pater tamen Romae habitabat. iuvenis igitur iter Romam saepe faciebat.

2. Iuno dea Aenean non amabat. Aeneas enim dux Troianorum erat. Iuno igitur consilium cepit et magnam <u>tempestatem</u> misit. Aeneas igitur in magno periculo erat. Venus tamen auxilium Troianis dedit.

tempestas -atis *f*   storm

Exercise 5.17

The eating of tables

A chance remark causes Aeneas to celebrate the fulfilment of a prophecy.

Aeneas et Troiani per oram Italiae navigabant. media nocte Neptunus navibus ventos secundos dedit et Troianos praeter insulam Circae sagae duxit. prima luce venti resiederunt et Aeneas terram vidit. magnam silvam et flumen Tiberim vidit. amicos ad terram navigare iussit; laeti ad flumen advenerunt et naves ad ripam
5 religaverunt. tum in ripa Aeneas et amici parvam cenam paraverunt. nautis poma libaque dura pro patellis dederunt. nautae poma et, adhuc esurientes, liba consumpserunt. tum Ascanius filius Aeneae risit et 'ecce, pater!' inquit 'etiam mensas consumimus!' Aeneas verba audivit et obstupefactus deos statim vocavit.

	ora -ae *f*	coast
	Italia -ae *f*	Italy
	Neptunus -i *m*	Neptune
	ventus -i *m*	wind
2	secundus -a -um	favourable, following
	praeter (+ *acc*)	past, beyond
	Circe -ae *f*	Circe (*goddess who turns men to beasts*)
	saga -ae *f*	witch
	lux lucis *f*	light
3	resido -ere -i	I become calm, I subside
	flumen -inis *n*	river
	Tiberis *acc* Tiberim *m*	the Tiber
	ripa -ae *f*	riverbank
	religo -are -avi	I tie up, I moor (a ship)
5	pomum -i *n*	fruit
	libum -i *n*	flat-bread board
	durus -a -um	tough
	pro (+ *abl*)	instead of
	patella -ae *f*	plate
6	adhuc	still
	esurientes	hungry (*m nom pl*)
	Ascanius -i *m*	Ascanius
	filius -i *m*	son
	etiam	(*here*) even
8	mensa -ae *f*	table
	obstupefactus -a -um	amazed, astounded

'salve, terra mihi <u>debita</u>! dei Troianorum, <u>salvete</u>! <u>hic</u> <u>domus</u> Troiana, <u>hic</u> patria
10 Troiana erit. pater meus* verba <u>arcana</u> mihi reliquit: "in terra <u>ignota</u> <u>fames</u> te
   <u>mensas</u> consumere <u>coget</u>. <u>ibi</u> mane! <u>ibi</u> urbem aedifica!" nunc <u>intellego</u>: ad
   <u>Hesperiam</u> tandem advenimus. Troiani, deos vocate! novam patriam tandem
   habemus.'

	salve! *pl* salvete!	hail!, hello!, greetings!
	debitus -a -um	owed, fated
	hic	here
	domus	home (*f nom sg*)
10	arcanus -a -um	secret
	ignotus -a -um	unknown
	fames -is *f*	hunger
	mensa -ae *f*	table
	cogo -ere	I force
11	ibi	there
	intellego -ere	I understand
	Hesperia -ae *f*	Hesperia (*the Trojans' promised land*)

* It was, in fact, the Harpy queen Celaeno who gave Aeneas this prophecy, as she
mocked him and warned him that he still had a long voyage to endure (see p85).
Why do you think Aeneas misremembers?

PERSONAL PRONOUNS AND POSSESSIVE ADJECTIVES (2): *nos, vos, noster, vester*

In Chapter Four we met the personal pronouns and possessive adjectives for the first
and second persons singular: *ego* and *tu*, *meus* and *tuus*. Here we meet the equivalents
for the first and second persons plural.

The personal pronouns decline as follows:

	we, us	you (*pl*)
nom	nos	vos
acc	nos	vos
gen	nostrum	vestrum
dat	nobis	vobis
abl	nobis	vobis

• Note the places where the same form is used for two cases – as usual, you
  must work out the case from the context.

• The vocative of *vos* is identical to the nominative. *nos* has no vocative.

e.g.   dominus multos libros nobis dedit.
       The master has given us many books.

vos heri in foro vidi.
I saw you (*pl*) yesterday in the marketplace.

As with *ego* and *tu*, *nos* and *vos* usually appear in the nominative only for emphasis or contrast, since the person endings of the verbs already reveal the subjects:

e.g.   vos fugistis, sed nos mansimus.
You (pl) fled, but *we* stayed.

Just as with *ego* and *tu*, if the ablative forms of *nos* and *vos* appear with *cum*, the words join up, with *cum* second:

e.g.   per agros vobiscum ambulabo, pueri.
I shall walk through the fields with you, boys.

The possessive adjectives *our(s)* and *your(s)* are 2-1-2 adjectives which decline like *pulcher -chra -chrum* (see p80). Note how the -*e*- drops out of the stem for both:

our, ours

		m	*f*	*n*
sg	*nom*	noster	nostr-a	nostr-um
	acc	nostr-um	nostr-am	nostr-um
		etc.		

your, yours (belonging to you *pl*)

sg	*nom*	vester	vestr-a	vestr-um
	acc	vestr-um	vestr-am	vestr-um
		etc.		

There is an overlap between parts of *noster* and *vester* and the genitive forms of *nos* (*nostrum*) and *vos* (*vestrum*). As a rule, the possessive adjective is used (in the appropriate number, gender and case) rather than the genitive of the pronoun. Study the following sentence, for example:

vinum nostrum bonum est.
Our wine is good.

Here *nostrum* is naturally read as the nominative neuter singular of the possessive adjective *noster* (i.e. *our wine*) rather than the genitive of the pronoun *nos* (i.e. *the wine of us*), though the forms are identical.

Exercise 5.18

Translate into English:

1. rex noster malus est; ad terram igitur vestram mox fugiemus.
2. milites nos ceperunt et ad ducem traxerunt.
3. mater pecuniam cibumque nobis tradidit.
4. mare nostrum est; naves nostrae semper vincunt.
5. pater noster nobiscum ad insulam navigavit.

Exercise 5.19

Translate into Latin:

1. The sailors heard our shouts and ran to the temple.
2. Surely the king has ordered you to defend the city, soldiers?
3. *You* be quiet, boys; *we* will ask father for money.
4. Have you seen our slaves, soldier? They have run away.
5. You fear your leader, Romans; we love our king.

REVISION CHECKPOINT

Make sure you know:

- the ten new verbs listed on p139, including their perfect tenses
- the meanings of time adverbs on p141
- how *enim*, *igitur* and *tamen* are used to link sentences
- how the personal pronouns *nos* and *vos* and their associated possessive adjectives *noster* and *vester* decline

Exercise 5.20

The future site of Rome

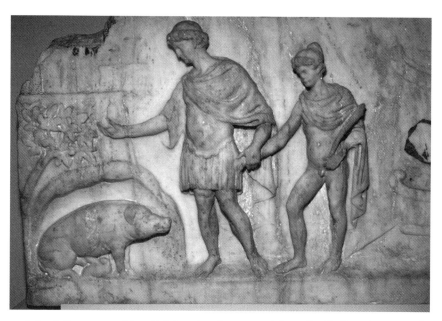

Figure 5.1 *A Roman marble relief showing Aeneas and Ascanius finding the sow with thirty piglets.* (Photo by CM Dixon/Print Collector(Getty Images)

Aeneas seeks allies in his war against the Latins, the tribe who dwell in the area where the Trojans have landed. He finds himself on the spot where Rome will one day stand.

erat in <u>Latio</u> bellum inter Troianos et <u>Latinos</u>. nox tamen nunc erat et milites tacebant. in <u>somnio</u> – ecce! – Aeneas <u>Tiberinum</u> deum vidit. Tiberinus statim 'Troiane,' inquit 'diu <u>exspectate</u>! bellum timere non debes. tu enim <u>tutus</u> eris, Troiani <u>tuti</u> erunt. in <u>ripa</u> ingentem <u>suem</u> <u>albam</u> cum <u>triginta</u> <u>porcellis</u> invenies. <u>ibi</u>

	Latium -i *n*	Latium (*region of central Italy*)
	Latini -orum *m pl*	the Latins (*tribe in Latium*)
	somnium -i *n*	sleep, dream
	Tiberinus -i *m*	Tiberinus (*river god of the Tiber*)
3	exspectatus -a -um	awaited
	tutus -a -um	safe
	ripa -ae *f*	riverbank
	sus suis *f*	sow, female pig
	albus -a -um	white
4	triginta *indecl*	thirty
	porcellus -i *m*	piglet
	ibi	there

5   post <u>triginta</u> annos filius tuus urbem, <u>Albam Longam</u> nomine, <u>condet</u>.* non <u>procul</u>
<u>socios</u> bonos invenies: <u>Evandrum</u> regem et <u>Pallanteum</u>, urbem <u>Graecam</u>.** Evander
cum Latinis semper <u>bellum gerit</u>. multum auxilium tibi dabit. ego te ad Evandrum
ducam; tu nunc <u>surge</u>!' Aeneas subito <u>surrexit</u>; <u>suem</u> mox invenit et deis <u>gratias egit</u>.

	Alba -ae Longa -ae *f*	Alba Longa (*forerunner to Rome*)
	condo -ere	(*here*) I found, I establish (a city)
	procul	far off, far away
	socius -i *m*	ally
6	Evander -ri *m*	Evander (*Greek now living in Latium*)
	Pallanteum -i *n*	Pallanteum (*settlement on site of Rome*)
	Graecus -a -um	Greek
	bellum gero -ere	I wage war
	surgo -ere surrexi	I rise, I get up
8	gratias ago -ere egi	I give thanks (to), I thank (+ *dat*)

* The name 'Alba' Longa is derived from *albus*.
** Recall that the Sibyl ordered Trojan Aeneas to seek help from, ironically, a Greek
city (see p137).

  deinde Troiani navem paraverunt et per <u>Tiberim</u> Pallanteum navigaverunt. muros,
10 <u>arcem</u>, villas <u>raras</u> tandem viderunt: urbs, nunc magna, tum parva erat. Evander
et filius, <u>Pallas</u> nomine, Troianos laeti salutaverunt. rex servos cibum Aeneae et
Troianis parare iussit. post cenam Evander cum Aenea per urbem ambulavit.

	Tiberis *acc* Tiberim *m*	the Tiber
	arx arcis *f*	citadel
	rarus -a -um	scattered
	Pallas -antis *m*	Pallas

Figure 5.2 *Cattle drovers near the Temple of Hercules Victor, Rome, 1890.* Photograph by
Count Primoli. (Photo by DeAgostini/Getty Images)

Evander multas <u>fabulas</u> loci <u>narrabat</u>: '<u>hic</u> est <u>antrum</u> <u>Caci</u>. Cacus <u>saevus</u> <u>vaccas</u>
<u>Herculis</u> cepit et in <u>antro</u> <u>celavit</u>. Hercules tamen <u>vaccas</u> invenit et Cacum morte
15 misera punivit. <u>hic</u> <u>Saturnus</u> viris <u>leges</u> et terrae Latium nomen dedit. <u>Fortuna</u>
<u>fatumque</u> me <u>exsulem</u> <u>huc</u> duxerunt.' rex Aeneasque ad <u>Capitolium</u> tandem
advenerunt: nunc <u>aureum</u>, tum <u>rusticum</u> erat. villa Evandri in foro Romano erat;
per vias ambulabant <u>vaccae</u>. nox tandem erat; Aeneas, loco <u>captus</u>, dormivit.
<u>postridie</u> Evander Aeneae milites et Pallantem <u>socium</u> dedit. Aeneas laetus discessit.

	fabula -ae *f*	story, tale
	narro -are	I tell, I narrate
	hic ... hic ...	here ... here ...
	antrum -i *n*	cave
13	Cacus -i *m*	Cacus
	saevus -a -um	savage, cruel
	vacca -ae *f*	cow, heifer
	Hercules -is *m*	Hercules
	celo -are -avi	I hide, I conceal
15	Saturnus -i *m*	Saturn (*god, father of Jupiter*)
	lex legis *f*	law
	Fortuna -ae *f*	Fortune
	fatum -i *n*	fate
	exsul -ulis *m/f*	exile, exiled person
16	huc	(to) here
	Capitolium -i *n*	the Capitol (*one of Rome's seven hills*)
	aureus -a -um	golden, refined
	rusticus -a -um	rustic, unadorned
	captus -a -um	(*here*) charmed, captivated
19	postridie	on the next day
	socius -i *m*	ally

ADJECTIVES (3): THIRD DECLENSION

So far we have met adjectives that use the endings of the first and second declensions in a 2-1-2 pattern (for the masculine, feminine and neuter): *laetus -a -um* and the slight variation *miser -era -erum*.

There are also many adjectives that use the endings of the third declension (see pp104–5). It is helpful to study two examples:

brave

		m/f	*n*
sg	nom	fort-is	fort-e
	acc	fort-em	fort-e
	gen	fort-is	fort-is
	dat	fort-i	fort-i
	abl	fort-i	fort-i
pl	nom	fort-es	fort-ia
	acc	fort-es	fort-ia
	gen	fort-ium	fort-ium
	dat	fort-ibus	fort-ibus
	abl	fort-ibus	fort-ibus

huge

		m/f	*n*
sg	nom	ingens	ingens
	acc	ingent-em	ingens
	gen	ingent-is	ingent-is
	dat	ingent-i	ingent-i
	abl	ingent-i	ingent-i
pl	nom	ingent-es	ingent-ia
	acc	ingent-es	ingent-ia
	gen	ingent-ium	ingent-ium
	dat	ingent-ibus	ingent-ibus
	abl	ingent-ibus	ingent-ibus

fortis and *ingens* represent two basic models:

1   Adjectives ending *-is* in the masculine and feminine nominative singular, like *fortis*. These have a different neuter nominative/accusative singular ending, *-e*.

2   Adjectives with other forms in the nominative singular, like *ingens*. For these adjectives the neuter nominative singular is identical to the masculine/ feminine. The genitive stem will usually change for these adjectives (e.g. *ingens*, stem *ingent-*).

Note the following points that apply to both models:

- As with third declension nouns, there is no separate set of feminine endings for third declension adjectives. We can therefore talk about these adjectives as 3-3 (shorthand for *3m&f – 3n*).
- The vocative is identical to the nominative.
- The ablative singular ends *-i* rather than *-e* as it does in third declension nouns. (For adjectives like *fortis*, the form *forte* is instead used for the neuter nominative and accusative singular.)
- The genitive plural is usually *-ium* (whereas it can be either *-um* or *-ium* for third declension nouns – see note on pp108–109)
- As always, in the neuter the nominative and accusative are identical in both singular and plural.
- The neuter nominative and accusative plural once again end in *-a*, but here there is an *-i-* added in, so the ending is *-ia*.

In word lists and dictionaries the information provided about a third declension adjective makes it clear which of the two models is being used.

- Adjectives like *fortis* will be listed with their separate neuter form. Take off *-is* from the masculine/feminine form to get the stem.
- Adjectives like *ingens* will be listed with the genitive form (removing *-is* from the genitive shows the stem, as with third declension nouns). There is no need to show the neuter form, since it is identical to the masculine/feminine. The stem, however, changes, so the genitive must be shown.

i.e.   fortis forte   *adj*
        ingens ingentis   *adj*

Alternatively this information may be given in abbreviated form:

        fortis -e *adj 3*
        ingens -entis *adj 3*

Here are some common third declension adjectives, listed with either the neuter nominative singular (if they go like *fortis*) or the genitive singular (if they go like *ingens*):

ferox -ocis	fierce, ferocious
gravis -e	heavy; serious
omnis -e	all, every
tristis -e	sad

Note too the following pair. The second is a compounded form of the first:

| facilis -e | easy | |
| difficilis -e | difficult | (originally *dis-facilis*: 'not-easy') |

Finally, *celer* (quick, fast) is unusual in that it behaves as if it started *celeris*, though the *-is* has dropped out of the nominative singular in the masculine. Thus the nominative singular is different in all three genders, though it goes just like *fortis* thereafter:

		m	*f*	*n*
sg	nom	celer	celeris	celere
	acc	celerem	celerem	celere
		etc.		

Exercise 5.21

Give an English derivative from:
1. facilis
2. celer
3. omnis
4. fortis
5. gravis

Exercise 5.22

Identify the number, gender and case (more than one possible answer exists for each of these; give one possibility):
1. ingentium
2. tristi
3. difficilibus
4. ferocem
5. omnes
6. celeria
7. facile
8. omnibus
9. celeris
10. graves

Exercise 5.23

Give the Latin for the following (noting the number, gender and case):

1. sad (*n nom pl*)
2. fierce (*f gen sg*)
3. difficult (*m abl sg*)
4. quick (*m acc pl*)
5. serious (*f acc sg*)

Exercise 5.24

Translate into English:

1. navis parva sed celeris est.
2. clamores puellarum tristium audivimus.
3. dux cum omnibus militibus mox adveniet.
4. facile est regem videre: ingens et pulcher est.
5. pater tuus vir gravis erat: numquam ridebat.
6. milites feroces fortesque sunt; a periculo non fugient.
7. servi dona gravia in hortum portaverunt.
8. mater nostra libros tristes legere non amat.
9. domina epistulam difficilem scribebat.
10. rex iussit omnes nautas statim oppugnare.

Exercise 5.25

Translate into Latin:

1. The brave young man loves the sad slave-girl.
2. I have read every book about the great war.
3. Send a quick messenger today, father!
4. It is easy to find a beautiful girl in Rome.
5. We shall build a huge temple in the middle of the city.

Exercise 5.26

A final duel

The Trojans, now helped by Pallas who leads a detachment of his father's soldiers, fight a bitter war of survival against the Latins. Eventually the matter is decided by a duel between Aeneas and Turnus; both men seek to marry Lavinia, the daughter of the local king. The brutal culmination of the duel represents the final act of Virgil's Aeneid.

bellum ferox erat. Aeneas auxilium <u>Pallantis</u> et milites <u>Evandri</u> nunc habebat. <u>Turnus</u> tamen, dux <u>Latinorum</u>, Pallantem <u>hasta</u> necavit et <u>balteum</u> a <u>corpore</u> cepit. sed vir stultus <u>spolio</u> <u>nimis</u> <u>gaudebat</u>; magna <u>ira</u> Aenean cepit; dux Troianus <u>fervidus</u> <u>ultionem</u> <u>promisit</u>. tandem <u>indutias</u> <u>conventum</u>que fecerunt. Aeneas et
5 Turnus 'nos <u>comminus</u>' inquiunt 'pugnabimus. <u>praemia</u> <u>victori</u> erunt urbs <u>Laurentum</u> et <u>filia</u> regis et regnum <u>Latium</u>! tum inter Troianos Latinosque <u>pax</u> erit.'

	Pallas -antis *m*	Pallas
	Evander -ri *m*	Evander
	Turnus -i *m*	Turnus
	Latini -orum *m pl*	the Latins
2	hasta -ae *f*	spear
	balteus -i *m*	sword-belt
	corpus -oris *n*	body
	spolium -i *n*	the spoil, the winnings
	nimis	too much, excessively
3	gaudeo -ere	I rejoice (in, + *abl*)
	ira -ae *f*	anger
	fervidus -a -um	seething, raging
	ultio -ionis *f*	revenge
	promitto -ere promisi	I promise
4	indutiae -arum *f pl*	truce
	conventum -i *n*	agreement
	comminus	(*here*) in single combat
	victor -oris *m*	victor
	praemium -i *n*	reward, prize
6	Laurentum -i *n*	Laurentum
	filia -ae *f*	daughter
	(*but dat & abl pl* filiabus; *compare* deabus)	
	Latium -i *n*	Latium
	pax pacis *f*	peace

diu pugnaverunt, dux contra ducem <u>sicut</u> <u>taurus</u> contra <u>taurum</u>. gladius Turno subito <u>defuit</u>; statim fugit; Aeneas tamen Turno <u>sicut</u> <u>venator</u> <u>cervo</u> <u>instabat</u>. tum in caelo <u>Iuno</u> <u>iram</u> tandem <u>deposuit</u> et <u>Iovi</u> 'cedo,' inquit 'marite. Latini nomen,
10 linguam, <u>vestes</u> retinebunt, sed Aeneas <u>victor</u> erit.' tum Aeneas Turnum <u>hasta</u> <u>percussit</u>. Turnus miser 'tu, Aenea,' clamavit 'vicisti! omnia tua sunt: urbs, uxor, regnum. sed mihi <u>parce</u>!' verba <u>animum</u> Aeneae nunc <u>flectebant</u>; tum tamen <u>balteum</u> Pallantis vidit et gladium in Turnum iratus <u>condidit</u>.

	sicut	just like
	taurus -i *m*	bull
	desum desse defui	I fail (someone), I let (someone) down (+ *dat*)
	venator -oris *m*	hunter
8	cervus -i *m*	stag
	insto -are	I chase, I press upon (+ *dat*)
	Iuno -onis *f*	Juno
	ira -ae *f*	anger
	depono -ere deposui	I let go
9	Iuppiter Iovis *m*	Jupiter
	cedo -ere	I yield, I give up
	lingua -ae *f*	language
	vestis -is *f*	clothing
	retineo -ere	I keep
10	hasta -ae *f*	spear
	percutio -ere percussi	I strike
	parco -ere	I spare (+ *dat*)
	animus -i *m*	mind
	flecto -ere	I alter, I bend
13	balteus -i *m*	sword-belt
	condo -ere -idi	(*here*) I bury

ADVERBS FROM ADJECTIVES

We have already met a number of adverbs, not formed from adjectives, which provide more information about *when* or *how* the action is happening, e.g. *diu, nunc, statim.*

Alternatively, adverbs can be formed from adjectives. To form the adverb, English often adds *-ly* to the adjective, though this is not always possible with longer adjectives: e.g. *bravely, happily, with difficulty,* etc.

Latin adjectives are turned into adverbs in one of two ways, according to their declension.

1   2-1-2 adjectives like *laetus* and *miser* add *-e* to the stem (found by removing *-i* from the masculine genitive singular).

e.g.   laetus   happy   *adj*   pulcher   beautiful   *adv*
       laete   happily   *adv*   pulchre   beautifully   *adv*

Note an irregular adverb formed from *bonus*, a regular 2-1-2 adjective:

       bene   well

2   Most 3-3 adjectives add *-iter* (or sometimes just *-ter)* to the stem (found by removing *-is* from the genitive singular).

e.g.   fortis   brave   *adjective*
       fortiter   bravely   *adverb*

so:	celeriter	quickly, fast (*as adv*)
	ferociter	fiercely, ferociously
	graviter	heavily; seriously

A few third declension adjectives, however, still form their adverbs with the ending -*e*: *facilis*, *difficilis* and *tristis* all do this.

so:	facile	easily
	difficile	with difficulty
	triste	sadly

If you meet one of these in a passage you will need to work out from the context whether it is the adverb or the neuter nominative or accusative singular of the adjective. Of the two, the adverb is more frequently found.

Finally, note the following new adverb:

forte   by chance

This looks like it comes from *fortis* (brave), but in fact has another root, *fors* (fortune), and a meaning quite different from that of *fortiter*. Although the form *forte* could be the neuter nominative or accusative singular of *fortis*, it is much more likely to be the adverb *by chance*.

Confusing *fortiter* with *forte* is an extremely common mistake at GCSE.

Unlike adjectives, adverbs do not decline, since they modify the verb and do not agree with any noun or pronoun in the sentence. Thus there are no sets of endings to learn.

It is important not to translate an adverb as if it were an adjective (another common mistake at GCSE). Take care to distinguish them. Compare:

e.g.   puer stultus librum non legit.
         The foolish boy did not read the book.   (*adjective*)

         puer amicum in periculum stulte duxit.
         The boy foolishly led his friend into danger.   (*adverb*)

In the first sentence, the boy himself is being described as foolish; in the second, it is his action that is being described as foolish.

As we have seen, however, it is sometimes acceptable to translate an adjective as if it were an adverb, e.g. *puer laetus clamavit* = *The happy boy shouted* or *The boy shouted happily*. Use your own judgement as to which translation is best. In summary: treating an adjective as an adverb is sometimes acceptable; treating an adverb as an adjective is not.

Exercise 5.27

Translate into English:

1. naves ad insulas celeriter navigaverunt.
2. dux 'cur, fratres, disceditis?' irate rogavit.
3. feminae amicos laete salutaverunt.
4. milites urbem fortiter diu defendebant; tandem fugerunt.
5. vos in foro heri forte vidimus.
6. post mortem mariti regina regnum multos annos bene regebat.
7. dux milites in silvam stulte duxit.
8. num Romae facile dormire potestis?
9. iuvenes laeti vinum in taberna bibebant.
10. nunc senex sum; verba difficile lego.

Exercise 5.28

S&C

Translate into Latin:

1. The freedman used to punish his slaves fiercely.
2. Our soldiers guarded the city bravely yesterday.
3. Your slaves are working well today, friends.
4. By chance I found the boys in the large crowd.
5. The girls walked slowly and sadly along the road.

REVISION CHECKPOINT

Make sure you know:

- the endings of third declension adjectives, and the two different models: *fortis* and *ingens*
- how to form adverbs from 2-1-2 and 3-3 adjectives
- the meanings of the irregular adverbs *bene* and *forte*

Background: from Aeneas to Romulus

Aeneas is, of course, a figure of myth rather than of history, but this didn't stop the Romans thinking of him as a founding father; it is unsatisfactory not to know where your nation comes from, and they sought some explanation of their own origins.

According to myth, Aeneas' killing of Turnus secured the survival of the Trojans in central Italy; the abandonment, however, of their native language, clothing and customs (as demanded by Juno in Ex. 5.26) conveniently explains why the Romans' culture was an Italian rather than Trojan one. Aeneas went on to marry the local princess Lavinia and to found the city of Lavinium, which he named after her. He was to live only three more years, but his son Ascanius succeeded him and reigned for thirty, founding Alba Longa as a new royal capital. Ascanius' own descendants would rule Alba Longa for three hundred more years: there is a suspicious elegance about the numbers (three/thirty/three hundred). As you will read in the next stories, a family crisis eventually led to Romulus' foundation of a third city, Rome, supposedly in the year we call 753 BC. Romans measured all dates from this point, *Ab Urbe Condita*: i.e. *from the city's foundation*. Might the sequence of numbers for the various stages of Roman development suggest that Rome itself is to last for 3000 years?

So much for the myth. In reality little is known about the early history of Rome and the surrounding region, Latium. No historical evidence exists for any of the characters named above, even Romulus: a figure of his name simply makes for a plausible founding hero. (Various theories have been offered to explain the actual origins of the name 'Rome'; it is probably linked to the language of the Etruscans, a local people who pre-dated the Romans.) As, however, with the myth of the Trojan War, the legend of Rome's foundation and growth contains a kernel of historical truth. Archaeolgical evidence shows traces of settlement on the site that would become Rome from as early as 5000 BC. Its topography made it a prime location: the hills on which Rome is famously built offered defence, while the River Tiber was narrow enough to be crossed safely but wide enough to be navigable from the sea, less than twenty miles away. The site was certainly inhabited by the tenth century BC, i.e. long before Romulus' supposed foundation in 753 BC. By the eighth century it seems there was an unremarkable village, *Rumi*, on the site; if there was any 'founding hero' around that date, he was perhaps symbolically re-founding an existing settlement in a bid to assert his own authority.

'Romulus' might be historically and archaeologically invisible, but to the Romans he was a central and inspirational part of the national story. Elements of his story, in particular the she-wolf who suckled Romulus and Remus as infants (compare the uncannily similar story of the bear suckling Paris, Ex. 2.15), became important visual symbols of the city. Romulus' leadership, meanwhile, was viewed as exemplary; the emperor Augustus liked to compare himself to Romulus as well as to Aeneas. Modern verdicts on the morality of Romulus' actions (see Ex. 5.30 and 5.39) are rather more complex.

Exercise 5.29

Romulus and Remus

Figure 5.3 *A bronze statue of the she-wolf suckling Romulus and Remus. c. 450–430 BC. Height 75 cm. Now in Capitoline Museum, Rome.* (Photo By DEA/G. NIMATALLAH/ De Agostini/Getty Images)

Several hundred years after Aeneas, twins are born to a princess. They are condemned to death, but their chance survival has lasting consequences.

Numitor et Amulius filii regis Albae Longae erant. post mortem patris, Numitor, frater natu maior, rex esse debebat. Amulius tamen multos milites habebat et fratrem ferociter expulit. Amulius igitur nunc rex erat, sed insidias semper timebat. filios Numitoris mox necavit; filiam tamen non necavit, sed Vestalem

5 fecit. 'femina igitur' inquit 'maritum filiosque numquam habebit.' femina tamen,

	Numitor -oris *m*	Numitor
	Amulius -i *m*	Amulius
	Alba -ae Longa -ae *f*	Alba Longa
	natu maior	elder
3	expello -ere expuli	I drive out
	insidiae -arum *f pl*	plotting, treachery
	Vestalis -is *f*	Vestal Virgin (*unmarried priestess*)

Rhea Silvia nomine, filios geminos, Romulum et Remum, mox peperit. Amulius
rex, ubi de pueris audivit, 'quis est pater geminorum?' irate rogavit. Rhea Silvia
'Mars' inquit 'pater est.' sed Amulius verbis matris non credebat. servum iussit
pueros in Tiberim iacere. servus tamen pueros in flumen non iecit sed in ripa
10 reliquit. deinde – ecce! – ad flumen forte advenit lupa. lupa pueros invenit et
lacte aluit. mox pastor geminos invenit et laete servavit.

	Rhea -ae Silvia -ae *f*	Rhea Silvia
	geminus -a -um	twin
	Romulus -i *m*	Romulus
	Remus -i *m*	Remus
6	pario -ere peperi	I give birth to
	ubi	(*here*) when
	quis?	who?
	Mars Martis *m*	Mars (*god of war*)
	credo -ere -idi	I believe, I trust (+ *dat*)
9	Tiberis *acc* Tiberim *m*	the Tiber
	iacio -ere ieci	I throw
	flumen -inis *n*	river
	ripa -ae *f*	riverbank
	lupa -ae *f*	she-wolf
11	lac lactis *m*	milk
	alo -ere -ui	I feed, I nourish
	pastor -oris *m*	shepherd
	servo -are -avi	I save

- *Romulus* and *Remus* will not be glossed again.

Exercise 5.30

The foundation of Rome

The twins exact their vengeance upon Aemulius before falling out themselves.

Romulus Remusque iuvenes fortes nunc erant. de matre et de Amulio
cognoverunt; regem punire constituerunt. Albam Longam iter fecerunt; Amulium
mox necaverunt et Numitorem regem restituerunt. tum novam urbem condere
constituerunt. erant prope Albam Longam septem colles. Romulus urbem in
5 Palatio aedificare cupiebat, Remus in Aventino. 'dei' inquiunt 'locum constituent.
nobis augurium mittent.' Romulus in Palatio manebat, Remus in Aventino. subito
super Aventinum sex vultures Remus vidit. 'in Aventino erit urbs mea!' laete
clamavit 'Rema erit nomen!' tum tamen super Palatium duodecim vultures
Romulus vidit. 'augurium tuum' clamavit 'primum fuit, frater, sed augurium meum
10 melius fuit. in Palatio urbem aedificabimus. urbem Romam vocabimus.' Romulus
urbem aedificare celeriter coepit. Remus tamen muros fratris vidit et risit. Romulus
iratus statim 'de urbe mea' inquit 'impune non ridebis!' diu pugnaverunt; tandem
Romulus Remum saeve necavit. ita Romulus cum morte fratris Romam condidit.

	Amulius -i *m*	Amulius
	cognosco -ere cognovi	I find out
	constituo -ere -ui	I decide
	Alba -ae Longa -ae *f*	Alba Longa
3	Numitor -oris *m*	Numitor
	restituo -ere -ui	I restore
	condo -ere	I found (a city)
	prope (+ *acc*)	near (to)
	septem	seven
4	collis -is *m*	hill
	Palatium -i *n*	the Palatine (*hill in Rome*)
	cupio -ere	I want, I desire
	Aventinum -i *n*	the Aventine (*hill in Rome*)
	augurium -i *n*	omen, augury
7	super (+ *acc*)	above
	sex	six
	vultur -uris *m*	vulture
	Rema -ae *f*	Reme
	duodecim	twelve
10	melius	better (*n nom sg*)
	coepi (*irreg pf*)	I began
	impune	freely, without being punished
	ita	thus, in this way

THIRD PERSON PRONOUNS (1): *is, ea, id*

We have so far met the personal pronouns for the first and second persons singular and plural: *ego, tu, nos, vos.*

Now we meet the third person pronoun. Unlike the other personal pronouns, this has forms in all three genders and in both the singular and the plural. As a result, it is very versatile, and can mean any of *he* (*him*), *she* (*her*), *it* or *they* (*them*). It is extremely common.

In addition to its role as a pronoun, forms of *is, ea, id* can also be used as an adjective meaning *that* (pl *those*); this will be covered in Chapter Seven, in Part 2.

he (him), she (her), it, they (them); that pl *those*

		m	*f*	*n*
sg	nom	is	ea	id
	acc	eum	eam	id
	gen	eius	eius	eius
	dat	ei	ei	ei
	abl	eo	ea	eo
pl	*nom*	ei	eae	ea
	acc	eos	eas	ea
	gen	eorum	earum	eorum
	dat	eis	eis	eis
	abl	eis	eis	eis

- Note the genitive and dative singular endings *-ius* and *-i* (underlined), which are the same for all three genders. You will see these endings again in the same parts of the many other pronouns.
- The plural forms have regular 2-1-2 endings.
- There is no vocative.
- As elsewhere, the number, gender and case of ambiguous forms need to be worked out from the context.

The gender and number of *is, ea, id* affect your translation: take care to identify these. You may need to supply the word *man, woman,* or *thing* (or their plural forms) when translating.

    e.g.   pueros inveni et eos ad regem duxi.
           I found the boys and led them to the king.

           eam in horto vidimus.
           We saw her in the garden.

           ea non audivi.
           I did not hear those things.

Exercise 5.31

Identify the number, gender and case of the following (give all possibilities):

1. eius (*three possibilities*)
2. ei (*four possibilites*)
3. eis (*six possibilities*)
4. eas
5. eorum (*two possibilites*)

Exercise 5.32

Give the Latin for:
1. to her (*dat*)
2. they (*m nom pl*)
3. her (*acc*)
4. them (*f acc pl*)
5. it (*nom*)

Exercise 5.33

Translate into English:
1. rex eos in villam vocavit.
2. ea facile legere non possum.
3. multam pecuniam eis dabo.
4. puella tristis eas in hortum duxit.
5. nomen eius non audivi.
6. Romanos deosque eorum amamus.
7. cum ea decem annos habitabamus.
8. erant forte inter eos multi milites fortes.
9. senem in silva cepimus. nunc eum ad regem trahemus.
10. femina laeta maritum vocavit et epistulam ei tradidit.

THIRD PERSON PRONOUNS (2): *se*

We saw that the pronouns *ego*, *tu*, *nos* and *vos* can be used reflexively:

e.g. *me terreo.* *num nos necabitis?*
      I frighten myself.   Surely you won't kill yourselves?

is, ea, id cannot be used as a reflexive in this way; as a pronoun it must always must refer to *someone other than the subject of the sentence.*

e.g. femina eam necavit.
      The woman killed her (i.e. someone else).

We therefore call *is*, *ea*, *id* the third person non-reflexive pronoun.

There is a **separate** third person reflexive pronoun: *se*.

himself, herself, itself, *pl* themselves

m/f/n, sg and *pl*

nom	-
acc	se
gen	sui
dat	sibi
abl	se

- The same forms are used for both the singular and plural of *se,* and for all three genders.
- There is no nominative.

se cannot be translated in isolation. It always refers back to the subject of the sentence, and agrees with it in gender and number.

e.g.   senex cibum sibi paravit.
       The old man prepared the food for himself.

       milites inter se pugnabant.
       The soldiers were fighting among themselves.

Take particular care to distinguish between *eum/eam/eos/eas* and *se:*

e.g.   ancilla eam necavit.
       The slave-girl killed her (i.e. someone else).

       ancilla se necavit.
       The slave-girl killed herself.

When used with the preposition *cum* (with), the ablative of *se* tags the preposition onto its end (so *secum*), just like the first and second person pronouns (e.g. *mecum, vobiscum*). Ablative forms of *is, ea, id* do not do this:

e.g.   dominus amicos secum duxit.
       The master took (*lit* led) his friends with him(self).

       cum eo ambulabamus.
       We were walking with him.

Exercise 5.34

Translate into English:

1. milites nostri se fortiter defendent.
2. dux noster cibum sibi numquam parat.
3. nautae stulti inter se diu clamabant.
4. senex saepe sibi ridet.
5. reges multas naves secum duxerunt.

Exercise 5.35

Translate into Latin:

1. After the war the Romans gave him a new name.
2. The leader will take all the soldiers with him.
3. We like the young men but we do not trust them.
4. The foolish kings were fighting among themselves.
5. The queen ruled them well for many years.

THIRD PERSON POSSESSIVES: *eius* and *suus*

In English there is room for ambiguity with the words *his, her, its, their(s)*, since they can be either reflexive or non-reflexive. In '*the boy saw his house*' we do not know whether the house being referred to is that of the boy (i.e. *his own* house) or that of somebody else (e.g. *his friend's*).

Latin avoids this problem by expressing the non-reflexive and the reflexive third person possessive in two different ways.

For the third person non-reflexive possessive, since there is no adjective meaning *his* (i.e. someone else's), we have to use the genitive of *is, ea, id* (*lit* of him/her/it).

Contrast for example the first person singular, where *meus* is available to express *my*, and so the genitive of the pronoun *ego* doesn't need to be used (e.g. we say *villa mea* instead of *villa mei*, lit *the house of me*).

his/her/its (*belonging to someone other than the subject of the sentence*)

	m	*f*	*n*
sg	eius	eius	eius

their (*belonging to people other than the subject of the sentence*)

pl	eorum	earum	eorum

When using the genitive of *is, ea, id* the number and gender are those of the possessor (though the singular forms are the same for all three genders, in any case). The forms do not depend on the number, gender and case of the thing owned.

> e.g.   matrem eius vidi.
>   I saw his (or her) mother.
>
>   feminae lacrimabant sed mox fratrem earum invenimus.
>   The women were crying but we soon found their brother.

Note that the *-us* ending of *eius* may give it the misleading appearance of a 2-1-2 adjective, but is actually the distinctive *-ius* genitive of a pronoun.

For the third person reflexive possessive (i.e. when the *his/her/its/their* refers back to the subject of the sentence) a specific adjective does exist: *suus -a -um*.

his/her/its/their (own) (*belonging to whoever is the subject of the sentence*)

		m	*f*	*n*	
sg	*nom*	suus	sua	suum	
	acc	suum	suam	suum	
		etc.	*etc.*	*etc.*	(regular 2-1-2)

suus (like e.g. *meus*) agrees in number, gender and case with the thing that is possessed, not with the possessor (therefore it works differently from *eius*: see above).

It is not the case that the masculine of *suus* means *his*, the feminine means *her*, and the neuter means *its* (or that the the plural means *their*). Any part of *suus* can mean any of these: the number, gender and case of *suus* are simply those of the noun it describes.

> e.g.   puer urbem suam amabat.   femina consilia sua amat.
>   The boy loved his (own) city.   The woman loves her (own) plans.

In these examples we translate using *his* or *her* depending on the gender of the possessor, but in the Latin the gender of *suus* depends on the gender of the thing possessed.

Compare the French possessive adjective for *his/her (own)*: *son, sa*. Like *suus* in Latin, the gender of *son/sa* depends on that of the thing possessed, not the possessor: e.g. *elle aime* <u>son</u> *père* (she loves <u>her</u> father); *il aime* <u>sa</u> *ville* (he loves <u>his</u> town).

Finally, note an important idiom involving *suos* (masculine plural, without a noun). In a military context it usually means *his men/soldiers*. In other contexts it can mean *his/her/their people/family*.

> e.g.   dux suos in periculum misit.   puella suos non amat.
>   The leader sent his men into danger. The girl does not like her family.

Exercise 5.36

Translate into English:

1. cives regi suo semper credebant.
2. amicos nostros et villam eorum amamus.
3. rex suos fortiter pugnare iussit.
4. post mortem senis filius eius regnum habebat.
5. milites ducem suum necaverunt et caput eius Romam miserunt.

Exercise 5.37

Translate into Latin:

1. The woman does not trust her own brother.
2. I love the girl but I fear her father.
3. A good leader never leaves his soliders.
4. We overcame the Romans and we killed their leader.
5. I have seen Rome and its beautiful temples.

REVISION CHECKPOINT

Make sure you know:

- how the non-reflexive *is, ea, id* and the reflexive *se* decline
- the difference in their meanings and usage
- the difference between the non-reflexive (*eius*) and the reflexive (*suus*) forms of the third person possessive
- what *suos* can mean if it appears without a noun

Exercise 5.38 (revision of all personal pronouns and possessive adjectives)

Translate into English:

1. id tibi statim dabo.
2. mater mea pecuniam suam vobis dedit.
3. villa nostra magna est: nobiscum manete, amici!
4. cur me de fratre tuo non monuisti?
5. frater vester cum ea diu habitabat.
6. Romani contra amicos suos numquam pugnant.
7. iuvenis amicum secum ad tabernam duxit.
8. unde venistis, pueri? ubi est urbs vestra?
9. tu vinum tuum bibe! ego meum bibam.
10. cives ducem suum necaverunt et caput eius per vias portabant.

Exercise 5.39

The Sabine women

Romulus' new city cannot grow without women; a brutal solution is found.

Romulus leges et magistratus urbi dedit. multi exsules et fugitivi Romae habitare
cupiebant. mox Palatium satis magnum non erat et cives villas suas in aliis collibus
aedificaverunt. plerique tamen novorum civium viri erant; feminae paucae erant.
urbs sine feminis crescere non poterat: rex igitur consilium cepit. Romulus ludos
5   in Circo Maximo fecit et Sabinos invitavit. viri Sabini cum uxoribus laete
advenerunt. Romulus tamen in turba milites celavit. milites signum exspectare
iussit. Romani Sabinis cibum vinumque dederunt; omnes bibebant et ridebant et
ludos laete spectabant. subito tamen Romulus signum dedit. milites Romani
feminas Sabinas ceperunt et eas e Circo traxerunt. viros Sabinos superaverunt.
10 Romani mox feminas Sabinas in matrimonium duxerunt. scelus malum fuit, sed
urbs nunc crescere poterat.

	lex legis *f*	law
	magistratus	magistrates (*m acc pl*)
	exsul -ulis *m/f*	exile, exiled person
	fugitivus -i *m*	fugitive, runaway
2	cupio -ere	I want, I desire
	Palatium -i *n*	the Palatine (*hill in Rome*)
	satis	enough, sufficiently
	civis -is *m/f*	citizen
	aliis	other (*m abl pl*)

2	collis -is *m*	hill
	plerique	the majority (*m n pl*)
	pauci -ae -a	few, few in number
	sine (+ *abl*)	without
	cresco -ere	I grow, I increase in size
4	ludi -orum *m pl*	games
	Circus -i Maximus -i *m*	Circus Maximus (*racecourse at Rome*)
	Sabini -orum *m pl*	Sabines (*people neighbouring Rome*)
	abinus -a -um	Sabine (*as adj*)
	celo -are -avi	I hide
6	signum -i *n*	sign, signal
	exspecto -are	I wait for
	in matrimonium duco	I marry (a woman; *lit* 'lead into marriage')
	scelus -eris *n*	crime

Exercise 5.40

The ascension of Romulus

Romulus mysteriously disappears; he later makes a surprising return.

Romulus Romanos multos annos bene regebat. multas <u>gentes</u> in bello vicit;
Romanis pacem dedit. olim cives in forum vocavit. magna turba civium et
<u>senatorum</u> advenit. deinde tamen ingens <u>nubes</u> cum multa <u>aqua</u> <u>grandineque</u> de
caelo ad terram <u>descendit</u>. cives <u>perterriti</u> erant et magna <u>voce</u> clamabant. <u>nubes</u>
5 tandem in caelum <u>iterum</u> ascendit. Romulus tamen in foro <u>non iam</u> erat. cives 'ubi'
inquiunt 'est rex noster? <u>quis</u> Romulum vidit?' <u>quamquam</u> omnes diu quaerebant,
<u>nemo</u> regem invenire potuit.

<u>postea</u> <u>senator</u> <u>Proclus</u> nomine per viam Romam ambulabat. subito – ecce! –
Romulus de caelo <u>descendit</u>. rex '<u>salve</u>, civis!' inquit. 'ego nunc in caelo cum deis

	gens gentis *f*	tribe, people
	senator -oris *m*	senator (*leading politician in Rome*)
	nubes -is *f*	cloud
	aqua -ae *f*	(*here*) rain
3	grando -inis *f*	hail, hail-storm
	descendo -ere -i	I descend, I come down
	perterritus -a -um	terrified
	vox vocis *f*	voice
	iterum	again
5	non iam	no longer
	quis?	who?
	quamquam	although
	nemo	no-one, nobody
	postea	later, afterwards
8	Proclus -i *m*	Proclus
	salve!	greetings! hello!

10 habito. iube cives templum mihi Romae aedificare! vobis magnam urbem aedificavi.
Roma omnes terras olim vincet. Romani <u>voluntate</u> deorum <u>orbem terrarum</u> regent.
<u>gens</u> <u>nulla</u> milites Romanos terrebit. festina! verba mea civibus <u>nuntia</u>!' tum rex in
caelum <u>iterum</u> ascendit. Proclus Romam celeriter cucurrit et cives vocavit. cives
nuntium audiverunt et laete lacrimaverunt.

voluntas -atis *f*	will, blessing
orbis -is *m* terrarum	the world
nulla	no (*f nom sg*)
nuntio -are	I announce

SUMMARY OF CHAPTER FIVE GRAMMAR

Future tense (*I shall/will . . .*):

- two sets of endings:

    1st and 2nd conj: *-bo, -bis, -bit, -bimus, -bitis, -bunt*

    (added to pres stem & characteristic vowel, e.g. *portabo, monebis*)

    3rd, 4th and mixed conj: *-am, -es, -et, -emus, -etis, -ent*

    (added to pres stem, e.g. *traham, audies*)

- future of *sum*:   ero, eris, erit, erimus, eritis, erunt
- future of *possum*:   potero, poteris, etc.

1st and 2nd person plural pronouns and possessives:

- we, us: *nos, nos, nostrum, nobis, nobis*   our: *noster -tra -trum*
- you (*pl*): *vos, vos, vestrum, vobis, vobis*   your (*pl*): *vester -tra -trum*
- N.B. order of *nobiscum, vobiscum*   (both 2-1-2)

Third person pronouns:

- non-reflexive: *is, ea, id*   e.g. *eum necavit*. (someone else)
- reflexive: *se*   e.g. *se necavit*.   (himself)

Third person possessives:

- non-reflexive: *eius/eorum/earum* (genitive of *is, ea, id*)
- reflexive: *suus -a -um* (2-1-2; agrees with thing possessed)
- e.g. *puer matrem eius vidit*.   (his = someone else's)

    puer matrem suam vidit.   (his = his own)

Third declension adjectives:

- two models:

    fortis: *n nom sg* different from *m/f*, i.e. *forte*

    ingens: *n nom sg* identical to *m/f*; *gen* stem changes (e.g. *ingent-*)

- use same endings as third declension nouns <u>except</u>: *abl sg* -i, *n nom/acc pl* -ia, *gen pl* usually -ium

Adverbs from adjectives:

- 2-1-2 adjectives form adverbs by adding *-e* to the stem   e.g. *laete*
- 3-3 adjectives usually add *-iter* or *-ter* to the stem   e.g. *fortiter*
- some 3-3 adjectives form adverbs in *-e*   e.g. *facile*

CHAPTER FIVE VOCABULARY

ascendo -ere -i	I climb
bene	well
celer -eris -ere	quick, fast
civis -is *m/f*	citizen
cras	tomorrow
credo -ere -idi	I believe, I trust (+ *dat*)
defendo -ere -i	I defend
difficilis -e	difficult
ecce!	look!
enim	for
facilis -e	easy
ferox -ocis	fierce, ferocious
filia -ae *f* (N.B. *dat/abl pl* filiabus)	daughter
filius -i *m*	son
forte	by chance
fortis -e	brave
gravis -e	heavy, serious
heri	yesterday
hodie	today
igitur	therefore, and so
ingens -entis	huge
is, ea, id	he, she, it, *pl* they
locus -i (*pl is n:* loca) *m/n*	place
mons montis *m*	mountain
mors mortis *f*	death
mox	soon
nos nostrum	we, us
noster -tra -trum	our, ours
numquam	never
olim	once, some time ago
omnis -e	all, every
pax pacis *f*	peace
pono -ere posui	I place, I put, I set up
rego -ere rexi	I rule
rogo -are -avi	I ask, I ask for
saepe	often
saevus -a -um	savage, cruel
se sui	himself, herself, itself, themselves (*refl*)
silva -ae *f*	wood
supero -are -avi	I overcome, I beat
suus -a -um	his, her, its, their (own) (*refl*)
taceo -ere -ui	I am silent, I am quiet
tamen	however

teneo -ere -ui	I hold
trado -ere -idi	I hand over, I hand down
tristis -e	sad
tum	then (i.e. at that time)
vester -tra -trum	your, yours (of you *pl*)
vinco -ere vici	I conquer, I win, I am victorious
vos vestrum	you (*pl*)

50 words

Chapter Six

VERBS: PLUPERFECT TENSE

We have already met four different verb tenses:

present	porto	I carry, I am carrying
future	portabo*	I shall carry, I am going to carry
imperfect	portabam	I was carrying, I used to carry
perfect	portavi	I carried, I have carried

> * Remember that verbs in the 3rd and 4th conjugations have a different set of endings in the future tense (*-am, -es, -et*, etc., e.g. *traham* = I shall drag).

When the action of a sentence is set in the past, and an event from even further back in time is referred to, the *pluperfect tense* is used. The term *pluperfect* literally means 'more than perfect', i.e. another stage back in time from the perfect tense. It is used to describe an action that *had already happened* by a certain point in the past.

Always use *had* when translating a pluperfect tense verb into English, e.g. *the king had ruled Rome for many years; the ship had arrived during the night.*

The pluperfect is formed by adding to the perfect stem a set of person endings identical to the imperfect tense of *sum* (i.e. *-eram, -eras, -erat* . . .).

Thus there are no new bits of learning: instead, this is a new arrangement of some of the building-blocks with which you are already familiar:

sg	*1*	perfect stem +	-eram	I had . . .
	2		-eras	you (*sg*) had . . .
	3		-erat	he/she/it had . . .
pl	*1*		-eramus	we had . . .
	2		-eratis	you (*pl*) had . . .
	3		-erant	they had . . .

hence:	*portaveram*	I had carried

Here is the pluperfect tense for each of the four main verb conjugations. All four attach the pluperfect endings to the perfect stem:

conj		1st I had carried	2nd I had warned	3rd I had dragged	4th I had heard
sg	1	portav-eram	monu-eram	trax-eram	audiv-eram
	2	portav-eras	monu-eras	trax-eras	audiv-eras
	3	portav-erat	monu-erat	trax-erat	audiv-erat
pl	1	portav-eramus	monu-eramus	trax-eramus	audiv-eramus
	2	portav-eratis	monu-eratis	trax-eratis	audiv-eratis
	3	portav-erant	monu-erant	trax-erant	audiv-erant

- Mixed conjugation verbs also attach the pluperfect endings to the perfect stem, hence: *ceperam, ceperas, ceperat* etc. for *capio*.

- The pluperfect of *sum* and *possum* are formed in the same way, hence: *fueram* and *potueram*.

- Take care to distinguish between the third person plural perfect (*-erunt*) and pluperfect (*-erant*). This is a common mistake at GCSE.

The pluperfect tense is often used to explain one action or situation as the result of an earlier one.

e.g. rex milites paravit. hostes enim viderat.
The king prepared his soldiers. For he had seen the enemy.

Exercise 6.1

Translate into English:

1. posuerant
2. rogaveramus
3. tenueram
4. superaverat
5. tradideratis
6. ceperas
7. fueram
8. crediderant
9. potueramus
10. reliquerat

Exercise 6.2

Translate into Latin:

1. We had climbed.
2. They had defended.
3. You (*sg*) had fallen.
4. I had conquered.
5. You (*pl*) had arrived.
6. They had fled.
7. He had laughed.
8. We had sought.
9. She had wept.
10. I had done.

Exercise 6.3 (mixed tenses)

Translate into English:

1. tenueramus
2. ponebam
3. credidistis
4. ascenditis
5. superaverant
6. tradiderunt
7. vincent
8. petiveras
9. feceram
10. ridebas

Exercise 6.4

Translate into English:

1. reges urbem Romam olim habuerant.
2. multos annos servi fueramus.
3. ancilla subito clamavit. nuntium enim tandem viderat.
4. maritum bonum invenire numquam potuerat.
5. ego manebam; tu tamen fugeras.
6. dux regnum filio tandem tradiderat.
7. servi omnem cibum in hortum portaverant.
8. iter longum difficileque fuit. iuvenes enim decem horas ambulaverant.
9. fuerat bellum saevum multos annos sed pacem tandem fecimus.
10. cur amicum vestrum de periculo non monueratis?

Exercise 6.5

Translate into Latin:

1. The ship had finally arrived at the island.
2. We had heard many things about the leader.
3. The good boys had read all the books.
4. The long walls had defended the city well for many years.
5. Had your father lived in Rome for a long time, girls?

REVISION CHECKPOINT

Make sure you know:

- the form and meaning of the pluperfect tense
- the sorts of situations in which a pluperfect tense might be used

Background: the early kings of Rome

From 753 to 509 BC Rome was supposedly ruled by seven kings, beginning with Romulus. Since, however, the Romans' own historical records were destroyed when the city was sacked by the Gauls in 390 BC, the stories about the kings cannot be treated as historical fact. Moreover, it seems somewhat implausible that the Romans had just seven kings during this period: their reigns would need to have been long (on average about 35 years each) and stable to account for the entire period. It is likely that the story of seven kings represents a considerable simplification of the reality.

In the absence of other explanations the Romans credited the kings with taking key steps in the early formation of the city: Romulus, for example, ensured a gender balance in the city with the capture of the Sabine women; Numa established a religious code; Tarquinius Superbus was responsible for purchasing the Sibylline Books, which would later be revered as a set of national prophecies. The tendency for major achievements to be ascribed to particular individuals was common in ancient times (the Spartans, for example, credited a lawgiver Lycurgus with creating their laws and culture, even though he may well have never existed).

Two of the last three kings had 'Tarquinius' as part of their name. This name derives from a neighbouring city, Tarquinii, which was an Etruscan settlement. The Etruscans were the major regional power prior to the growth of Rome. It is likely that the Etruscans did in fact control Rome for a period prior to 509 BC, and that the Roman legend of two kings with Etruscan names is a memory of this period of subjugation. The eventual overthrow of the last king, Tarquinius Superbus, in 509 BC may well therefore have been, in reality, a Roman liberation from foreign Etruscan control rather than simply a Roman popular uprising against their own monarchy.

The Romans celebrated this overthrow as a landmark date: when the kings were evicted the state became a *republic* in which power was shared between two *consuls* who were elected each year. It was under this system that Rome grew from a small village into the cosmopolitan capital city of an empire that ruled most of the known world. The term *rex* became, in the Roman mind, a tainted byword for moral corruption; both Julius Caesar and Augustus would later go to great lengths to deny that they were kings, even though in many ways that is precisely what they were.

Exercise 6.6

The reluctant ruler

After Romulus' ascension the Romans struggle to find a new king.

Romulus in caelum nunc ascenderat; in terra tamen <u>senatores</u> de regno inter se pugnabant. viri <u>Sabini</u> regem Sabinum <u>cupiebant</u>; viri Romani regem Romanum <u>cupiebant</u>. <u>nemo</u> tamen <u>magnopere eminebat</u>: fuit <u>annuum interregnum</u> et <u>senatores</u> urbem regebant. cives regem tandem rogabant. 'vos, senatores,' inquiunt 'novum

5   regem Romae legite!'

	senator -oris *m*	senator (*leading politician in Rome*)
	Sabinus -a -um	Sabine (*or as m pl noun* = the Sabines)
	cupio -ere -ivi	I want, I desire
	nemo	no-one (*nom*)
3	magnopere	greatly

emineo -ere	I stand out, I am pre-eminent
annuus -a -um	year-long
interregnum -i *n*	interregnum (*period without a monarch*)

vir bonus <u>clarus</u>que, <u>Numa</u> nomine, in agris habitabat. Numa magnam <u>virtutem</u>, multam <u>doctrinam</u>, <u>animum</u> <u>temperatum</u> habebat; omnes <u>leges</u> deorum <u>sciebat</u>. <u>senatores</u> Romani igitur Numam novum regem legerunt. nuntios ad Numam statim miserunt. nuntii 'Numa bone,' inquiunt 'Romam veni civesque Romanos rege!'

10 Numa Romam mox advenit. 'Romani,' inquit 'non <u>cupio</u> rex vester esse. dei <u>signum</u> mittent <u>si</u> me regem esse <u>cupiunt</u>.' <u>augur</u> igitur <u>Iovem</u> vocavit: 'Iuppiter pater, <u>signum</u> Romanis mitte!' rex deorum <u>signum</u> statim dedit; Numa rex fuit.

	clarus -a -um	famous
	Numa -ae *m*	Numa
	virtus -utis *f*	excellence, goodness, virtue
	doctrina -ae *f*	learning
7	animus -i *m*	mind
	temperatus -a -um	sensible, even-tempered
	lex legis *f*	law
	scio -ire	I know
	signum -i *n*	sign, signal
11	si	if
	augur -uris *m/f*	augur, soothsayer
	Iuppiter Iovis *m*	Jupiter

BECAUSE AND *ALTHOUGH*:
quod and *quamquam*

A *subordinate clause* is a group of words that contains a verb but is not the *main clause* in a sentence. Subordinate clauses could be bracketed off and the sentence would still make sense.

Because and *although* introduce two types of subordinate clause. Both of these analyse events: *because* gives a reason why something occurs (a causal clause); *although* gives a reason why it might have been expected not to (a concessive clause: *although* one fact is *conceded*, another is still true).

These clauses are introduced by indeclinable conjunctions:

| quod | because |
| quamquam | although |

These clauses often contain a verb in the pluperfect tense, describing an action that had already happened by the time of the sentence.

Exercise 6.7

Translate into English:

1. pater ridebat quod verba senis audiverat.
2. pueri quamquam perterriti erant ad portam manebant.
3. filia mea laeta est quod multas epistulas hodie accepit.
4. difficile est credere feminae quamquam eam amo.
5. quamquam milites viderat senex non timebat.

Exercise 6.8

S&C

Translate into Latin:

1. I am sad because you (*sg*) did not send gift.
2. Father climbed the mountain although he cannot easily walk.
3. We are miserable because the Romans have overcome us in war.
4. Because we are Romans we shall never flee.
5. Although my son never writes letters, I send letters to him.

Exercise 6.9

Numa, thunderbolts and fish

Numa presides over a peaceful and devout city. One day he demonstrates his intellect by defeating Jupiter in a battle of wits.

Numa regnum multos annos bene servaverat. pacem cum hostibus Romanorum fecerat; multa templa in urbe aedificaverat; leges civibus dederat; libros scripserat. rex (fama est) cum dea pulchra, Egeria nomine, habitabat. Egeria Numae verba deorum dicebat; deinde Numa ea civibus dicebat; cives verbis regis semper
5   credebant. quamquam Romani bellum multos annos amaverant, Numa cives pacem amare docuit. hostes igitur Romam amare coeperunt. Romulus hostes bello superaverat, Numa pace.

	Numa -ae *m*	Numa (*second king of Rome*)
	servo -are -avi	I save, I protect, I keep
	hostis -is *m*	enemy (*usually plural*)
	lex legis *f*	law
3	fama -ae *f*	rumour, story
	Egeria -ae *f*	Egeria (*a nymph i.e. a minor goddess*)
	dico -ere dixi	I say, I speak, I tell

doceo -ere -ui	I teach
coepi (*irreg pf*)	I began

rex magnam <u>sapientiam</u> habebat. <u>Iuppiter</u> ad terram de caelo olim venit. Numam ad se irate vocavit. deus 'rex' inquit '<u>sapientiam</u> tuam <u>proba</u>! <u>averte</u> <u>fulmina</u> mea
10 ab urbe tua!' Numa '<u>quomodo</u>?' rogavit. deus 'capitibus' inquit. 'capitibus <u>caeparum</u>?' Numa rogavit. 'virorum' Iuppiter inquit. Numa '<u>capillis</u>?' rogavit. Iuppiter inquit '<u>vitas posco</u>'. '<u>pisces</u> igitur dabimus,' Numa inquit. Romani <u>adhuc</u> <u>fulmina</u> <u>caepis</u> et <u>capillis</u> et <u>piscibus</u> <u>avertunt</u>.

	sapientia -ae *f*	wisdom
	Iuppiter Iovis *m*	Jupiter
	probo -are	I prove, I demonstrate
	averto -ere	I ward off, I repel
9	fulmen -inis *n*	lightning, thunderbolt
	quomodo	how?
	caepa -ae *f*	onion (*note the play-on-words: caput/caepa*)
	capilli -orum *m pl*	hair
	vita -ae *f*	life
12	posco -ere	I demand
	piscis -is *m*	fish (*note the play-on-words: posco/piscis*)
	adhuc	still, to this day

THE RELATIVE PRONOUN AND RELATIVE CLAUSES: *qui, quae, quod*

The *relative pronoun* is the name for the pronoun *who* or *which*, and declines according to number, gender and case:

who, which

		m	*f*	*n*
sg	*nom*	qui	quae	quod
	acc	quem	quam	quod
	gen	<u>cuius</u>	<u>cuius</u>	<u>cuius</u>
	dat	<u>cui</u>	<u>cui</u>	<u>cui</u>
	abl	quo	qua	quo
pl	*nom*	qui	quae	quae
	acc	quos	quas	quae
	gen	quorum	quarum	quorum
	dat	quibus	quibus	quibus
	abl	quibus	quibus	quibus

Note the following:

- Some of the endings resemble those of 2-1-2 adjectives (i.e. the ablative singular, and the nominative, accusative and genitive plural); elsewhere endings resemble those of the third declension (e.g. the dative and ablative plural).

- The genitive and dative singular start with a distinctive *c* rather than *q*. Their endings *-ius* and *-i* (underlined above) are the same for all genders. These distinctive endings are used in many pronouns; we have already seen them, for example, in *is, ea, id: eius, ei* (see p162).

Exercise 6.10

Identify the number, gender and case of the following (give all possibilities):

1. quas
2. cui
3. quod
4. quarum
5. quibus
6. quo
7. quorum
8. quae
9. qui
10. cuius

Exercise 6.11

Give the Latin for (noting the required number, gender and case):

1. to whom (*m pl*)*
2. whom (*f acc pl*)
3. which (*n acc sg*)
4. whose (*f sg*)
5. by which (*f sg*)

* English properly uses *whom* for all cases apart from the nominative (*who*) and the genitive (which is best translated *whose*): e.g. *whom* (acc) *did you see in the forum?* However, *whom* is now rather old-fashioned and you will often find *who* being used instead: i.e. *who did you see in the forum?* With its various endings (*who, whom* and *whose*) the relative pronoun is one of the few places where English still uses some inflection (personal pronouns are another, as we have seen).

The appropriate form of *qui, quae, quod* is used to introduce a *relative clause*, which is a subordinate clause that gives us more information about a noun already mentioned in the sentence.

e.g.   The man who was walking along the road was sad.

Here the main clause is *the man . . . was sad*. The relative clause is *who was walking along the road*, and gives us more information about the man. The noun that the relative pronoun refers to is called the *antecedent*. The relative clause refers or *relates* back to the antecedent.

Using a relative clause is one way of incorporating the information provided by one sentence into another:

e.g   puer in foro est. is puellam amat.
      The boy is in the forum. He loves the girl.

      puer qui puellam amat in foro est.
      The boy who loves the girl is in the forum.

The main focus of the second example is that the boy is in the forum: *puer . . . in foro est* is the *main clause*. Now, however, with the addition of the *relative clause* (i.e. *qui puellam amat*) we learn more information about the boy, or find out which boy the author is talking about.

The relative pronoun takes its number and gender from the thing it is describing (the antecedent).

Conversely, it takes its case from the job which it itself is doing within the relative clause. The relative pronoun does not have to be the same case as the antecedent (though this may happen by coincidence); often, it is not. To analyse another example:

libertus quem heri vidi in foro est.
The freedman whom I saw yesterday is in the forum.

antecedent	=	*libertus*
relative pronoun =		*quem*
number:	singular	(agreeing with *libertus*)
gender:	masculine	(agreeing with *libertus*)
case:	accusative	(because the freedman is the object in the relative clause: *I saw him*)

Some forms of the relative pronoun are confusable with *quod* and *quamquam*. Take care to distinguish the following:

quod	*indeclinable conjunction*	because
quod	*n nom/acc sg* of relative	which
quamquam	*indecl conj*	although
quam	*f acc sg* of relative	who/whom/which

Exercise 6.12

Translate into English, identifying the case of the relative pronoun:

1. puer cui donum dedi in foro est.
2. puer qui pecuniam habet in foro est.
3. puer a quo fugio in foro est.
4. puer cuius clamorem audivi in foro est.*
5. puer quem puella amat in foro est.

* Beware of confusing *whose* (= *of whom*) and *who's* (= *who is* or *who has*) in English.

The third person pronoun and the relative pronoun can appear together:

e.g. ei qui Romam defendunt fortes sunt.
      Those who defend Rome are brave.

Exercise 6.13

Translate into English, indentifying the number, gender and case of the relative pronoun in each sentence:

1. ancillam quae regem necaverat invenimus.
2. vidistisne milites qui ad urbem heri advenerunt?
3. navis in qua Romam navigabimus magna et celeris est.
4. amasne eum qui in horto nunc est?
5. templa quae Romani nunc aedificant ingentia erunt.
6. vir pecuniam quam in via invenerat filiabus tradidit.
7. timetisne turbam cuius clamores audire possumus?
8. nautae capita Romanorum quos necaverunt ad regem portant.
9. milites quibus dux pecuniam dedit muros fortiter defendent.
10. femina ad portam per quam maritus festinaverat diu lacrimabat.

Exercise 6.14

S&C

Translate into Latin:

1. The old man who is walking to the forum is my father.
2. The man whom I saw in the street was crying.
3. Give the sword to the man who is now arriving, slave!
4. Do you have the books which my husband sent?
5. The master from whom I am fleeing is savage.

THE INTERROGATIVE PRONOUN: *quis?, quid?*

A slightly modified version of the relative pronoun is used for the question version, *who?, what?*; this is called the *interrogative pronoun*. The term *interrogative* is derived from *rogo*: a question is being *asked*.

Its form only differs from the relative pronoun in the nominative and accusative singular:

who? what?

		m	*f*	*n*
sg	*nom*	quis?	quis?	quid?
	acc	quem?	quam?	quid?
	gen	cuius?	cuius?	cuius?

etc.: same as the relative pronoun

e.g. quis nunc advenit?   quid est nomen tuum?
     Who is now arriving?   What is your name?

     quae video?   cuius clamorem audio?
     What (things) am I seeing?   Whose shouting do I hear?

Exercise 6.15

Translate into English:

1. quis portam nunc defendet?
2. cuius est liber quem teneo? estne tuus, fili?
3. quem in turba vidisti, marite?
4. quae tenes, puer? cur taces?
5. cum quibus ad urbem ambulabis, filia?

REVISION CHECKPOINT

Make sure you know:

- the meaning and use of *quod* and *quamquam*
- how the relative pronoun *qui, quae, quod* declines
- how a relative clause works, and what the *antecedent* is
- the forms and use of the the interrogative pronoun

NUMERALS

Cardinal numbers (one, two, etc.) tell you how many there are of something.

Ordinal numbers (first, second, etc.) tell you the order things come in. The only ordinal number you need for GCSE is *primus* (first).

The cardinal numbers 1–10, 100 and 1000 and their corresponding Roman numerals are given below. They have numerous derivatives in modern European languages.

unus una unum	one	I
duo duae duo	two	II
tres tria	three	III
quattuor	four	IV or IIII
quinque	five	V
sex	six	VI
septem	seven	VII
octo	eight	VIII
novem	nine	IX
decem	ten	X
centum	100	C
mille *pl* milia	1000	M

unus, *duo* and *tres* decline as below; the other numbers do not decline, except *mille*, which declines in the plural.

one

	m	*f*	*n*
nom	unus	una	unum
acc	unum	unam	unum
gen	unius	unius	unius
dat	uni	uni	uni
abl	uno	una	uno

unus is 2-1-2 except in the genitive and dative, which have in all three genders the distinctive *-ius* and *-i* endings we met with the pronouns *is* (*eius* and *ei*) and *qui* (*cuius* and *cui*).

two

	m	*f*	*n*
nom	duo	duae	duo
acc	duos	duas	duo
gen	duorum	duarum	duorum
dat	duobus	duabus	duobus
abl	duobus	duabus	duobus

duo has a few parts in common with 2-1-2.

three

	m/f	*n*
nom	tres	tria
acc	tres	tria
gen	trium	trium
dat	tribus	tribus
abl	tribus	tribus

tres is 3-3 in declension.

Numbers normally come before their nouns, as in English: e.g. *duae feminae*, *quattuor villae*, etc.

mille in the singular can be used with a noun in any case, but its plural *milia* is followed by a genitive (literally *thousands of . . .*). *milia* declines like the neuter of *tres*.

e.g.   Romani mille milites ceperunt.
       The Romans captured a thousand soldiers.

       Romani decem milia militum ceperunt.
       The Romans captured ten thousand soldiers.

       Hannibal cum milibus militum advenit.
       Hannibal arrived with thousands of soldiers.

Exercise 6.16

Give as many derivatives as you can from:

1. octo
2. centum
3. tres
4. unus
5. quinque

Exercise 6.17

Translate into English:

1. fratres nostri novem horas dormiebant.
2. servus malus sex cives bonos necavit.
3. senex laetus tria milia librorum in villa sua habet.
4. Roma regnum unius viri numquam erit.
5. vidistine decem naves quae heri advenerunt?
6. prima hora Roma discessimus.
7. statim tradite mihi duos gladios, pueri!
8. de bellis Romanorum centum libros legi.
9. erant in insula quattuor magna templa.
10. septem duces ad septem portas urbis pugnabant.

Exercise 6.18

Translate into Latin:

1. The soldiers fought bravely for five hours.
2. I will soon arrive with four thousand soldiers.
3. We shall be able to defend the city for one year.
4. The woman lived in Rome with her two daughters.
5. Did you find the eight horses which suddenly fled, slave?

Exercise 6.19

Servius Tullius: flaming child

During the reign of the fifth king of Rome a dramatic omen marks out a slave-boy as heir to the throne.

erat inter servos regis puer cuius nomen <u>Servius Tullius</u> erat. puer olim in <u>regia</u>
dormiebat. servi media nocte? ecce!? <u>flammas</u> circum caput eius subito viderunt.
servi <u>perterriti</u> erant et clamores eorum regem <u>uxorem</u>que eius mox <u>excitaverunt</u>.
puer tamen tacebat et <u>adhuc</u> dormiebat. servus unus aquam ad puerum portabat.
5 regina tamen eum <u>retinuit</u>. '<u>noli</u>' clamavit '<u>flammas</u> <u>restinguere</u>! <u>noli</u> timere! <u>noli</u>
eum <u>movere</u>! <u>flammae</u> <u>signum</u> a deis sunt.' <u>flammae</u> a puero mox discesserunt.

	Servius -i Tullius -i *m*	Servius Tullius
	regia -ae *f*	palace
	flamma -ae *f*	flame
	perterritus -a -um	terrified
3	uxor -oris *f*	wife
	excito -are -avi	I stir, I wake (someone) up
	adhuc	still
	retineo -ere -ui	I hold (someone) back
	noli + *inf*	don't . . .!
5	restinguo -ere	I put out, I extinguish
	moveo -ere	I move
	signum -i *n*	sign, signal

post <u>miraculum</u> regina regi 'videsne, marite,' inquit '<u>hunc</u> puerum, cui dei
<u>flammas</u> miserunt? donum a deis est. <u>lux</u> regno nostro olim erit patriamque
suam servabit. <u>regiam</u> fortiter custodiet. eum igitur statim <u>libera</u>! eum inter filios
10 nostros <u>educare</u> debemus.' puer igitur in <u>regia</u> <u>velut</u> filius regis habitabat. omnia
<u>discebat</u> quae filius regis <u>discere</u> debet. filiam regis tandem <u>in matrimonium duxit</u>
et post mortem regis cives Romani Servium Tullium novum regem legerunt.
regnum multos annos bene regebat.

	miraculum -i *n*	miracle, omen
	hunc	this (*m acc sg*)
	lux lucis *f*	light
	libero -are -avi	I set free
10	educo -are	I bring up, I educate
	velut	just like, as if
	disco -ere	I learn
	in matrimonium duco	I marry

TIME EXPRESSIONS (3): 'TIME WITHIN WHICH'

We saw in Chapter Two that a *time how long* expression uses the accusative:

e.g.   septem horas dormiebam.
         I was sleeping for seven hours.

In Chapter Four we met *time when* expressions, which use the ablative:

e.g.   cives media nocte fugerunt.
         The citizens fled in the middle of the night.

There is a third type of time expression: *time within which*. This kind of expression is best translated into English using *within* or *during*. Like *time when*, *time within which* is expressed with the ablative.

e.g.   urbem tribus horis capiemus.
         We shall capture the city within three hours.

         uno anno duo itinera longa feci.
         I made two long journeys during one year.

Although they both use the ablative case, *time when* and *time within which* expressions are clearly distinguishable if they use numbers: *time when* uses an *ordinal* number like *primus* whereas *time within which* uses a *cardinal* number like *unus*.

e.g   feminae prima hora advenient.
        The women will arrive at the first hour.* (time when)

        feminae una hora advenient.
        The women will arrive within one hour.   (time within which)

* The Romans divided up the day into twenty-four hours, twelve of daylight and twelve of night. The length of the hours therefore changed according to the season: a daylight 'hour' was, for example, c. 75 minutes in midsummer and c. 45 minutes in midwinter.

Note how none of these expressions use prepositions for the words *for, in, during, within* (etc.): they simply use the different cases. (One exception is that *per* can be added to accusatives for emphasis: *per decem horas dormiebam* = I was asleep for ten whole hours.)

Exercise 6.20

Translate into English:

1. multas terras decem annis vincetis.
2. Romanos quattuor horis superavimus.
3. regnum tuum nobis uno anno trade, rex!
4. omnes cives duabus horis fugere iussi.
5. iuvenis laetus sex epistulas una nocte scripsit.

Exercise 6.21

Translate into Latin:

1. The sailors will arrive at the island within three hours.
2. The Romans built new walls within two years.
3. Our friends sent help within five hours.
4. The evil men killed the king during the night.
5. A crowd of angry citizens destroyed the temple within one hour.

REVISION CHECKPOINT

Make sure you know:

- the numbers 1–10, 100 and 1000
- how the numbers 1–4 and the plural of *mille* decline
- the difference between a cardinal number and an ordinal number
- the case used for *time within which* expressions

THE VERB *I GO*: *eo*

The verb *eo* (I go) is very common and is irregular, as in many other languages (compare English: *I go, I went*). This irregularity is most obvious in the present tense.

present tense

sg	1	eo	I go	*or*	I am going
	2	is	you (*sg*) go		you (*sg*) are going
	3	it	he/she/it goes		he/she/it is going
pl	1	imus	we go		we are going
	2	itis	you (*pl*) go		you (*pl*) are going
	3	eunt	they go		they are going

imperative	2 sg	i	go (*sg*)!
	2 pl	ite	go (*pl*)!

infinitive	ire	to go

Other tenses use the usual endings with the stem *i-*:

future	ibo, ibis, ibit, *etc.*
imperfect	ibam, ibas, ibat, *etc.*

The perfect stem (which the pluperfect uses too) can be either *i-* or *iv-*. When *eo* is used in compound verbs, the shorter form is always used.

perfect	ii, iisti, iit, *etc.*	*or*	ivi, ivisti, ivit, *etc.*
pluperfect	ieram, ieras, ierat, *etc.*	*or*	iveram, iveras, iverat, *etc.*

Exercise 6.22

Translate into English:

1. ibimus
2. eunt
3. iit
4. iverant
5. ite
6. ibam
7. imus
8. iimus
9. i
10. ibunt

Exercise 6.23

Translate into Latin:
1. She goes.
2. They went.
3. We go.
4. He will go.
5. We had gone.
6. You (*sg*) will go.
7. You (*sg*) go.
8. To go.
9. They were going.
10. I went.

Exercise 6.24

Translate into English:
1. nonne Romam cras ibimus?
2. iuvenis miser per vias lente it.
3. ad parvam insulam numquam iveramus.
4. magna turba civium saevorum in forum celeriter ivit.
5. ecce! tres milites in villam senis eunt. quid invenient?

Exercise 6.25

Translate into Latin:
1. Go into the garden at once, mistress!
2. My sons were afraid to go to new places.
3. Many of the citizens are going towards the gate.
4. Surely you won't go to the city today, daughter?
5. Where did you go yesterday, husband?

Exercise 6.26

Tarquinius seizes the throne

A disgruntled son of the former king plots to wrest the kingdom away from Servius Tullius, the slave-boy who had been blessed by the omen of the fire.

Servius Tullius rex Romae erat. bene regebat et Romani eum amabant. Lucius Tarquinius tamen, filius Tarquinii Prisci, qui rex antea fuerat, ei invidebat. uxor eius, Tullia nomine – filia Servii Tullii erat – iram iuvenis incitabat. 'pater tuus, marite,' inquit 'rex Romae erat. tu igitur rex esse debebas. pater meus tamen servus
5   olim erat. regnum tuum recipe! Romam libera!' verba ferocia uxoris Tarquinio facile persuaserunt.

	Servius -i Tullius -i *m*	Servius Tullius (*sixth king of Rome*)
	Lucius -i Tarquinius -i *m*	Lucius Tarquinius
	Tarquinius -i Priscus -i *m*	Tarquinius Priscus (*fifth king*)
	antea	before, earlier
2	invideo -ere	I envy (+ *dat*)
	Tullia -ae *f*	Tullia
	ira -ae *f*	anger
	incito -are	I rouse, I stir up
	recipio -ere	I take back
6	persuadeo -ere -suasi	I persuade (+ *dat*)

Tarquinius regem publice iudicare et dona senatoribus divitibus dare coepit. deinde milites collegit et ad curiam iit. in sella sedit et senatores iussit ad se regem vocare. 'Servius' irate clamavit 'servus et filius servi est. ego princeps et filius regis sum. vos,
10   senatores, eum regem non legistis: femina mala, mater mea, eum regem fecit. Servius agros vestros plebi dare cupit. regnum Romanum delebit!'

	publice	publicly, in public
	iudico -are	I criticise
	dives -itis	rich
	coepi (*irreg pf*)	I began
8	collego -ere collegi	I collect, I gather (people) together
	curia -ae *f*	senate-house
	sella -ae *f*	throne
	princeps -ipis *m*	(*here*) prince
	plebs plebis *f*	the common people, the masses

Servius rex de verbis malis Tarquinii audivit et ad curiam festinavit. iuvenis tamen senem cepit et ad terram ferociter iecit. amici regis statim fugerunt; amici iuvenis Servium celeriter necaverunt. tum Tullia ad curiam currum agebat. maritum regem
15   salutare cupivit. auriga eius subito corpus Servii in via vidit. 'consiste, domina!' clamavit 'patrem tuum in via video.' Tullia tamen non constitit; equos flagellavit; currum super corpus patris egit.

	iacio -ere ieci	I thow
	currum	chariot (*acc sg*)
	ago agere egi	I drive
	auriga -ae *m*	charioteer, driver
15	corpus -oris *n*	body
	consisto -ere constiti	I halt, I stop
	flagello -are -avi	I whip
	super (+ *acc*)	over

nomen viae hodie <u>Vicus Sceleratus</u> est: <u>scelere</u> saevo Tarquinius regnum
<u>obtinuerat</u>, <u>scelere</u> saevo Tullia patrem suam <u>foedaverat</u>. Tarquinius iussit cives
20 <u>corpus</u> Servii in via relinquere. 'necabo eum qui senem malum <u>sepeliet</u>' irate
clamavit. Romani igitur Tarquinio regi <u>cognomen</u> <u>Superbum</u> dederunt.

	Vicus Sceleratus	Street of Crime
	scelus -eris *n*	crime
	obtineo -ere -ui	I obtain, I gain
	foedo -are -avi	I defile, I mistreat
20	sepelio -ire	I bury
	cognomen -inis *n*	extra name
	Superbus -i *m*	Superbus (the Proud, the Arrogant)

PREFIXES AND COMPOUNDS (1)

Latin often joins a prefix onto another word (most frequently a verb) to focus its
meaning, creating a *compound*. We have already met several:

venio	I come	
invenio	I find	*lit* I come into/upon
advenio	I arrive	*lit* I come to
pugno	I fight	
oppugno	I attack	originally *ob-pugno*: *lit* I bring the fight to
sum	I am	
possum	I can, I am able	originally *potis-sum*, shortened to *pot-sum*: *lit* I am powerful enough to
facilis	easy	
difficilis	difficult	originally *dis-facilis*: *lit* not-easy; note the vowel change from *fac-* to *-fic-*

Some common prefixes are as follows; we have already met many of these as
prepositions:

a-/ab-	away, from	
ad-	to, towards	
e-/ex-	out of, from, out	
in-	into, in, onto	
re-	back	(only used as a prefix)
trans-	across	(also used as a preposition, + *acc*)

At GCSE you are expected to be able to work out compound verbs formed when these prefixes are attached to verbs you already know:

e.g.	reduco	I lead back
	ineo	I go in(to), I enter
	transeo	I go across, I cross

It is common to find both a preposition and the corresponding prefix used in quick succession. In such instances, the preposition and the prefix simply reinforce each another, and only one is translated:

nuntius in villam iniit.
lit   The messenger went in into the villa.
i.e.   The messenger went into the villa.

Alternatively, the prefix in a compound verb can supply new information that is not revealed by the rest of the sentence:

pueri in viam exierunt.
The boys went out (e.g. of the house) into the street.

Exercise 6.27

Translate into English:

1. puellas in hortum statim exire iussi.
2. dux multos milites trans mare secum transportavit.
3. quae sunt nomina duorum senum qui in templum nunc ineunt?
4. fratrem stultum a taberna puellisque abduximus.
5. pater servum in villam revocavit.

Figure 6.1 *Tullia drives her chariot over the body of her father.* After a painting of
E. Hildebrandt (Photo by ullstein bild/ullstein bild via Getty Images)

Exercise 6.28

S&C

Translate into Latin:

1. Go away, boys! Your mother is now asleep.
2. Why did the women not enter the temple?
3. Lead me back to my country, boy!
4. My son will order the old men to go out into the forum.
5. Did you lead the soldiers towards the wood, messenger?

PREFIXES AND COMPOUNDS (2): NEW VERBS

Below is a table of new compound verbs listed beneath their parent verbs.

The logic behind the meaning of a compound verb is usually fairly straightforward. Occasionally though the meaning is not just the sum of the prefix and the verb, and needs to be explained.

For example, *pereo* means *I die, I perish* rather than *I go through*, as you might have expected: the thought process is that you have *gone through your life* when you perish.

capio	capere	cepi	I take, I catch, I capture
accipio	accipere	accepi	I accept, I take in, I receive
			(*lit* I take to [myself])
eo	ire	ii *or* ivi	I go
pereo	perire	perii*	I die, I perish
			(*lit* I go through [life])
redeo	redire	redii*	I go back, I come back, I return
fugio	fugere	fugi	I run away, I flee
effugio	effugere	effugi	I escape
			(*lit* I flee out [to a successful conclusion])
specto	spectare	spectavi	I look at, I watch
exspecto	exspectare	exspectavi	I wait for, I expect (*lit* I watch out [for])
sum	esse	fui	I am
absum	abesse	afui	I am absent, I am away, I am distant from
adsum	adesse	adfui	I am here, I am present
venio	venire	veni	I come
convenio	convenire	conveni	I come together, I gather, I meet
			(=*cum* + *venio*; *cum* changes to *con*)

* Remember that although uncompounded forms of *eo* can have either *i-* or *iv-* as the perfect stem, compounded forms of *eo* always have the shorter version.

As you will have noticed from the above table, adding a prefix to a verb often results in a slight modification of spelling.

Note the following changes that make pronunciation easier:

ad + capio = accipio
re + eo   = redeo
ex + fugio = effugio

Note too the vowel change that has taken place in forming *accipio*: the *-a-* of *capio* has become *-i-* in the compound form: *-cipio*. Compare the same vowel change between *facilis* and its compound form *difficilis*.

This vowel change also occurs with compouds of *iacio* (I throw), which we met in the last story:

iacio	iacere	ieci	I throw
inicio	inicere	inieci	I throw in(to)/on(to)
eicio	eicere	eieci	I throw out

Exercise 6.29

Translate into English:

1. domina dona pulchra laete accepit.
2. filii mei diu afuerant, sed tandem redierunt.
3. turba irata ad villam ducis conveniebat: is effugere non poterat.
4. omnes qui aderant clamores senis tristis audiverunt.
5. nuntium multas horas exspectabamus. is tandem advenit. 'rex' inquit 'periit et cives eum in <u>Tiberim</u> iniecerunt.'

Tiberis *acc* Tiberim   *m*   the Tiber (*river in Rome*)

Exercise 6.30

Translate into Latin:

1. Many brave soldiers had gathered in the forum.
2. Four young men perished in the middle of the night.
3. We shall receive help from the gods.
4. I escaped, but the Romans captured my brother.
5. Your husband will be here tomorrow, mistress.

PREFIXES AND COMPOUNDS (3)

Note the following, which are all compounds of one sort or another. Some are based on new items of vocabulary. Others are based on words you already know, or are alternative compound forms of the same parent verb:

ascendo -ere -i	I climb
descendo -ere -i	I go down, I come down
prope (+ *acc*)	near
appropinquo -are -avi	I approach, I come near to (usually + *dat*)
terreo -ere -ui	I frighten
perterritus -a -um	terrified (*lit* thoroughly* frightened)

* The meaning *thoroughly* here comes from *per*, which normally means *through*. The two meanings are not as unconnected as it first appears: compare the phrase *wet through*, which means *thoroughly wet*. Something done *thoroughly* has been done *right through*.

intellego -ere intellexi   I understand, I realise
   (inter-lego, *lit* I distinguish/choose between [things])

interficio -ere interfeci   I kill
   (inter-facio, *lit* I make someone be amongst [the dead]; note the vowel change)

Finally, some compound verbs are encountered more frequently than their parent verbs:

conspicio -ere conspexi	I catch sight of, I notice
constituo -ere constitui	I decide
persuadeo -ere persuasi	I persuade (+ *dat*)
respondeo -ere -i	I reply

Note that out of the compound verbs we have now met, the following are mixed conjugation (see p119): accipio, effugio, (iacio), inicio, eicio, interficio, conspicio.

Exercise 6.31

Translate into English:

1. ancilla perterrita 'hostes nunc adsunt, domine!' subito clamavit.
2. verba quae rex dixerat intellegere non poteramus.
3. puella fratrem prope portam exspectabat.
4. cur silvae numquam appropinquas, puer?
5. omnes de monte cras descendemus.
6. iuvenis malus in villam cucurrit et dominum interfecit.
7. conspexistine milites Romanos, pater?
8. insulam relinquere et Romae habitare constitueramus.
9. epistula amicorum patri meo non persuadebit.
10. frater 'Romam ibo' inquit 'et ducem interficiam'. ego non respondi.

Exercise 6.32

S&C

Translate into Latin:

1. I quickly approached the huge temple.
2. My mother's serious words persuaded me.
3. Our mistress is building a large house near the wood.
4. We suddenly caught sight of the soldiers and decided to flee.
5. The foolish young man will not understand the leader's plan.

REVISION CHECKPOINT

Make sure you know:

*   how the verb *I go* (eo) is conjugated
*   that Latin often forms a compound verb by adding a prefix to a verb
*   the lists of new compound verbs on pp198–200
*   the ways in which spelling can be modified in compound verbs

Exercise 6.33

Tarquinius Superbus buys some odd books

A visitor arrives at the palace claiming that the books she wants to sell contain divine prophecies.

anus pauper incognitaque olim villam Tarquinii Superbi intravit. militibus 'donum'
inquit 'habeo quod regi dare cupio. donum regnum eius servabit.' milites verbis eius
non credebant. eam tamen ad regem duxerunt. anus diu tacebat. tum e sacco suo
novem libros extraxit. 'o rex magne,' inquit 'hos libros in quibus sunt
5   verba deorum vendere cupio. libri regnum tuum per multos annos defendent
patriamque contra hostes feroces custodient. eos emere cupis?' Tarquinius ei non
credebat. rex tamen propter paupertatem feminae benigne respondit. 'quantam
pecuniam cupis, femina bona?' rogavit. anus magnum pretium poposcit. rex diu
risit. anus igitur tres libros in ignem statim iniecit. 'sex' inquit 'libros eodem pretio
10 emes?' Tarquinius magna voce iterum risit. deinde anus tres alios libros in ignem
iniecit. 'libros reliquos eodem pretio emere cupis?' constantia feminae regi tandem
persuasit. Tarquinius igitur tres libros magno pretio emit. anus laeta discessit. rex
libros in templo posuit. Romani consilium eorum in magnis periculis semper
petebant.

	anus	old woman (*f nom sg*)
	pauper -eris	poor
	incognitus -a -um	unknown
	Tarquinius -i Superbus -i *m*	Tarquinius Superbus (*7th king of Rome*)
1	intro -are -avi	I enter
	saccus -i *m*	bag
	hos	these (*m acc pl*)
	vendo -ere -idi	I sell
	emere -ere emi	I buy
7	propter (+ *acc*)	on account of
	paupertas -atis *f*	poverty
	benignus -a -um	kind
	quantus -a -um	how much . . .?
	pretium -i *n*	price
8	posco -ere poposci	I demand
	ignis -is *m*	fire
	eodem	the same (*n abl sg*)
	vox vocis *f*	voice
	iterum	again
10	alios	other (*m acc pl*)
	reliquus -a -um	remaining
	constantia -ae *f*	persistence, determination

•   *Tarquinius Superbus* will not be glossed again.

Exercise 6.34

Tarquinius Superbus gives some advice

A father sends a message to his son by actions rather than words.

erat bellum longum inter Romanos Gabinosque. Romani Gabios superare non
poterant. tum Tarquinius Superbus rex et Sextus filius eius consilium callidum
ceperunt. Sextus Gabios transfugit. civibus Gabinis 'Roma' inquit 'fugio quod
pater meus me saeve punit. accipite me, cives!' Gabini verbis eius credebant et
5   eum in urbem accipere constituerunt. iuvenis mox multos amicos multamque
potestatem inter Gabinos habebat.

	Gabini -orum *m pl*	Gabians (*people of Gabii*)
	Gabii -orum *m pl*	Gabii (*city near Rome*)
	callidus -a -um	clever
	transfugio -ere -i	I go over to, I flee to
6	potestas -atis *f*	power

filius nuntium ad patrem suum mox misit quod nova mandata cupiebat. nuntius
Romam festinavit et in regiam Tarquinii venit. 'filius tuus, rex,' inquit 'omnia
paravit; quid nunc facere debet?' Tarquinius non respondit sed in hortum exiit.
deinde per hortum ambulavit et baculo longo summa capita papaverum decussit.
10 nulla verba dixit. deinde nuntium ad filium remisit. nuntius non intellexit sed
Gabios rediit. Sexto facta regis nuntiavit. filius ambages patris statim intellexit.
postridie milites iussit principes Gabinorum colligere. tum omnes necavit.

	mandatum -i *n*	order, instruction
	regia -ae *f*	palace
	baculum -i *n*	stick
	summus -a -um	highest, top (of)
9	papaver -eris *n*	poppy
	decutio -ere decussi	I knock off
	nulla	no (*adj*; *n acc pl*)
	factum -i *n*	deed
	nuntio -are -avi	I announce
11	ambages -um *f pl*	hints, obscure indications
	postridie	(on) the next day
	princeps -ipis *m*	leader, chief
	colligo -ere	I collect, I gather together

TIME CLAUSES: *ubi* and *postquam*

We have already met several types of subordinate clause:

- causal clauses with *quod* (because)
- concessive clauses with *quamquam* (although)
- relative clauses with *qui, quae, quod* (who, which)

Another type of subordinate clause is a *time clause*. Two words commonly used to introduce a time clause are:

ubi	when (*also* where)*
postquam	after (*an action*)

> * We have already met ubi as a question word meaning *where?*. When not in a question, *ubi* can mean either *when* or *where*. If you see *ubi* in a sentence that is not a question, work out from the context whether it means *when* or *where*.

    e.g.   ubi verba nuntii audivi ad villam ambulavi.
          When I heard the messenger's words I walked to the house.

          ad villam ubi senex habitabat ambulavi.
          I walked to the house where the old man lived.

A first important point to note is that *ubi* and *postquam* are not followed by a pluperfect tense verb in Latin, even though you may choose to translate using one in English: the logic is simply *after X happened, Y happened* (not *In a situation where X had already happened . . .*). Rather than the pluperfect, Latin uses the perfect tense:

    e.g.   postquam rex advenit cives ad forum festinaverunt.
          After the king (had) arrived the citizens hurried to the forum.

Secondly, if a time clause refers to the future, Latin uses a future tense (showing, logically, when the action happens), but this is translated into natural English with a present tense. We call this a *hidden future*.

    e.g.   ubi ad insulam navigabit, templum inveniet.
    lit   When he will sail to the island, he will find a temple.
    i.e.   When he sails to the island he will find a temple.

Exercise 6.35

Translate into English:

1. postquam regem interfecimus ab urbe statim discessimus.
2. ubi ea intelleges, perterrita eris.
3. domina lacrimavit ubi epistulam tristem legit.
4. ad silvam ubi milites me exspectabant celeriter cucurri.
5. dei postquam verba regis audiverunt irati erant.

Exercise 6.36

Translate into Latin:

1. After I received the letter I decided to go to Rome.
2. When we arrive at the island we are always happy.
3. The boys ran into the house after their father shouted angrily.
4. When you arrive in Rome, soldier, you will want to stay for a long time.
5. The young men were able to understand everything after they read the book.

REVISION CHECKPOINT

Make sure you know:

- that *ubi* when not in a question can mean either *when* or *where*
- that *ubi* and *postquam* are never followed by a pluperfect tense
- the way in which English often uses a *hidden future* (resembling the present tense) when talking about future events: e.g. *when you go . . .*

Exercise 6.37

Tarquinius Superbus sends his sons to Delphi

*An omen in Rome leads to a consultation of the oracle, but a second question
weighs more heavily on the minds of those consulting.*

Tarquinius Superbus rex et servi sui ingentem <u>serpentem</u> in <u>regia</u> olim viderunt.
omnes qui aderant perterriti statim fugerunt. deinde rex duos filios ad se vocavit.
'iram deorum' inquit 'timeo. ad <u>Graeciam</u> ite, filii! <u>Delphos</u> petite et consilium
<u>Apollinis</u> quaerite!' rex amicum cum eis misit <u>Brutum</u>, filium <u>sororis</u> suae.
5 quamquam filii regis Brutum <u>propter</u> <u>stultitiam</u> eius non amabant, tres iuvenes
<u>una</u> discesserunt. trans mare ad Graeciam celeriter navigaverunt.

	serpens -entis *m/f*	snake
	regia -ae *f*	palace
	Graecia -ae *f*	Greece
	Delphi -orum *m pl*	Delphi (*oracle in central Greece*)
4	Apollo -inis *m*	Apollo (*god of prophecy*)
	Brutus -i *m*	Brutus
	soror -oris *f*	sister
	propter (+ *acc*)	on account of
	stultitia -ae *f*	stupidity, foolishness
6	una	together

Figure 6.2 *Denarius issued in 54 BC by Marcus Junius Brutus, descendant of the
Brutus in Exercises 6.37 and 6.38, depicting his ancestor as consul and surrounded by
lictors (bodyguards).* (Photo by: Photo12/UIG via Getty Images)

ubi Delphos advenerunt templum Apollinis statim intraverunt. <u>oraculum</u> de
<u>serpente</u> <u>consulerunt</u>. tum filii ad patrem redire debebant. <u>invidia</u> tamen eos vicit
et 'magne deus,' rogaverunt 'quis ex nobis post mortem patris rex Romae erit?'
10 <u>sacerdos</u> statim respondit: 'is <u>summum</u> <u>imperium</u> Romae habebit qui primus
<u>osculum</u> matri dabit.' fratres igitur, postquam verba dei audiverunt, Romam ad
matrem suam celeriter redierunt. Brutus tamen, qui verba dei audiverat et
consilium Apollinis intellexerat, ad terram cecidit et terrae <u>osculum</u> dedit. 'terra'
sibi inquit 'mater omnium est.' deinde Romam rediit.

	oraculum -i *n*	oracle
	consulo -ere -ui	I consult, I seek the advice of
	invidia -ae *f*	envy
	sacerdos -otis *f*	priestess
10	summus -a -um	(*here*) greatest
	imperium -i *n*	power
	osculum -i *n*	kiss

Exercise 6.38

The birth of the Roman Republic

A terrible crime leads to a popular uprising against Tarquinius Superbus.

Tarquinius Superbus multos hostes viceret, multa templa aedificaverat. <u>propter</u>
tamen ingentes <u>impensas</u> cives Romani laeti non erant. rex <u>Rutulos</u> oppugnare
constituit quod Rutuli multum pecuniae habebant. tum tamen regis filius, cuius
nomen <u>Sextus Tarquinius</u> erat, <u>scelus</u> malum fecit. iuvenis feminam <u>nobilem</u>,
5 <u>Lucretiam</u> nomine, saeve <u>stupravit</u>. quamquam maritus <u>veniam</u> ei <u>dedit</u>, Lucretia
<u>propter</u> magnum <u>pudorem</u> se necavit. maritus igitur et amici eius, inter quos fuit
<u>Brutus</u>, <u>ultionem</u> <u>iuraverunt</u>. Brutus 'ecce!' irate clamavit '<u>quam</u> mali sunt reges!

	propter (+ *acc*)	on account of
	impensa -ae *f*	expenditure, expense
	Rutuli -orum *m pl*	Rutulians (*people near Rome*)
	Sextus -i Tarquinius -i *m*	Sextus Tarquinius
4	scelus -eris *n*	crime
	nobilis -e	noble, aristocratic
	Lucretia -ae *f*	Lucretia
	stupro -are -avi	I rape
	veniam do	I forgive, I pardon (+ *dat*)
6	pudor -oris *m*	shame, sense of shame
	Brutus -i *m*	Brutus
	ultio -onis *f*	revenge
	iuro -are -avi	I swear
	quam!	how . . .! (*exclamation*)

cives Romani, <u>iuro</u>, regem <u>alium</u> non habebunt.' Brutus Romanos celeriter
<u>incitavit</u>. cives ad se vocavit qui Tarquinium nunc <u>oderant</u>. milites qui cum rege
10 Rutulos oppugnabant mox eum reliquerunt. Tarquinius timebat et Romam
festinavit. Romani tamen portas <u>clauserunt</u> et eum <u>reppulerunt</u>. 'Roma nostra
nunc est,' laete clamaverunt, 'et nos cives urbem nunc regemus.' <u>pro</u> rege igitur
legerunt duos <u>consules</u>, inter quos fuit Brutus. Romani <u>libertatem</u> <u>obtinuerant</u>.

	alium	another (*m acc sg*)
	incito -are -avi	I stir up, I rouse
	oderant (*irreg*)	(they) hated
	claudo -ere clausi	I close, I shut
11	repello -ere reppuli	I drive back, I drive away
	pro (+ *abl*)	(*here*) instead of
	consul -ulis *m*	consul (*one of two chief magistrates in Rome*)
	libertas -atis *f*	freedom
13	obtineo -ere -ui	I obtain

SUMMARY OF CHAPTER SIX GRAMMAR

Pluperfect tense (*I had . . .*):

- endings: *-eram, -eras, -erat, -eramus, -eratis, -erant*
- endings added to perfect stem (= third principal part minus *-i*)
- describes events that *had already happened* by a certain point in past

quod, quamquam, ubi, postquam:

- used to introduce different types of *subordinate clause*: causal (*quod*), concessive (*quamquam*) or temporal (*ubi, postquam*)

Relative pronoun (*qui, quae, quod*) and relative clause:

- meaning: *who, which*; forms on p181
- used in relative clause which gives more detail about a noun already mentioned (the *antecedent*)
- must agree with the antecedent in *number* and *gender*; but *case* depends on role it is doing within the relative clause
- interrogative version *quis?, quid?* used in questions: *who?, what?*

Numerals:

- one (*unus*), two (*duo*), three (*tres*) and plural of thousand (*mille*, pl *milia*) decline; others do not

'Time within which' expressions:

- use ablative case, e.g. *septem annis* = within seven years

eo (I go):

present:	eo, is, it, imus, itis, eunt
future:	ibo *etc.*
imperfect:	ibam *etc.*
perfect:	ivi *or* ii (-ii *in compounds*) *etc.*
pluperfect:	iveram *or* ieram (-ieram *in compounds*) *etc.*
infinitive:	ire
imperative:	i! (*sg*); ite! (*pl*)

Prefixes & compounds:

- compounds sometimes require spelling changes e.g. *redeo, accipio*
- corresponding preposition can be used as well as prefix to reinforce the meaning
- prefix can add a new detail not already in sentence e.g. *I ran out into the street.*

CHAPTER SIX VOCABULARY

absum abesse afui	I am absent, I am away, I am distant (from)
accipio -ere accepi	I accept, I take in, I receive
adsum adesse adfui	I am here, I am present
appropinquo -are -avi	I approach, I come near (to, + *dat*)
conspicio -ere conspexi	I catch sight of, I notice
constituo -uere -ui	I decide
convenio -ire -i	I come together, I gather, I meet
cupio -ere -ivi	I want, I desire
descendo -ere -i	I go down, I come down
dico -ere dixi	I say, I speak, I tell
effugio -ere -i	I escape
emo -ere emi	I buy
eo ire i(v)i	I go
exspecto -are -avi	I wait for, I expect
hostis -is *m*	enemy (*usu pl*)
iacio -ere ieci	I throw
(*in compounds* -icio, *e.g.* eicio [I throw out], inicio [I throw in])	
intellego -ere intellexi	I understand, I realise
interficio -ere interfeci	I kill
intro -are -avi	I enter
ira -ae *f*	anger
libero -are -avi	I set free
nuntio -are -avi	I announce, I report
pereo -ire -ii	I die, I perish
persuadeo -ere persuasi	I persuade (+ *dat*)
perterritus -a -um	terrified
postquam	after, when
prope (+ *acc*)	near
quamquam	although
qui quae quod	who, which
quis? quid?	who?, what?
quod	because
re-	. . . back (*prefix for verbs*)
redeo -ire -ii	I go back, I come back, I return
respondeo -ere -i	I reply
senator -oris *m*	senator
servo -are -avi	I save, I protect, I keep
trans (+ *acc, or as prefix*)	across
ubi	(*not question*) when, where
uxor -oris *f*	wife
vendo -ere -idi	I sell

unus una unum	I	one
duo duae duo	II	two
tres *n* tria	III	three
quattuor	IV or IIII	four
quinque	V	five
sex	VI	six
septem	VII	seven
octo	VIII	eight
novem	IX	nine
decem	X	ten
centum	C	hundred
mille *pl* milia	M	thousand

50 new words

ENGLISH TO LATIN
PRACTICE SENTENCES

The GCSE Latin exam will include the option of translating some simple sentences into Latin.

The vocabulary tested in this section will come from a list of 125 Latin words, all of which you have now met. A summary list is below; you should check grammar details for each word in the Latin–English vocabulary at the back of the book.

a/ab (+ *abl*)	dico	longus	rogo
ad (+ *acc*)	diu	magnus	saepe
advenio	domina	malus	saevus
aedifico	dominus	maritus	saluto
ager	donum	mitto	scribo
ambulo	dormio	multus	semper
amicus	duco	murus	servo
ancilla	e/ex (+ *abl*)	nauta	servus
annus	epistula	navigo	silva
aqua	et	neco	statim
arma	facio	non	subito
audio	femina	novus	sum
auxilium	festino	nuntio	supero
bene	filia	nuntius	taberna
bibo	filius	paro	taceo
bonus	forum	parvus	tandem
cado	fugio	patria	templum
capio	gladius	pecunia	teneo
cena	habeo	periculum	terreo
cibus	habito	peto	timeo
clamo	hora	pono	trado
consilium	hortus	porta	traho
conspicio	in (+ *acc*)	porto	venio
constituo	in (+ *abl*)	possum	via
contra (+ *acc*)	intro	puella	villa
cum (+ *abl*)	invenio	puer	vinco
cur?	invito	quando?	vinum
curro	ira	-que	vir
custodio	iratus	regina	voco
dea	laboro	regnum	
defendo	laetus	rego	
deus	libertus	relinquo	

The sentences will test the following areas of grammar:

Accidence (word forms):

- The forms of regular verbs in the present, imperfect and perfect tenses
- The infinitive of regular verbs
- The present and imperfect tenses of the verbs *sum* and *possum*
- The forms of regular nouns of the first and second declensions
- The forms of 2-1-2 adjectives like *laetus -a -um*

Syntax (grammatical rules):

- Standard uses of the cases
- Use of the accusative case to express 'time how long'
- The cases taken by prepositions contained in the list above
- Direct statements and direct questions

The following exercises provide practice for this part of the GCSE exam. Each sentence is marked out of either 3 or 4, as shown. (One mark per word; but a prepositional phrase, e.g. *in the garden*, counts as one mark.)

Exercise EL.1

a) The slaves are not working. (3)

b) We suddenly ran into the temple. (3)

c) The husband was writing a letter in the garden. (4)

Exercise EL.2

a) I am not able to sleep. (3)

b) You (*sg*) immediately entered the house. (3)

c) Many messengers were in the marketplace. (4)

Exercise EL.3

a) I caught sight of the woman in the street. (3)

b) We caught sight of the great danger. (3)

c) The freedmen defended the gate with swords. (4)

Exercise EL.4

a) Why are you (*pl*) afraid of the mistress?   (3)

b) They carried the food into the wood.   (3)

c) We often used to drink wine in the inn.   (4)

Exercise EL.5

a) He was silent for many hours.   (3)

b) You (*sg*) have sent a good gift.   (3)

c) I protected the master's money for a long time.   (4)

Exercise EL.6

a) The plan is bad.   (3)

b) You (*pl*) were building the new temple.   (3)

c) We decided to hand over the weapons to the boy.   (4)

Exercise EL.7

a) The goddesses are cruel.   (3)

b) I greeted the happy master.   (3)

c) The angry men called the slave-girls.   (4)

Exercise EL.8

a) The girl suddenly fell.   (3)

b) You (*sg*) always prepare the dinner.   (3)

c) The master's anger was savage.   (4)

Exercise EL.9

a) The women walked into the fields.   (3)

b) We ask the gods for help.   (3)

c) He ruled well for many years.   (4)

Exercise EL.10

a) The queen often shouts.   (3)

b) When did the sailors arrive?   (3)

c) The bad water killed the girl.   (4)

Exercise EL.11

a) You (*pl*) have conquered a large kingdom.   (3)

b) He leads the daughter into the garden.   (3)

c) I was guarding the small gate against the men.   (4)

Exercise EL.12

a) We built long walls.   (3)

b) I am seeking help from the man.   (3)

c) He was finally able to drink the wine.   (4)

REFERENCE GRAMMAR

NOUNS

First and second declensions

		first declension			second declension		
		girl			master	war	
		f	*endings*		*m*	*n*	*endings*
sg	*nom*	puella	-a		dominus*	bellum	-us (-um *if n*)
	acc	puellam	-am		dominum	bellum	-um
	gen	puellae	-ae		domini	belli	-i
	dat	puellae	-ae		domino	bello	-o
	abl	puella	-a (*long*)		domino	bello	-o
					(**voc* domine)		
pl	*nom*	puellae	-ae		domini	bella	-i (-a *if n*)
	acc	puellas	-as		dominos	bella	-os (-a *if n*)
	gen	puellarum	-arum		dominorum	bellorum	-orum
	dat	puellis	-is		dominis	bellis	-is
	abl	puellis	-is		dominis	bellis	-is

- First declension nouns are nearly all feminine, but *nauta* (sailor) is masculine. There is no neuter variant in the first declension.
- *dea* (goddess) and *filia* (daughter) have dative and ablative plural *deabus*, *filiabus*, to distinguish from equivalent parts of *deus* (god) and *filius* (son).
- Second declension nouns ending *-us* or *-ius* are the only ones with a vocative singular different from the nominative.
- *filius* has vocative *fili*, *nuntius* has vocative *nunti*.
- Second declension masculine nouns with nominative singular ending in *-r* behave as if *-us* has disappeared. Hence *vir* (man), acc *virum*; *puer* (boy), acc *puerum*. Most others ending in *-er* drop the *e* in the other cases (reflecting pronunciation in practice): *ager* (field), acc *agrum*; *liber* (book), *librum*.

Third declension

		king	shout	ship	name	
		m	*m*	*f*	*n*	*endings*
sg	nom	rex	clamor	navis	nomen	-
	acc	regem	clamorem	navem	nomen	-em (*as nom if n*)
	gen	regis	clamoris	navis	nominis	-is
	dat	regi	clamori	navi	nomini	-i
	abl	rege	clamore	nave	nomine	-e
pl	nom	reges	clamores	naves	nomina	-es (-a *if n*)
	acc	reges	clamores	naves	nomina	-es (-a *if n*)
	gen	regum	clamorum	navium	nominum	-um *or* -ium
	dat	regibus	clamoribus	navibus	nominibus	-ibus
	abl	regibus	clamoribus	navibus	nominibus	-ibus

There is a wide range of possibilities for the nominative singular, but other endings attach to the *genitive stem*. This and the gender need to be learned.

- The genitive plural is normally *-um*, but sometimes *-ium*. The genitive plural usually ends up one syllable longer than the nominative singular. If the noun 'increases' by a syllable from the nominative to the genitive singular (as most do), it does not increase again in the plural, so the genitive plural is *-um*. If (like *navis*) it does not increase in the singular, it does so in the plural, so the genitive plural is *-ium*. But there are exceptions:

  i) single-syllable nouns ending in two consonants increase twice: *urbs* (city), *urbis*, gen pl *urbium*; similarly *mons* (mountain), *nox* (night) [*x* counts double]; but not *rex*.
  ii) a few nouns that would be expected to increase in the genitive plural do not do so: *frater* (brother), gen sg *fratris*, gen pl *fratrum*; similarly *iuvenis* (young man), *mater* (mother), *pater* (pater), *senex* (old man).

- Note that *mare* (sea) is slightly irregular, having abl sg *mari* (to avoid confusion with nom/acc) and nom/acc pl *maria*.

ADJECTIVES

first and second declension (2-1-2, i.e. like *dominus – puella – bellum*)

happy

		m	*f*	*n*
sg	nom	laetus*	laeta	laetum
	acc	laetum	laetam	laetum
	gen	laeti	laetae	laeti
	dat	laeto	laetae	laeto
	abl	laeto	laeta	laeto
		(*voc laete)		
pl	nom	laeti	laetae	laeta
	acc	laetos	laetas	laeta
	gen	laetorum	laetarum	laetorum
	dat	laetis	laetis	laetis
	abl	laetis	laetis	laetis

- *miser* (miserable) keeps the *e* like *puer* does, hence m acc sg *miserum*, f nom sg *misera*;
- *pulcher* (beautiful) drops the *e* like *liber* does, hence m acc sg *pulchrum*, f nom sg *pulchra*.

third declension (3-3)

brave   huge

		m/f	*n*	*m/f*	*n*
sg	nom	fortis	forte	ingens	ingens
	acc	fortem	forte	ingentem	ingens
	gen	fortis	fortis	ingentis	ingentis
	dat	forti	forti	ingenti	ingenti
	abl	forti	forti	ingenti	ingenti
pl	nom	fortes	fortia	ingentes	ingentia
	acc	fortes	fortia	ingentes	ingentia
	gen	fortium	fortium	ingentium	ingentium
	dat	fortibus	fortibus	ingentibus	ingentibus
	abl	fortibus	fortibus	ingentibus	ingentibus

- Note that the ablative singular ending is *-i*, not *-e* as in third declension nouns.
- *celer* (swift) behaves as if it had started *celeris* (and does so in the feminine, here unusually different from the masculine):

		m	*f*	*n*
sg	nom	celer	celeris	celere
	acc	celerem	celerem	celere

ADVERBS

2-1-2 adjectives form their adverb by adding *-e* to the stem:

adjective	*adverb*	
laetus	laete	happily

Third declension adjectives normally add *-iter* to the stem:

fortis	fortiter	bravely

A few third declension adjectives ending *-is* instead use their neuter singular (*-e*) as adverb:

facilis	facile	easily

Note the following irregular adverb:

bene	well

NUMERALS

Arabic	Roman	
1	I	unus, una, unum
2	II	duo, duae, duo
3	III	tres, tria
4	IV (*or* IIII)	quattuor
5	V	quinque
6	VI	sex
7	VII	septem
8	VIII	octo
9	IX	novem
10	X	decem
100	C	centum
1000	M	mille, *pl* milia

The small numbers *unus*, *duo* and *tres* decline as follows:

one

	m	*f*	*n*
nom	unus	una	unum
acc	unum	unam	unum
gen	unius	unius	unius
dat	uni	uni	uni
abl	uno	una	uno

• This is basically 2-1-2, but with the distinctive genitive -*ius* and dative -*i* across all three genders (like most pronouns).

two

	m	*f*	*n*
nom	duo	duae	duo
acc	duos (*or* duo)	duas	duo
gen	duorum	duarum	duorum
dat	duobus	duabus	duobus
abl	duobus	duabus	duobus

• This has a few parts in common with 2-1-2 pl.

three

	m and f	*n*
nom	tres	tria
acc	tres	tria
gen	trium	trium
dat	tribus	tribus
abl	tribus	tribus

• This is third declension plural.

• *milia* (plural of *mille* = 1000) declines like *tria*.

PRONOUNS

Summary of pronouns for basic recognition:

ego (*acc* me)	I (me)
nos	we (us)
tu	you (*sg*)
vos	you (*pl*)
is, ea, id	he, she, it (*pl* they, them)
se	himself/herself/itself/themselves (*reflexive*)
qui	who (*relative*)
quis?	who?
quid?	what?

Personal pronouns

	person:	*first*	*second*	*third reflexive*
		I, me, we, us	you	him/her/it(self), *pl* themselves
sg	*nom*	ego	tu	-
	acc	me	te	se
	gen	mei	tui	sui
	dat	mihi	tibi	sibi
	abl	me	te	se
pl	*nom*	nos	vos	-
	acc	nos	vos	se
	gen	nostrum	vestrum	sui
	dat	nobis	vobis	sibi
	abl	nobis	vobis	se

- For the associated possessives *meus*, *noster*, *tuus*, *vester*, *suus* and *eius* see pp222–3.
- Note that *se* cannot be translated in isolation, but only in context: it refers back to the subject of the sentence.

third person non-reflexive

he, she, it, *pl* they, them

		m	*f*	*n*
sg	*nom*	is	ea	id
	acc	eum	eam	id
	gen	eius	eius	eius
	dat	ei	eiei	
	abl	eo	ea	eo
pl	*nom*	ei	eae	ea
	acc	eos	eas	ea
	gen	eorum	earum	eorum
	dat	eis	eis	eis
	abl	eis	eis	eis

- Note the distinctive genitive and dative singular endings (*-ius* and *-i*) across all three genders (used also for other pronouns).

Possessives

A possessive indicates who something belongs to (e.g. *my*, *your*, *his*). Most of these are 2-1-2 adjectives, which agree in number/gender/case with the thing possessed (not the possessor).

first person

my

		m	*f*	*n*
sg	*nom*	meus*	mea	meum
	acc	meum	meam	meum
		etc	*etc*	*etc*
		(**voc* mi)		

our

		m	*f*	*n*
sg	*nom*	noster	nostra	nostrum
	acc	nostrum	nostram	nostrum
		etc	*etc*	*etc*

second person

your (belonging to you *sg*)

		m	*f*	*n*
sg	*nom*	tuus	tua	tuum
	acc	tuum	tuam	tuum
		etc	*etc*	*etc*

your (belonging to you *pl*)

		m	f	n
sg	*nom*	vester	vestra	vestrum
	acc	vestrum	vestram	vestrum
		etc	*etc*	*etc*

In the third person it is a bit more complicated.

(1) If the possessive refers back to the subject of the sentence or clause, the 2-1-2 adjective *suus* is used (like the associated reflexive pronoun *se*, *suus* cannot be translated in isolation but only in context):

third person reflexive

his/her/its/their (own) (*belonging to the subject of the sentence/clause*)

		m	f	n
sg	*nom*	suus	sua	suum
	acc	suum	suam	suum
		etc	*etc*	*etc*

- As with the first and second person possessive adjectives, the number and gender are those of the thing possessed, not the possessor. (Thus it is NOT the case that the masculine means *his*, the feminine *her*, and the plural *their*: any part of *suus* can mean any of these, depending on the number and gender of the subject.)

(2) If *his/her/its/their* refers to someone other than the subject of the sentence or clause, there is no adjective available and so the genitive of the pronoun *is, ea, id* is used instead: literally *of him, of her, of it, of them*. This time the number and gender are those of the possessor (not the thing possessed), though in the singular all three genders are the same anyway (*eius*).

- Note carefully that the ending of the possessive *eius* is the distinctive -*ius* genitive of a pronoun (not the masculine nominative singular of a 2-1-2 adjective, as it is with *suus*).

third person non-reflexive

his/her/its (*belonging to someone not the subject of the sentence/clause*)

	m	f	n
sg	eius	eius	eius

their (*belonging to people not the subject of the sentence/clause*)

	m	f	n
pl	eorum	earum	eorum

Relative pronoun: *who, which*

who, which

		m	f	n
sg	nom	qui	quae	quod
	acc	quem	quam	quod
	gen	cuius	cuius	cuius
	dat	cui	cui	cui
	abl	quo	qua	quo
pl	nom	qui	quae	quae
	acc	quos	quas	quae
	gen	quorum	quarum	quorum
	dat	quibus	quibus	quibus
	abl	quibus	quibus	quibus

- This is used in relative clauses (*servus quem heri vidi* = the slave whom I saw yesterday).

Interrogative pronoun: *who? what?*

who?   what?

		m	f	n
sg	nom	quis	quis	quid
	acc	quem	quam	quid

(other parts the same as the relative pronoun *qui, quae, quod*)

- This is used in direct questions (where it comes first word in the sentence).

PREPOSITIONS

Prepositions are followed by either the accusative or the ablative. They often focus more closely a meaning the case already has. Prepositions with the accusative mostly indicate *motion towards* or *through*, whilst those with the ablative mostly indicate either *a position of rest in* a place or *going away from* it.

(1) Prepositions with the accusative:

ad	to, towards, at
circum	around
contra	against
in	into, onto
inter	among, between
per	through, along
post	after, behind
prope	near
trans	across

(2) Prepositions with the ablative:

a/ab*	from, away from, by
cum	with
de	from, down from, about
e/ex*	from, out of
in	in, on

　　* the forms *ab* and *ex* are used if the next word begins with a vowel or *h*

- Note that *in* can be used with either accusative or ablative according to meaning.

- With the names of towns and cities, no preposition is used, but the case is what it would have been if the preposition had been there: hence *Romam* (acc) = to Rome, *Roma* (abl) = from Rome. This idiom must be distinguished from the use of the *locative*, meaning *in/at* a place, e.g. *Romae* (in Rome).

- Many prepositions are also used as prefixes to form compound verbs: *a/ab-, ad-, e/ex-, in-, trans-*. Note also a prefix that is not found as a preposition: *re-* (back), e.g. *revenimus* = we came back.

VERBS

- The present tense describes something that is happening now or is currently true.

- The future tense describes something that will happen in the future.

- The imperfect and perfect tenses both describe something that happened in the past. The imperfect typically denotes an incomplete, repeated or long-lasting action (*X was happening/used to happen*). The perfect is either a simple past tense describing a completed action (*X happened*); or a 'true perfect' (*X has happened*, implying that the effects continue).

- The pluperfect describes something that *had* already happened by some point in the past.

- Regular verbs of all conjugations use the imperfect endings *-bam, -bas, -bat* etc. but there are two different ways of forming the future: first and second use *-bo, -bis, -bit* etc. (hence *portabo, monebo*); third and fourth use *-am, -es, -et* etc. (hence *traham, audiam*).

- The characteristic vowel(s) for each conjugation precede *-bam* in the imperfect tense (first *a*, second *e*, third *e*, fourth *ie*).

- The perfect and pluperfect of all verbs use the perfect stem (the third principal part minus *-i*) with perfect endings *-i, -isti, -it, -imus, -istis, -erunt*, and pluperfect *-eram, -eras, -erat, -eramus, -eratis, -erant*.

- Verbs of 'mixed' third/fourth conjugation (e.g. *capio*, sometimes called 'three and a half'), count as third because of their infinitive (*-ere*), and often also have perfect stems, which look like third (e.g. *cep-*), but form their present (3 pl *capiunt*), future (*capiam, capies* etc.) and imperfect (*capiebam*) like fourth.

Verb tenses

conjugation		1st	2nd	3rd	4th	mixed 3rd/4th
present		I carry	I warn	I drag	I hear	I take
sg	1	porto	moneo	traho	audio	capio
	2	portas	mones	trahis	audis	capis
	3	portat	monet	trahit	audit	capit
pl	1	portamus	monemus	trahimus	audimus	capimus
	2	portatis	monetis	trahitis	auditis	capitis
	3	portant	monent	trahunt	audiunt	capiunt
future		I shall carry	I shall warn	I shall drag	I shall hear	I shall take
sg	1	portabo	monebo	traham	audiam	capiam
	2	portabis	monebis	trahes	audies	capies
	3	portabit	monebit	trahet	audiet	capiet
pl	1	portabimus	monebimus	trahemus	audiemus	capiemus
	2	portabitis	monebitis	trahetis	audietis	capietis
	3	portabunt	monebunt	trahent	audient	capient
imperfect		I was carrying	I was warning	I was dragging	I was hearing	I was taking
sg	1	portabam	monebam	trahebam	audiebam	capiebam
	2	portabas	monebas	trahebas	audiebas	capiebas
	3	portabat	monebat	trahebat	audiebat	capiebat
pl	1	portabamus	monebamus	trahebamus	audiebamus	capiebamus
	2	portabatis	monebatis	trahebatis	audiebatis	capiebatis
	3	portabant	monebant	trahebant	audiebant	capiebant
perfect		I (have) carried	I (have) warned	I (have) dragged	I (have) heard	I took, I have taken
sg	1	portavi	monui	traxi	audivi	cepi
	2	portavisti	monuisiti	traxisti	audivisti	cepisti
	3	portavit	monuit	traxit	audivit	cepit
pl	1	portavimus	monuimus	traximus	audivimus	cepimus
	2	portavistis	monuistis	traxistis	audivistis	cepistis
	3	portaverunt	monuerunt	traxerunt	audiverunt	ceperunt
pluperfect		I had carried	I had warned	I had dragged	I had heard	I had taken
sg	1	portaveram	monueram	traxeram	audiveram	ceperam
	2	portaveras	monueras	traxeras	audiveras	ceperas
	3	portaverat	monuerat	traxerat	audiverat	ceperat
pl	1	portaveramus	monueramus	traxeramus	audiveramus	ceperamus
	2	portaveratis	monueratis	traxeratis	audiveratis	ceperatis
	3	portaverant	monuerant	traxerant	audiverant	ceperant

Imperatives

conjugation	1st	2nd	3rd	4th	mixed 3rd/4th
	carry!	warn!	drag!	hear!	take!
sg	porta	mone	trahe	audi	cape
pl	portate	monete	trahite	audite	capite

Infinitives

conjugation	1st	2nd	3rd	4th	mixed 3rd/4th
	to carry	to warn	to drag	to hear	to take
	portare	monere	trahere	audire	capere

- The infinitives of second and third conjugations look the same, but note that the first *e* is long in second conjugation, short in third.

Irregular verbs

			sum = I am (the verb to be)	possum = I am able	eo = I go
present					
	sg	1	sum	possum	eo
		2	es	potes	is
		3	est	potest	it
	pl	1	sumus	possumus	imus
		2	estis	potestis	itis
		3	sunt	possunt	eunt
infinitive			esse	posse	ire
future					
	sg	1	ero	potero	ibo
		2	eris	poteris	ibis
		3	erit	poterit	ibit
	pl	1	erimus	poterimus	ibimus
		2	eritis	poteritis	ibitis
		3	erunt	poterunt	ibunt
imperfect					
	sg	1	eram	poteram	ibam
		2	eras	poteras	ibas
		3	erat	poterat	ibat
	pl	1	eramus	poteramus	ibamus
		2	eratis	poteratis	ibatis
		3	erant	poterant	ibant

perfect

	sg	1	fui		potui	i(v)i
		2	fuisti		potuisti	i(vi)sti
			etc		*etc*	*etc*

pluperfect

	sg	1	fueram		potueram	i(v)eram
		2	fueras		potueras	i(v)eras
			etc		*etc*	*etc*

- *possum* is a compound of *sum*, using as prefix an original adjective *potis* (able), abbreviated to *pot-*, which changes to *pos-* before another *s*; the perfect and pluperfect of both verbs are regular (*possum* has perfect *potui*, abbreviated from original *potfui*).
- the imperative forms of *eo* are: *i* (sg), *ite* (pl).

Important irregular principal parts

accipio	accipere	accepi	I accept, I receive
ascendo	ascendere	ascendi	I climb
cado	cadere	cecidi	I fall
capio	capere	cepi	I take, I capture
conspicio	conspicere	conspexi	I catch sight of
constituo	constituere	constitui	I decide
credo	credere	credidi	I believe, I trust (+ *dat*)
curro	currere	cucurri	I run
defendo	defendere	defendi	I defend
deleo	delere	delevi	I destroy
dico	dicere	dixi	I say
discedo	discedere	discessi	I depart, I leave
do	dare	dedi	I give
duco	ducere	duxi	I lead
emo	emere	emi	I buy
eo	ire	i(v)i	I go
facio	facere	feci	I make, I do
fugio	fugere	fugi	I run away
iacio	iacere	ieci	I throw
intellego	intellegere	intellexi	I understand
iubeo	iubere	iussi	I order
lego	legere	legi	I read, I choose
maneo	manere	mansi	I remain, I stay
mitto	mittere	misi	I send
persuadeo	persuadere	persuasi	I persuade (+ *dat*)
peto	petere	petivi	I seek
pono	ponere	posui	I place
possum	posse	potui	I am able
promitto	promittere	promisi	I promise
quaero	quaerere	quaesivi	I search for, I ask
rego	regere	rexi	I rule
relinquo	relinquere	reliqui	I leave
respondeo	respondere	respondi	I reply
rideo	ridere	risi	I laugh, I smile
scribo	scribere	scripsi	I write
sedeo	sedere	sedi	I sit

sum	esse	fui	I am
traho	trahere	traxi	I drag
venio	venire	veni	I come
video	videre	vidi	I see
vinco	vincere	vici	I conquer

GLOSSARY OF GRAMMAR TERMS

ablative case expressing *by*, *with*, *from*; used with prepositions expressing motion away from, or being in a place.

accusative case of direct object; used with prepositions expressing motion towards.

adjective word describing a noun (with which in Latin it agrees in number, gender and case).

adverb word describing a verb (or an adjective, or another adverb).

agree have the same number (agreement of subject and verb); have the same number, gender and case (agreement of noun and adjective).

ambiguous can mean more than one thing.

antecedent noun or pronoun in main clause to which relative pronoun refers back.

case form of a noun, pronoun or adjective that shows the job it does in the sentence (e.g. accusative for direct object); cases are arranged in the order nominative, (vocative), accusative, genitive, dative, ablative.

causal clause subordinate clause stating why something happened, introduced by *quod* (= because).

clause part of a sentence with its own subject and verb.

complement another nominative word or phrase describing the subject, usually with the verb *to be*.

compound verb with prefix (e.g. *exire* = to go out).

concessive clause subordinate clause stating why something might have been expected not to happen (but nevertheless did), introduced by *quamquam* (= although).

conjugate go through the different parts of a verb (e.g. *porto*, *portas*, *portat* etc).

conjugation one of the four main patterns by which verbs change their endings.

conjunction word joining clauses, phrases or words together (e.g. *and*, *but*, *therefore*).

consonant letter representing a sound that can only be used together with a vowel.

dative case of indirect object, often translated *to* or *for*.

declension one of the patterns (three main ones, also used for adjectives) by which nouns change their endings.

decline go through the different parts of a noun, pronoun or adjective in case order.

direct object noun or pronoun on the receiving end of action of verb.

direct speech actual words of a speaker, usually enclosed by inverted commas.

ending last part of a word, added to the stem to give more information and show its job in the sentence.

feminine one of the three genders, for females or things imagined as female.

future tense of verb referring to something that will happen in the future.

gender one of three categories (masculine, feminine, neuter) into which nouns and pronouns are put according to their actual or imagined sex or lack of it.

genitive case expressing possession or definition, often translated *of*.

gerundive adjective formed from verb, expressing the idea *needing to be done*; used with *ad* to express purpose.

imperative form of verb used for direct command.

imperfect tense of verb referring to incomplete, extended or repeated action in the past.

indeclinable does not change its endings.

indirect indirect object is person or thing in the dative indirectly affected by object of verb, e.g. *I gave the money* (direct object) *to the old man* (indirect object).

infinitive form of verb introduced by *to*, expressing the basic meaning (e.g. *currere* = to run).

irregular word that does not follow one of the standard declensions or conjugations.

literally translated in a way corresponding closely to the Latin words, but which needs to be modified to produce natural English.

locative special case ending of some nouns (usually names of cities) expressing *at* or *in*.

main clause clause that makes sense on its own, and expresses the main point of a sentence (as distinct from subordinate clause).

masculine one of the three genders, for males or things imagined as male.

negative expressing that something is not the case or should not happen.

neuter one of the three genders, for things imagined as neither male nor female.

nominative case used for subject of sentence.

noun word naming a person, place or thing (e.g. *urbs* = city; a *proper* noun with a capital letter gives its actual name e.g. *Roma* = Rome).

number singular or plural.

numerals numbers.

object noun or pronoun acted upon by a verb.

part of speech category of word (noun, adjective, pronoun, verb, adverb, preposition, conjunction).

perfect tense of verb referring to a completed action in the past.

person term for the subject of verb: first person = *I*, *we*; second person = *you*, third person = *he*, *she*, *it*, *they* (or a noun replacing one of these).

phrase group of words not containing a finite verb (as distinct from clause).

pluperfect tense of verb referring to something that had already happened by a particular point in the past.

plural more than one.

possessive adjective or pronoun expressing who or what something belongs to.

prefix word or syllable added to the beginning of another word.

preposition word used with a noun or pronoun in the accusative or ablative to focus more closely the meaning of the case (e.g. *into*).

present tense of a verb referring to something that is happening now.

principal parts set of parts of a verb from which you can work out all necessary information about it. So far we have met three: present tense (first person singular), infinitive, perfect tense (first person singular).

pronoun word that stands instead of a noun (e.g. *he*, *she*, *they*), avoiding the need to repeat it.

reflexive word referring back to the subject of the verb.

relative clause subordinate clause describing or giving further information about a person or thing just mentioned in the main clause, introduced by the relative pronoun *qui, quae, quod*.

sentence group of words with subject and verb (and often other elements), which can stand on its own (as distinct from phrase or subordinate clause).

singular just one (as distinct from plural).

stem the part of a word that stays the same: different endings are added to give more information and show the job it does in the sentence.

subject noun or pronoun in the nominative case, expressing who or what does the action.

subordinate of secondary importance to something else; a subordinate clause cannot stand alone but only makes sense in relation to the main clause.

supply provide in translation a word that is not separately represented in Latin but worked out from the grammar and context (e.g. *multa dixit* = he said many *things*).

syllable part of a word forming a spoken unit, usually consisting of a vowel with consonants before or after or both.

tense form of a verb showing when the action takes place (in the past, present or future).

verb word expressing an action.

vocative case used for addressing someone or something.

vowel letter representing a sound that can be spoken by itself: *a, e, i, o, u, y* (but *y* is rare in Latin).

ENGLISH TO LATIN VOCABULARY

For further information about a word, check it in the Latin to English vocabulary.

able, be	possum, posse, potui
about	de (+ *abl*)
absent, be	absum, abesse, afui
accept	accipio, accipere, accepi
across	trans (+ *acc*)
advice	consilium -i *n 2*
advise	moneo, monere, monui
afraid (of), be	timeo, timere, timui
after (*prep*)	post (+ *acc*)
after (*conj*)	postquam
against	contra (+ *acc*)
all	omnis -e
along	per (+ *acc*)
although	quamquam
always	semper
among	inter (+ *acc*)
and	et; -que (*attached to the second word*)
and so	igitur (*not first word*)
anger	ira -ae *f 1*
angry	iratus -a -um
announce	nuntio, nuntiare, nuntiavi
answer (reply)	respondeo, respondere, respondi
approach	appropinquo, appropinquare, appropinquavi (+ *dat*)
arms, armour	arma -orum *n 2 pl*
around	circum (+ *acc*)
arrive	advenio, advenire, adveni
ask (a question)	rogo, rogare, rogavi
ask for	rogo, rogare, rogavi; peto, petere, petivi
at	ad (+ *acc*)
at last	tandem
at once	statim
attack	oppugno, oppugnare, oppugnavi
away, be	absum, abesse, afui
away from	a/ab (+ *abl*)
back (*prefix*)	re-, e.g. revenio (come back)
bad	malus -a -um
be	sum, esse, fui

be absent/away	absum, abesse, afui
be here/present	adsum, adesse, adfui
beautiful	pulcher -chra -chrum
because	quod
behind	post (+ *acc*)
believe	credo, credere, credidi (+ *dat*)
between	inter (+ *acc*)
big	magnus -a -um
block of flats	insula -ae *f 1*
book	liber -bri *m 2*
boy	puer -eri *m 2*
brave	fortis -e
bravely	fortiter
brother	frater -tris *m 3*
build	aedifico, aedificare, aedificavi
but	sed
buy	emo, emere, emi
by	a/ab (+ *abl*)
call	voco, vocare, vocavi
camp	castra -orum *n 2 pl*
can (be able)	possum, posse, potui
capture	capio, capere, cepi
carry	porto, portare, portavi
catch	capio, capere, cepi
catch sight of	conspicio, conspicere, conspexi
chance, by	forte
choose	lego, legere, legi
citizen	civis -is *m/f 3*
city	urbs, urbis *f 3*
climb	ascendo, ascendere, ascendi
come	venio, venire, veni
come down	descendo, descendere, descendi
come near to	appropinquo, appropinquare, appropinquavi (+ *dat*)
come together	convenio, covenire, conveni
conquer	vinco, vincere, vici
country (native land)	patria -ae *f 1*
crowd	turba -ae *f 1*
cruel	crudelis -e; saevus -a -um
cry	lacrimo, lacrimare, lacrimavi
danger	periculum -i *n 2*
daughter	filia -ae (*dat/abl pl* filiabus) *f 1*
death	mors, mortis *f 3*
decide	constituo, constituere, constitui
defeat	vinco, vincere, vici
defend	defendo, defendere, defendi
depart (from)	discedo, discedere, discessi (+ *prep* + *abl*)
descend	descendo, descendere, descendi
desire	cupio, cupere, cupivi
destroy	deleo, delere, delevi

difficult	difficilis -e
dinner	cena -ae *f 1*
discover	invenio, invenire, inveni
distant (from), be	absum, abesse, afui (+ *abl*)
do	facio, facere, feci
down from	de (+ *abl*)
drag	traho, trahere, traxi
drink	bibo, bibere, bibi
earth	terra -ae *f 1*
easily	facile
easy	facilis -e
eat	consumo, consumere, consumpsi
eight	octo
enemy	hostis -is *m 3* (*usu pl*)
enter	intro, intrare, intravi
escape	effugio, effugere, effugi
every	omnis -e
everyone (all the people)	omnes -ium *pl*
everything (all things)	omnia -ium *pl*
evil	malus -a -um
ex-slave	libertus -i *m 2*
fall	cado, cadere, cecidi
fast	celer -eris -ere
father	pater -tris *m 3*
fear	timeo, timere, timui
ferocious	ferox *gen* -ocis
field	ager, agri *m 2*
fierce	ferox *gen* -ocis
fight	pugno, pugnare, pugnavi
finally	tandem
find	invenio, invenire, inveni
first (*adj*)	primus -a -um
five	quinque
flee	fugio, fugere, fugi
food	cibus -i *m 2*
foolish	stultus -a -um
for (*giving explanation*)	enim (*not first word*)
for (*length of time*)	*use acc*
for (the benefit of)	*use dat*
forum	forum -i *n 2*
four	quattuor
freedman	libertus -i *m 2*
friend	amicus -i *m 2*
frighten	terreo, terrere, terrui
frightened, very	perterritus -a -um
from	a/ab (+ *abl*); de (+ *abl*); e/ex (+ *abl*)
garden	hortus -i *m 2*
gate	porta -ae *f 1*

gather (meet, assemble)	convenio, convenire, conveni
gift	donum -i *n 2*
girl	puella -ae *f 1*
give	do, dare, dedi
go	eo, ire, i(v)i
go back	redeo, redire, redii
go down	descendo, descendere, descendi
go out	exeo, exire, exii
god	deus -i *m 2*
goddess	dea -ae (*dat/abl pl* deabus) *f 1*
good	bonus -a -um
great	magnus -a -um
greet	saluto, salutare, salutavi
ground	terra -ae *f 1*
guard	custodio, custodire, custodivi
hand over	trado, tradere, tradidi
handsome	pulcher -chra -chrum
happy	laetus -a -um
have	habeo, habere, habui
he	is, *gen* eius
head	caput -itis *n 3*
hear	audio, audire, audivi
heaven	caelum -i *n 2*
heavy	gravis -e
help	auxilium -i *n 2*
her, her own (*refl*)	suus -a -um
herself (*refl*)	se
here, be	adsum, adesse, adfui
highest (part of)	summus -a -um
himself (*refl*)	se
his, his own (*refl*)	suus -a -um
hold	teneo, tenere, tenui; habeo, habere, habui
homeland	patria -ae *f 1*
horse	equus -i *m 2*
hour	hora -ae *f 1*
house	villa -ae *f 1*
however	tamen (*not first word*)
huge	ingens *gen* -entis
hundred	centum
hurry	festino, festinare, festinavi
husband	maritus -i *m 2*
I	ego, *gen* mei
idea	consilium -i *n 2*
immediately	statim
in	in (+ *abl*)
inn	taberna -ae *f 1*
into	in (+ *acc*)
invite	invito, invitare, invitavi
is it (the case that)?	-ne (*attached to first word of question*)

island	insula -ae *f 1*
it	id, *gen* eius
journey	iter -ineris *n 3*
keep	servo, servare, servavi
kill	neco, necare, necavi; interficio, interficere, interfeci
king	rex, regis *m 3*
kingdom	regnum -i *n 2*
land	terra -ae *f 1*
large	magnus -a -um
laugh	rideo, ridere, risi
lead	duco, ducere, duxi
leader	dux, ducis *m 3*
leave (something behind)	relinquo, relinquere, reliqui
leave (depart from)	discedo, discedere, discessi (+ *prep* + *abl*)
letter	epistula -ae *f 1*
life	vita -ae *f 1*
like	amo, amare, amavi
listen (to)	audio, audire, audivi
little	parvus -a -um
live (dwell)	habito, habitare, habitavi
long	longus -a -um
long time, for a	diu
look!	ecce
look at	specto, spectare, spectavi
look for	quaero, quaerere, quaesivi
love (*verb*)	amo, amare, amavi
love (*noun*)	amor -oris *m 3*
make	facio, facere, feci
make for	peto, petere, petivi
man	vir, viri *m 2*
many	multi -ae -a
market-place	forum -i *n 2*
master	dominus -i *m 2*
meal	cena -ae *f 1*
meet	convenio, convenire, conveni
message	nuntius -i *m 2*
messenger	nuntius -i *m 2*
middle (mid part of, *adj*)	medius -a -um
miserable	miser -era -erum
mistress	domina -ae *f 1*
money	pecunia -ae *f 1*
mother	mater -tris *f 3*
mountain	mons, montis *m 3*
much (*adj*)	multus -a -um; *or as n noun* + *gen, e.g.* multum pecuniae (much money)
must	debeo, debere, debui
my	meus -a -um

name	nomen -inis *n 3*
near	prope (+ *acc*)
never	numquam
new	novus -a -um
next (then, after that)	deinde
night	nox, noctis *f 3*
nine	novem
noise	clamor -oris *m 3*
not	non
notice	conspicio, conspicere, conspexi
now	nunc
often	saepe
old man	senex -is *m 3*
on	in (+ *abl*)
once (some time ago)	olim
once, at	statim
one	unus -a -um
onto	in (+ *acc*)
order (to do something)	iubeo, iubere, iussi *(+ acc + inf)*
ought	debeo, debere, debui
our	noster -tra -trum
out of	e/ex (+ *abl*)
overcome, overpower	supero, superare, superavi
owe	debeo, debere, debui
peace	pax, pacis *f 3*
perish	pereo, perire, perii
persuade	persuadeo, persuadere, persuasi (+ *dat*)
place (*verb*)	pono, ponere, posui
place (*noun*)	locus -i *m 2, with n 2 pl* loca
plan	consilium -i *n 2*
prepare	paro, parare, paravi
present (gift)	donum -i *n 2*
present, be	adsum, adesse, adfui
protect	servo, servare, servavi
provide	paro, parare, paravi
punish	punio, punire, punivi
put	pono, ponere, posui
queen	regina -ae *f 1*
quick	celer -eris -ere
quickly	celeriter
quiet, be	taceo, tacere, tacui
read	lego, legere, legi
realise	intellego, intellegere, intellexi
receive	accipio, accipere, accepi
remain	maneo, manere, mansi
reply	respondeo, respondere, respondi
report	nuntio, nuntiare, nuntiavi

return (go back)	redeo, redire, redii
road	via -ae *f 1*
Roman	Romanus -a -um
Romans	Romani -orum *m 2 pl*
Rome	Roma -ae *loc* Romae (in/at Rome) *f 1*
rule (be king)	rego, regere, rexi
run	curro, currere, cucurri
run away	fugio, fugere, fugi
sad	tristis -e; miser -era -erum
sail	navigo, navigare, navigavi
sailor	nauta -ae *m 1*
savage	saevus -a -um
save	servo, servare, servavi
say	dico, dicere, dixi
says/said, he/she	inquit, *pl* inquiunt (*interrupting quoted speech*)
sea	mare, maris *n 3*
search for	quaero, quaerere, quaesivi
see	video, videre, vidi
see!	ecce
seek	peto, petere, petivi
sell	vendo, vendere, vendidi
senator	senator -oris *m 3*
send	mitto, mittere, misi
serious	gravis -e
set free	libero, liberare, liberavi
set up	pono, ponere, posui
seven	septem
she	ea, *gen* eius
ship	navis -is *f 3*
shop	taberna -ae *f 1*
should	debeo, debere, debui
shout (*verb*)	clamo, clamare, clamavi
shout, shouting (*noun*)	clamor -oris *m 3*
silent, be	taceo, tacere, tacui
sit	sedeo, sedere, sedi
six	sex
sky	caelum -i *n 2*
slave	servus -i *m 2*
slave-girl, slave-woman	ancilla -ae *f 1*
sleep	dormio, dormire, dormivi
small	parvus -a -um
smile	rideo, ridere, risi
soldier	miles -itis *m 3*
son	filius -i *m 2*
soon	mox
speak	dico, dicere, dixi
stay	maneo, manere, mansi
street	via -ae *f 1*
stupid	stultus -a -um
suddenly	subito

surely?	nonne
surely . . . not?	num
sword	gladius -i *m 2*
take	capio, capere, cepi
take (someone somewhere)	duco, ducere, duxi
tell (inform)	dico, dicere, dixi (+ *dat*)
tell (order)	iubeo, iubere, iussi (+ *acc* + *inf*)
temple	templum -i *n 2*
ten	decem
terrified	perterritus -a -um
their, their own (*refl*)	suus -a -um
themselves (*refl*)	se
then (at that time)	tum
then (next)	deinde
therefore	igitur (*not first word*)
thousand	mille, *pl* milia
three	tres, tria
through	per (+ *acc*)
throw	iacio, iacere, ieci
to	ad (+ *acc*)
today	hodie
tomorrow	cras
top (part of, *adj*)	summus -a -um
towards	ad (+ *acc*)
trust	credo, credere, credidi (+ *dat*)
two	duo, duae, duo
understand	intellego, intellegere, intellexi
used to	*use imperfect tense*
victorious, be	vinco, vincere, vici
villa	villa -ae *f 1*
wait	maneo, manere, mansi
wait for	exspecto, exspectare, exspectavi
walk	ambulo, ambulare, ambulavi
wall	murus -i *m 2*
want	cupio, cupere, cupivi
war	bellum -i *n 2*
warn	moneo, monere, monui
watch	specto, spectare, spectavi
water	aqua -ae *f 1*
way	via -ae *f 1*
we	nos, *gen* nostrum
weapons	arma -orum *n 2 pl*
weep	lacrimo, lacrimare, lacrimavi
well	bene
what?	quid
when?	quando
when (at the time when)	ubi

when (after)	postquam
where (at)?, (in the place) where	ubi
where from?	unde
where to?	quo
which (the one which)	qui, quae, quod
who?	quis
who (the one who)	qui, quae, quod
why?	cur
wife	uxor -oris *f 3*
win (be victorious)	vinco, vincere, vici
wine	vinum -i *n 2*
with (accompanied by)	cum (+ *abl*)
with (using, by means of)	*use abl, without prep*
within (a length of time)	*use abl, without prep*
woman	femina -ae *f 1*
wood (forest)	silva -ae *f 1*
word	verbum -i *n 2*
work	laboro, laborare, laboravi
wretched	miser -era -erum
write	scribo, scribere, scripsi
year	annus -i *m 2*
yesterday	heri
you (*sg*)	tu, *gen* tui
you (*pl*)	vos, *gen* vestrum
young man	iuvenis -is *m 3*
your (of you *sg*)	tuus -a -um
your (of you *pl*)	vester -tra -trum

LATIN TO ENGLISH
VOCABULARY

The second column has further information about each word:

- Verbs are shown with principal parts: present tense (first person singular) in the first column, then infinitive (showing conjugation, e.g. 3rd) and perfect tense (first person singular). Note that 3rd* = mixed 3rd/4th conjugation: these verbs count as 3rd because of infinitive *-ere*, but form present, imperfect and future tenses like 4th.

- Nouns are shown with genitive singular, gender, and declension (e.g. 3).

- Adjectives are given with feminine and neuter. If only one other form is given, it is the neuter (and the feminine is the same as the masculine). Third declension adjectives of the *ingens* type are shown instead with the genitive singular (for the stem).

- Common irregular forms are cross-referenced.

- The chapter where the word forms part of the learning vocabulary is shown in square brackets.

- For explanation of abbreviations, see the list on pages xiv–xv.

a/ab	+ *abl, or as prefix*	*prep*	from, away from, by (*as prefix* = away)	[2]
absum	abesse, afui	*verb irreg*	be absent, be away, be distant from	[6]
accepi		(*perfect of* accipio)		
accipio	accipere, accepi	*verb 3rd**	accept, take in, receive	[6]
ad	+ *acc, or as prefix*	*prep*	to, towards, at	[1]
adsum	adesse, adfui	*verb irreg*	be here, be present	[6]
advenio	advenire, adveni	*verb 4th*	arrive	[3]
aedifico	aedificare, aedificavi	*verb 1st*	build	[3]
ager	agri	*noun m 2*	field	[2]
ambulo	ambulare, ambulavi	*verb 1st*	walk	[1]
amicus	amici	*noun m 2*	friend	[1]
amo	amare, amavi	*verb 1st*	love, like	[1]
amor	amoris	*noun m 3*	love	[4]
ancilla	ancillae	*noun f 1*	slave-girl, slave-woman	[1]
annus	anni	*noun m 2*	year	[2]

appropinquo	appropinquare, appropinquavi	*verb 1st*	approach, come near to (*usu + dat*)	[6]
aqua	aquae	*noun f 1*	water	[2]
arma	armorum	*noun n 2 pl*	arms, weapons	[2]
ascendo	ascendere, ascendi	*verb 3rd*	climb	[5]
audio	audire, audivi	*verb 4th*	hear, listen to	[2]
auxilium	auxilii	*noun n 2*	help	[2]
bellum	belli	*noun n 2*	war	[2]
bene	*indecl*	*adv*	well	[5]
bibo	bibere, bibi	*verb 3rd*	drink	[2]
bonus	bona, bonum	*adj*	good	[3]
cado	cadere, cecidi	*verb 3rd*	fall	[3]
caelum	caeli	*noun n 2*	sky, heaven	[4]
capio	capere, cepi	*verb 3rd**	take, catch, capture	[4]
caput	capitis	*noun n 3*	head	[4]
cecidi		*(perfect of* cado)		
celer	celeris, celere	*adj*	quick, fast	[5]
cena	cenae	*noun f 1*	dinner, meal	[3]
centum	*indecl*	*num*	100	[6]
cepi		*(perfect of* capio)		
cibus	cibi	*noun m 2*	food	[1]
circum	+ *acc*	*prep*	around	[1]
civis	civis	*noun m/f 3*	citizen	[5]
clamo	clamare, clamavi	*verb 1st*	shout	[1]
clamor	clamoris	*noun m 3*	shout, shouting, noise	[4]
consilium	consilii	*noun n 2*	plan, idea, advice	[3]
conspexi		*(perfect of* conspicio)		
conspicio	conspicere, conspexi	*verb 3rd**	catch sight of, notice	[6]
constituo	constituere, constitui	*verb 3rd*	decide	[6]
consumo	consumere, consumpsi	*verb 3rd*	eat	[3]
contra	+ *acc*	*prep*	against	[1]
convenio	convenire, conveni	*verb 4th*	come together, gather, meet	[6]
cras	*indecl*	*adv*	tomorrow	[5]
credo	credere, credidi	*verb 3rd*	believe, trust (+ *dat*)	[5]
cucurri		*(perfect of* curro)		
cum	+ *abl*	*prep*	with	[2]
cupio	cupere, cupivi	*verb 3rd**	want, desire	[6]
cur?	*indecl*	*adv*	why?	[4]
curro	currere, cucurri	*verb 3rd*	run	[3]
custodio	custodire, custodivi	*verb 4th*	guard	[2]
de	+ *abl*	*prep*	from, down from, about	[2]
dea	deae	*noun f 1*	goddess	[1]
debeo	debere, debui	*verb 2nd*	ought, should, must; owe	[3]
decem	*indecl*	*num*	ten	[2]

dedi		*(perfect of* do)		
defendo	defendere, defendi	*verb 3rd*	defend	[5]
deinde	*indecl*	*adv*	then, next	[3]
deleo	delere, delevi	*verb 2nd*	destroy	[3]
descendo	descendere, descendi	*verb 3rd*	go down, come down	[6]
deus	dei	*noun m 2*	god	[1]
dico	dicere, dixi	*verb 3rd*	say, speak, tell	[6]
difficilis	difficile	*adj*	difficult	[5]
discedo	discedere, discessi	*verb 3rd*	depart, leave	[3]
diu	*indecl*	*adv*	for a long time	[3]
dixi		*(perfect of* dico)		
do	dare, dedi	*verb 1st*	give	[2]
domina	dominae	*noun f 1*	mistress	[3]
dominus	domini	*noun m 2*	master	[1]
donum	doni	*noun n 2*	gift, present	[2]
dormio	dormire, dormivi	*verb 4th*	sleep	[2]
duco	ducere, duxi	*verb 3rd*	lead, take	[2]
duo	duae, duo	*num*	two	[6]
dux	ducis	*noun m 3*	leader	[4]
duxi		*(perfect of* duco)		
e/ex	*+ abl, or as prefix*	*prep*	from, out of, out	[2]
ecce!	*indecl*	*interjection*	look! see!	[5]
effugio	effugere, effugi	*verb 3rd**	escape	[6]
ego	mei	*pron*	I, me	[4]
emo	emere, emi	*verb 3rd*	buy	[6]
enim	*indecl*	*conj*	for	[5]
eo	ire, i(v)i	*verb irreg*	go	[6]
epistula	epistulae	*noun f 1*	letter	[1]
equus	equi	*noun m 2*	horse	[1]
et	*indecl*	*conj*	and, even	[1]
exspecto	exspectare, exspectavi	*verb 1st*	wait for, expect	[6]
facilis	facile	*adj*	easy	[5]
facio	facere, feci	*verb 3rd**	make, do	[4]
feci		*(perfect of* facio)		
femina	feminae	*noun f 1*	woman	[1]
ferox	*gen* ferocis	*adj*	fierce, ferocious	[5]
festino	festinare, festinavi	*verb 1st*	hurry	[3]
filia	filiae	*noun f 1*	daughter	[5]
filius	filii	*noun m 2*	son	[5]
forte	*indecl*	*adv*	by chance	[5]
fortis	forte	*adj*	brave	[5]
forum	fori	*noun n 2*	forum, marketplace	[3]
frater	fratris	*noun m 3*	brother	[4]
fugio	fugere, fugi	*verb 3rd**	run away, flee	[4]
fui		*(perfect of* sum)		
gladius	gladii	*noun m 2*	sword	[1]
gravis	grave	*adj*	heavy, serious	[5]

habeo	habere, habui	*verb 2nd*	have, hold	[2]
habito	habitare, habitavi	*verb 1st*	live, dwell	[3]
heri	*indecl*	*adv*	yesterday	[5]
hodie	*indecl*	*adv*	today	[5]
hora	horae	*noun f 1*	hour	[2]
hortus	horti	*noun m 2*	garden	[1]
hostis	hostis	*noun m 3*	enemy (*usu pl*)	[6]
iacio	iacere, ieci	*verb 3rd**	throw	[6]
	(*in compounds* -icio, e.g. eicio [throw out], inicio [throw in])			
ieci		(*perfect of* iacio)		
igitur	*indecl*	*conj*	therefore, and so	[5]
ii		(= ivi, *perfect of* eo)		
in	+ *acc/abl, or as prefix*	*prep*	(+ *acc*) into, onto;	[1]
			(+ *abl*) in, on	[2]
ingens	*gen* ingentis	*adj*	huge	[5]
inquit	*pl* inquiunt	*verb irreg*	(s/he) says, (s/he) said	[2]
insula	insulae	*noun f 1*	island; block of flats	[1]
intellego	intellegere, intellexi	*verb 3rd*	understand, realise	[6]
inter	+ *acc*	*prep*	among, between	[3]
interficio	interficere, interfeci	*verb 3rd**	kill	[6]
intro	intrare, intravi	*verb 1st*	enter	[6]
invenio	invenire, inveni	*verb 4th*	find	[2]
invito	invitare, invitavi	*verb 1st*	invite	[3]
ira	irae	*noun f 1*	anger	[6]
iratus	irata, iratum	*adj*	angry	[3]
is	ea, id	*pron*	he, she, it, *pl* they	[5]
iter	itineris	*noun n 3*	journey	[4]
iubeo	iubere, iussi	*verb 2nd*	order	[2]
iussi		(*perfect of* iubeo)		
iuvenis	iuvenis	*noun m 3*	young man	[4]
ivi		(*perfect of* eo)		
laboro	laborare, laboravi	*verb 1st*	work, toil	[1]
lacrimo	lacrimare, lacrimavi	*verb 1st*	weep, cry	[3]
laetus	laeta, laetum	*adj*	happy	[3]
lego	legere, legi	*verb 3rd*	read, choose	[2]
liber	libri	*noun m 2*	book	[2]
libero	liberare, liberavi	*verb 1st*	set free	[6]
libertus	liberti	*noun m 2*	freedman, ex-slave	[3]
locus	loci (*pl is n:* loca)	*noun m/n 2*	place	[5]
longus	longa, longum	*adj*	long	[4]
magnus	magna, magnum	*adj*	big, large, great	[3]
malus	mala, malum	*adj*	bad, evil	[3]
maneo	manere, mansi	*verb 2nd*	remain, stay	[3]
mansi		(*perfect of* maneo)		
mare	maris	*noun n 3*	sea	[4]
maritus	mariti	*noun m 2*	husband	[4]
mater	matris	*noun f 3*	mother	[4]

medius	media, medium	*adj*	middle (of)	[4]
meus	mea, meum	*adj*	my	[4]
miles	militis	*noun m 3*	soldier	[4]
mille	*pl* milia	*num*	1000	[6]
miser	misera, miserum	*adj*	miserable, wretched, sad	[3]
misi		(*perfect of* mitto)		
mitto	mittere, misi	*verb 3rd*	send	[2]
moneo	monere, monui	*verb 2nd*	warn, advise	[2]
mons	montis	*noun m 3*	mountain	[6]
mors	mortis	*noun f 3*	death	[5]
mox	*indecl*	*adv*	soon	[5]
multus	multa, multum	*adj*	much, *pl* many	[3]
murus	muri	*noun m 2*	wall	[2]
nauta	nautae	*noun m 1*	sailor	[3]
navigo	navigare, navigavi	*verb 1st*	sail	[1]
navis	navis	*noun f 3*	ship	[4]
-ne . . . ?	*indecl*	*adv*	makes a question, e.g. is it?	[4]
neco	necare, necavi	*verb 1st*	kill	[1]
nomen	nominis	*noun n 3*	name	[4]
non	*indecl*	*adv*	not	[1]
nonne . . . ?	*indecl*	*adv*	surely . . . ?	[4]
nos	nostrum	*pron*	we, us	[5]
noster	nostra, nostrum	*adj*	our	[5]
novem	*indecl*	*num*	nine	[6]
novus	nova, novum	*adj*	new	[3]
nox	noctis	*noun f 3*	night	[4]
num . . . ?	*indecl*	*adv*	surely . . . not?	[4]
numquam	*indecl*	*adv*	never	[5]
nunc	*indecl*	*adv*	now	[1]
nuntio	nuntiare, nuntiavi	*verb 1st*	announce, report	[6]
nuntius	nuntii	*noun m 2*	messenger, message, news	[1]
octo	*indecl*	*num*	eight	[6]
olim	*indecl*	*adv*	once, some time ago	[5]
omnis	omne	*adj*	all, every	[5]
oppugno	oppugnare, oppugnavi	*verb 1st*	attack	[3]
paro	parare, paravi	*verb 1st*	prepare, provide	[1]
parvus	parva, parvum	*adj*	small	[3]
pater	patris	*noun m 3*	father	[4]
patria	patriae	*noun f 1*	country, homeland	[3]
pax	pacis	*noun f 3*	peace	[5]
pecunia	pecuniae	*noun f 1*	money	[1]
per	+ *acc*	*prep*	through, along	[1]
pereo	perire, perii	*verb irreg*	die, perish	[6]
periculum	periculi	*noun n 2*	danger	[2]
persuadeo	persuadere, persuasi	*verb 2nd*	persuade (+ *dat*)	[6]
perterritus	perterrita, perterritum	*adj*	terrified	[6]

peto	petere, petivi	*verb 3rd*	seek, beg/ask for, make for	[4]
pono	ponere, posui	*verb 3rd*	place, put, set up	[5]
porta	portae	*noun f 1*	gate	[3]
porto	portare, portavi	*verb 1st*	carry, bear, take	[1]
possum	posse, potui	*verb irreg*	can, be able	[3]
post	+ *acc*	*prep*	after, behind	[4]
postquam	*indecl*	*conj*	after, when	[6]
posui		(*perfect of* pono)		
potui		(*perfect of* possum)		
primus	prima, primum	*adj*	first	[4]
prope	+ *acc*	*prep*	near	[6]
puella	puellae	*noun f 1*	girl	[1]
puer	pueri	*noun m 2*	boy	[2]
pugno	pugnare, pugnavi	*verb 1st*	fight	[1]
pulcher	pulchra, pulchrum	*adj*	beautiful, handsome	[3]
punio	punire, punivi	*verb 4th*	punish	[2]
quaero	quaerere, quaesivi	*verb 3rd*	search for, look for, ask	[3]
quamquam	*indecl*	*conj*	although	[6]
quando?	*indecl*	*adv*	when?	[4]
quattuor	*indecl*	*num*	four	[6]
-que	*indecl*	*conj*	and (*before word it is attached to*)	[3]
qui	quae, quod	*pron*	who, which	[6]
quinque	*indecl*	*num*	five	[2]
quis?	quid?	*pron*	who? what?	[6]
quo?	*indecl*	*adv*	(*question*) where to?	[4]
quod	*indecl*	*conj*	because	[6]
re-	*indecl*	*prefix*	. . . back	[6]
redeo	redire, redii	*verb irreg*	go back, come back, return	[6]
regina	reginae	*noun f 1*	queen	[4]
regnum	regni	*noun n 2*	kingdom	[4]
rego	regere, rexi	*verb 3rd*	rule, reign	[5]
relinquo	relinquere, reliqui	*verb 3rd*	leave, leave behind	[4]
respondeo	respondere, respondi	*verb 2nd*	reply	[6]
rex	regis	*noun 3 m*	king	[4]
rideo	ridere, risi	*verb 2nd*	laugh, smile	[4]
risi		(*perfect of* rideo)		
rogo	rogare, rogavi	*verb 1st*	ask, ask for	[5]
Roma	Romae (Romae = at/in Rome)	*noun f 1*	Rome	[1]
Romanus	Romana, Romanum	*adj*	Roman	[3]
saepe	*indecl*	*adv*	often	[5]
saevus	saeva, saevum	*adj*	savage, cruel	[5]
saluto	salutare, salutavi	*verb 1st*	greet	[1]
scribo	scribere, scripsi	*verb 3rd*	write	[2]
scripsi		(*perfect of* scribo)		

se	sui	*refl pron*	himself, herself, itself, themselves	[5]
sed	*indecl*	*conj*	but	[1]
sedeo	sedere, sedi	*verb 2nd*	sit	[2]
semper	*indecl*	*adv*	always	[1]
senator	senatoris	*noun m 3*	senator	[6]
senex	senis	*noun m 3*	old man	[4]
septem	*indecl*	*num*	seven	[6]
servo	servare, servavi	*verb 1st*	save, protect, keep	[6]
servus	servi	*noun m 2*	slave	[1]
sex	*indecl*	*num*	six	[6]
silva	silvae	*noun f 1*	wood, forest	[5]
specto	spectare, spectavi	*verb 1st*	look at, watch	[4]
statim	*indecl*	*adv*	at once, immediately	[3]
stultus	stulta, stultum	*adj*	stupid, foolish	[3]
subito	*indecl*	*adv*	suddenly	[3]
sum	esse, fui	*verb irreg*	be	[1]
supero	superare, superavi	*verb 1st*	overcome, overpower	[5]
suus	sua, suum	*adj*	his, her, its, their (own) (*refl*)	[5]
taberna	tabernae	*noun f 1*	shop, inn	[2]
taceo	tacere, tacui	*verb 2nd*	be silent, be quiet	[5]
tamen	*indecl*	*adv*	however	[5]
tandem	*indecl*	*adv*	at last, finally	[3]
templum	templi	*noun n 2*	temple	[2]
teneo	tenere, tenui	*verb 2nd*	hold	[5]
terra	terrae	*noun f 1*	earth, ground, land, country	[3]
terreo	terrere, terrui	*verb 2nd*	frighten	[2]
timeo	timere, timui	*verb 2nd*	fear, be afraid	[2]
trado	tradere, tradidi	*verb 3rd*	hand over, hand down	[5]
traho	trahere, traxi	*verb 3rd*	drag	[2]
trans	+ *acc, or as prefix*	*prep*	across	[6]
traxi		(*perfect of* traho)		
tres	tria	*num*	three	[6]
tristis	triste	*adj*	sad	[5]
tu	tui	*pron*	you (*sg*)	[4]
tum	*indecl*	*adv*	then, at that time	[5]
turba	turbae	*noun f 1*	crowd	[4]
tuus	tua, tuum	*adj*	your (of you *sg*), yours	[4]
ubi	*indecl*	*adv*	(*question*) where? (*not question*) when, where	[4] [6]
unde	*indecl*	*adv*	(*question*) where from?	[4]
unus	una, unum	*num*	one	[6]
urbs	urbis	*noun f 3*	city, town	[4]

uxor	uxoris	*noun f 3*	wife	[6]
vendo	vendere, vendidi	*verb 3rd*	sell	[6]
venio	venire, veni	*verb 4th*	come	[2]
verbum	verbi	*noun n 2*	word	[2]
vester	vestra, vestrum	*adj*	your (of you *pl*), yours	[5]
via	viae	*noun f 1*	road, street, way	[3]
vici		(*perfect of* vinco)		
video	videre, vidi	*verb 2nd*	see	[2]
villa	villae	*noun f 1*	house, country villa	[1]
vinco	vincere, vici	*verb 3rd*	conquer, win, be victorious	[5]
vinum	vini	*noun n 2*	wine	[2]
vir	viri	*noun m 2*	man, male	[2]
voco	vocare, vocavi	*verb 1st*	call	[1]
vos	vestrum	*pron*	you (*pl*)	[5]

INDEX